OF FORESTS AND FIELDS

LATINIDAD

Transnational Cultures in the United States

This series publishes books that deepen and expand our understanding of Latina/o populations, especially in the context of their transnational relationships within the Americas. Focusing on borders and boundary-crossings, broadly conceived, the series is committed to publishing scholarship in history, film and media, literary and cultural studies, public policy, economics, sociology, and anthropology. Inspired by interdisciplinary approaches, methods, and theories developed out of the study of transborder lives, cultures, and experiences, titles enrich our understanding of transnational dynamics.

Matthew Garcia, Series Editor, School of Historical, Philosophical, and Religious Studies; and Director of Comparative Border Studies, Arizona State University.

For a list of titles in the series, see the last page of the book.

OF FORESTS AND FIELDS

Mexican Labor in the Pacific Northwest

MARIO JIMENEZ SIFUENTEZ

RUTGERS UNIVERSITY PRESS

New Brunswick, New Jersey, and London

Library of Congress Cataloging-in-Publication Data

Names: Sifuentez, Mario Jimenez, 1979–
    Title: Of forest and fields : Mexican labor in the Pacific Northwest /
Mario Jimenez Sifuentez.
    Description: New Brunswick, New Jersey : Rutgers University Press, 2016. |
    Series: Latinidad : transnational cultures in the United States | Includes
bibliographical references and index.
    Identifiers: LCCN 2015024443| ISBN 9780813576909 (hardcover : alkaline
paper) | ISBN 9780813576893 (paperback : alkaline paper) | ISBN 9780813576916
(ePub) | ISBN 9780813576923 (Web PDF)
    Subjects: LCSH: Migrant agricultural laborers—Northwest, Pacific—
History. | Foreign workers, Mexican—Northwest, Pacific—History. | Mexican
Americans—Northwest, Pacific—History. | Mexicans—Northwest, Pacific—
History. | Immigrants—Northwest, Pacific—History. | Working class—
Northwest, Pacific—History. | PCUN—History. | Agricultural laborers—Labor
unions—Northwest, Pacific—History. | Northwest, Pacific—Economic conditions. |
Northwest, Pacific—Ethnic relations.

    Classification: LCC HD1527.N87 S54 2016 | DDC 331.5/4408968720795—dc23
    LC record available at http://lccn.loc.gov/2015024443

A British Cataloging-in-Publication record for this book is available from the British
Library.

Visit our website: http://rutgerspress.rutgers.edu

Manufactured in the United States of America

For my parents Mario and Lilia
and
in memory of Tam Ngoc Tran

CONTENTS

ACKNOWLEDGMENTS

I would like to begin by thanking the most important people in my life, Mario and Lilia Sifuentez. My parents are two of the hardest-working people I have ever known, and I am grateful that I have inherited a small portion of their work ethic. My sister Brenda has been an instrumental part of my success. I know of no other siblings who share the same bond as we do. I would like to thank my enormous extended family. They have labored in the fields for over five decades, and I am indebted to the sacrifices they made so that future generations could take advantage of opportunities they never had. My grandmothers have been an inspiration to me. Although they are very different from one another, I have never met two more powerful forces of nature.

Next to my family members, my advisor and mentor Matt Garcia has played the most influential role in my life. He continues to mentor me through a profession that I am ill-equipped to handle. As the son of migrant farmworkers and a first generation college student, I had no idea what the writing of a book entailed. Matt Garcia has guided me through the transition from consuming knowledge to producing it.

I would like to thank Karl Jacoby and Evelyn Hu-DeHart for their mentorship and guidance during my time at Brown University, and my colleagues in academe, Jerry Cadava, Marcia Chatelain, Matt Delmont, Maria Hwang, Hilary Jenks, Heather Lee, Erin Linell, Mireya Loza, Mark Padoongpatt, Felicia Salinas-Moniz, Sarah Wald, and Julie Weise, who at one point or another offered invaluable advice, comments, sources, and suggestions. Grey Osterud played a crucial part in helping me turn the dissertation into a manuscript, Her expertise in labor and the Pacific Northwest were invaluable. I would like to thank my copyeditor, Gary Von Euer, whose careful attention to detail have made this text more readable, engaging, and accurate.

My special thanks goes to Larry Kleinman and the people at PCUN. They have been gracious with their time, memory, and archives. I am grateful for their trust and for their work in the farmworker community. Larry Kleinman was essential to the completion of this book. His insight, candor, and connections led me down a fruitful path of discovery. This book could not have been written without his expertise and generosity.

No less important were the staffs at the University of Oregon special collections, the Four Rivers Cultural Center, Malheur County Library, University of Texas El Paso Oral History Project, Oregon State University Libraries Special Collections and Archives Research Center and the Smithsonian. A special acknowledgment goes to my support system, Keith Allen, Richard Butler and Cecilia Butler, Desiree Garcia, Huy Ong, Ryan Shaw, Ty and Alex Shaw, and Gloria Wong. All of you played a special part in my life outside of academia.

The University of California, Merced has been instrumental in the publication of this book. Their institutional support has been that of a first-class research institution. Just as important are my colleagues in history, Susan Amussen, Kevin Dawson, Sean Malloy, Ruth Mostern, Sholeh Quinn, and David Torres-Rouff, who have mentored me, encouraged me, jealously guarded my time, and protected me from many of the pitfalls of junior faculty. But above all I want to thank the students because they remind me on a daily basis why I wanted to be in this profession in the first place.

My editor Leslie Mitchner and the rest of the staff at Rutgers University Press have taken much of the stress and tension out of the process. They have been a pleasure to work with and have been timely, conscientious, and engaged. I can't imagine working with a better publisher. The anonymous readers who offered insightful comments and support for my manuscript have been invaluable.

Finally and most importantly I want to thank my wife Sarah Garcia Sifuentez. Your companionship, comfort, and love are immeasurable. You are one of the most compassionate, caring, genuine, and understanding people I have ever met. You are truly selfless. Not only could I not have finished this book without you, I look forward to never having to do anything without you again. ¡Hasta La Victoria Siempre!

OF FORESTS AND FIELDS

⤳ INTRODUCTION

In 1975 Ernest Callenbach's novel *Ecotopia*, which depicted a seces-sionist, ecologically stable Pacific Northwest, attracted national attention. One of the first attempts to portray a sustainable society, the novel influenced genera-tions of environmental activists. It has sold over a million copies in nine different languages, was reissued in 2005 on the thirtieth anniversary of its release, and is a staple in environmental studies courses across the country.

Callenbach imagined the Pacific Northwest of the future as the locale for solu-tions to the ecological consequences of capitalism. Ecotopia's high-speed rails, recycling programs, energy-efficient buildings, and population control have all become essential aspects of the "green" movement. Callenbach's world has one other defining feature: people of color are essentially absent. Blacks have "self-segregated." Native Americans are relics of the past that allow Ecotopia's residents to "play Indian," going so far as giving themselves "Indian" names and partaking in ritualized warfare. Mexicans simply do not exist in this ecological wonderland. In Ecotopia the workweek has been cut to twenty hours. People who want to use the abundant timber supplies must travel to the forest and contribute a month of labor to make up for their consumption. The residents of Ecotopia grow their own food on community farms and hunt for meat. For "Ecotopians," work is not labor but a pleasurable exercise in sustainability. Perhaps Ecotopia does not need any Mexicans because it does not need any workers.

For my family, the Northwest represented something very different: work. Although born in Mexico, my father and the majority of his relatives considered themselves Tejanos. His father was born in Houston and left Texas "voluntarily" during the Depression. Twenty years later he returned with his brothers to the United States. As early as the 1950s my father's family, along with other Tejanos, worked in the fields, lived in the labor camps, and enjoyed themselves in the dance halls of Nyssa, Oregon. My mother, a Mexican immigrant, came with her family to Ontario, Oregon, much later. As the oldest child of seven, she labored in the free-zone factories known as maquiladoras just south of the border and in Texas cotton fields before making her way to Oregon, where she met, fell in love with, and married my father. My parents represent two distinct waves of Mexican immigrants to Oregon: the Tejano migration that lasted from the 1950s to the early 1970s, and the migration of Mexican nationals that followed in their wake. As children, my cousins and I worked in the fields alongside our parents until the agricultural sector in eastern Oregon mechanized and no longer needed so much labor.

This book examines the role that ethnic Mexican labor played in fashioning the Northwest into one of the most productive regions in the country after the Second World War. Expanding water development projects, accelerated timber harvests, and a booming agricultural sector owe their success in large part to the labor of braceros, Tejano migrants, and Mexican immigrants, both documented and undocumented. Like Callenbach's Ecotopia, the residents of the Pacific Northwest attempted to obscure the presence of ethnic Mexicans in the region and relegated them to being invisible and temporary laborers. Yet ethnic Mexicans refused to be erased from the landscape. They struggled against their marginalization with whatever method was available to them. Their methods ranged from what James Scott calls "the weapons of the weak," such as skipping out on contracts and sabotage, to more recognizable forms of resistance, such as forming a labor union.[1]

I follow the trajectory of worker resistance both unorganized and organized in the Pacific Northwest. It began with individual braceros and their isolated efforts to win respect, dignity, higher wages, and fairer treatment. Next came the Tejanos. I argue that their resistance came not in the form of traditional labor militancy but in the maintenance of a Tejano culture in the Northwest that often challenged Anglo notions of superiority. Finally, I turn to the efforts of activists in Oregon, who built one of the only long-lasting and successful farmworker unions in the country. Their success was based primarily on a strategy that at the time was generally considered anathema to success—organizing undocumented immigrants.

This history of ethnic Mexican immigration to the Pacific Northwest is important in the context of a larger Chicana/o history for a number of reasons. Numerous scholarly books and articles have been written about the "Mexicanization" of rural communities across the country. For the most part these are examinations of relatively recent transformations of small-town largely Anglo communities into predominantly Mexican towns. My work, however, traces that movement back to the bracero program and its effects not only on the Southwest but on the creation of a migrant network to the Pacific Northwest that began a transformation of rural communities as early as the 1950s. Thus the "Mexicanization" covered in this book is taking place, in the case of the Northwest, much earlier in time than what is studied in most scholarly works.

I also demonstrate that place matters. The great distance between Mexican communities in the Northwest and other Mexican communities in the Southwest and Mexico provided challenges and opportunities for ethnic Mexicans. For example, the bracero program and farmworker unionization took on different characteristics in the Northwest than they did in California.

Political culture in the Northwest created unique enemies and allies for ethnic Mexican farmworkers. Farmworkers found themselves at odds with white reforestation workers who were ostensibly anticapitalist, yet reverted to the rhetoric of ownership when faced with undocumented workers in the forests. Conversely, they also found a strong ally in the Nisei growers, who were often the only people willing to rent homes and provide year-round work to them. Thus the Northwest is not just important because it is not the Southwest but because unique patterns of migration, settlement, and resistance arose out of its specific location.

In some ways, the exploitation of the braceros in the Northwest was similar to that in California. Housing and food were substandard, contracts were often violated, violence was prevalent, and workdays were long. On the other hand, braceros in the Pacific Northwest received somewhat better wages, in part because they took a more militant stance towards their employers and went on strike more often. This book complicates the conversation about the Bracero Program by examining the bittersweet experiences of those who participated in the bilateral labor program in the Northwest. Although as a whole the program was exploitative and inhumane, the men who engaged in the work saw themselves as agents of their own labor and performed with dignity. Erasmo Gamboa's *Mexican Labor and World War II: Braceros in the Pacific Northwest 1942–1947* details the numerous strikes, slowdowns, and walkouts braceros conducted. In addition to the contemporary documents on which Gamboa relies, I use oral interviews with braceros that worked in the region. Taken together, these sources provide a vivid and detailed account of braceros' lives that testifies to the special character the program assumed in the Northwest.

Studying Mexican immigration to the Pacific Northwest requires an engagement with the environmental history of the region as well. Major dam projects during World War II brought millions of previously arid acres under cultivation in eastern Oregon, Washington, and western Idaho. The national forests of the Pacific Northwest have long been essential to the region's economy. William Robbins's *Landscapes of Promise* delineates the transformation wrought by dams and changing agricultural practices on Native American ecosystems in Oregon. In *Landscapes of Conflict*, he argues that the movement to the suburbs, the automobile, and the increasing fascination with outdoor recreation reshaped Oregon's landscape. The intense use of land and timber was not slowed until the 1970s, when pressure from environmental activists resulted in state regulations regarding land use, federal environmental standards, and the Endangered Species Act.[2]

This book locates new points of intersection among Chicano/a, labor, and environmental history.[3] Older environmental histories often told stories that focused on literary treatments of "nature," the corporations that destroy the natural environment, and the state apparatus that shapes policy. Historians such as Richard White, William Cronon, and Andrew Hurley have made concerted efforts to link labor and environmental history.[4] White's work on the Columbia River, for example, connects natural history and human history, examining the labor organization of Native Americans on the river and the connections that fishermen and boat captains have with the river. I extend this marriage of landscape and laborers to Mexicans who worked in the forest as well as the fields and explore the meaning that they gave to their work with nature.

Despite these efforts, as Gunther Peck points out, "there remains little 'nature' in labor history and few working-class subjects in environmental history."[5] This book highlights the immigrant workers themselves and maintains that reforestation should be considered part of agricultural labor. This book places major themes of environmental history, such as land use, the concept of "wilderness," national forests, and pesticide use, in the context of race, labor, and social justice.

The geographical focus highlights the importance of the national forests and the agricultural fields to immigrants' work experiences. In addition to working in traditional row crops, undocumented Mexican immigrants labored in the national forests of the Pacific Northwest. While felling trees and working in sawmills are notoriously dangerous occupations, little attention has been paid to the work of those who toiled in planting trees. Indeed, timber escaped classification as a crop until the mid-1980s. My research demonstrates that the federal government sees the national forests as yielding a crop. Consequently, those who labor in the forests should be thought of as agricultural laborers.

A crucial component of that struggle is the history of the Pineros y Campesinos Unidos Noroeste (Northwest Treeplanters and Farm Workers United), known by its Spanish acronym PCUN (pronounced "Pe-Coon") and their early incarnation as the Willamette Valley Immigration Project (WVIP). The goals of the reforestation, nursery, and farmworkers' union are to empower agricultural laborers and eliminate their systematic oppression and exploitation through collective bargaining, boycotts, legislative campaigns, and, most importantly, immigrant organizing. PCUN challenged the idea that the absence of citizenship made undocumented workers vulnerable to deportation and thus unorganizable. Its commitment to organizing all workers regardless of citizenship made PCUN a leader among groups that were rethinking the relationship between farm work and immigrant rights.[6]

The story of PCUN contributes to an already substantial body of work concerning farmworkers and the farmworker movement. This book demonstrates that PCUN utilized strategies similar to those of the United Farm Workers, yet defined its own criteria for success. In sharp contrast to the UFW, PCUN developed an internationalist critique of imperialism, capitalism, and militarism reminiscent of those of the International Workers of the World (IWW) and Centro de Acción Social Autónomo (CASA). PCUN's strategies, tactics, and vision were influenced by the UFW, but it also learned from the larger group's failures and embraced a more inclusive viewpoint.

In the early 1970s, the UFW had an initial presence in Oregon but failed to establish a solid union, effectively abandoning the state. Its departure created a vacuum that PCUN later filled. The union has succeeded and sustained itself as a movement, even during the antilabor Reagan years when organized labor lost numerous battles and declined precipitously in many sectors of the economy.[7] PCUN's success came partly as a result of their formation of a separate union, independent from the UFW and the AFL-CIO. Three factors contributed to their ability to emerge from UFW's shadow: the leadership of Cipriano Ferrel, a former UFW organizer and close friend of Chavez who learned from his mentor's mistakes; the UFW's war with the Teamsters Union and their commitment to organizing all immigrant workers.

I examine the attitudes, circumstances, and influences that led to PCUN's decision to organize workers within the context of immigrant rights, and show how that decision has led to their long-standing success as a union. My focus on PCUN contributes not only to the historiography of farmworkers but also to the burgeoning scholarship on the immigrant rights movements, immigrant organizing, and transnational labor.[8]

SOURCES AND METHODS

This book draws on archival documents and oral histories to illuminate the daily lives and struggles of ethnic Mexicans in the Northwest. While the archival sources contextualize and historicize workers' situations, the official record often tells us more about what bureaucrats thought about Mexicans than about their lived experiences. The dearth of written records left by guest workers, migrants, and immigrants makes it difficult to ascertain their thoughts, desires, anguish, and dreams. For this reason, oral histories by others and myself form a substantial portion of my source material.

The interviews in the first chapter were primarily conducted when I was a member of the Smithsonian's National Museum of American History's Bracero Oral History Project. A team of graduate and undergraduate students, under the directorship of Matt Garcia and Kristine Navarro, traveled around the country conducting oral histories with former braceros. These oral histories were coded and uploaded to a digital archive available for public use. The Bracero History Archive has proven an invaluable resource for this book, and received the 2010 Public History Project Award from the National Council on Public History. The remainder of the interviews took place in various locations throughout Oregon over the span of six years (2004–2010). I knew the interviewees through personal connections; for instance, many of the labor contractors I interviewed agreed to participate because they had originally contracted my family to come and work in Oregon. Some of the migrant workers came in the same migrant stream as my relatives and labored in the fields next to them. Others I met through word of mouth and my connection to other migrants in the community. The activists interviewed also agreed to participate because of their familiarity with me as a student activist. Additionally, this gave me access to the previously private archives of the union. They have since been donated to the University of Oregon Special Collections. I told each interviewee that I was writing a history of Mexican migration to the Pacific Northwest and framed the interview as a contribution to an oral history collection.

I acknowledge that relying on oral histories entails certain obstacles to writing a comprehensive history. The interaction between the interviewer and the interviewee produces a subjective view of history. People remember and interpret things through their own historical lens, based upon their ideas and position at the time they are interviewed rather than as they understood them in the past. Recognizing those potential problems, I examined the oral histories critically and placed them within historical context. Most of the interviews I conducted were in Spanish. The subjects felt much freer and better able to articulate their thoughts and feelings to a person who shared their language and ethnocultural background. I have translated the interviews into English for this work. While this process leaves some room for distortion or misrepresentation, I consulted colleagues, native Spanish speakers, and texts for assistance. Despite the potential pitfalls of oral history, I have chosen to use it because I believe that the insights of my interviewees far outweigh the potential for distortion. Ultimately, I side with Gary Okihiro, who argues: "the collective voice of the people once silenced has a right to be heard. Oral history is not only a tool or method for recovering history; it is also a theory of history which maintains that the common folk and the dispossessed have a history and that this history must be written."[9] Over the years, as I conducted interviews with individuals who lived through the circumstances that I write about, they conveyed to me the importance they placed on having their history recorded. Elders often complained that the younger generation did not know about their struggles, the indignities they had suffered, and the victories they had achieved as youth and young adults.

Although the book relies significantly on oral histories, I use newspapers, government reports, and other official documents to further buttress the interviews. For a region where Mexican immigrants have been largely ignored in the official record, these sources are not as plentiful as they might be in the Southwest. Oftentimes the nature of documents pertaining to Mexican immigrants make obscure references to their presence while commenting on some other more "pertinent" issue.

If we lose these stories we risk perpetuating the myth that the economy of the Pacific Northwest is nature's gift and not a product of human labor. We seldom interrogate the origins of the food on our table, the roof over our heads, and the other comforts that immigrant workers provide for most Americans. Including their voices in this book preserves their memories and yields irreplaceable insights into how they experienced their own lives.

The interviews complicate the findings of research in archival documents. For example, they demonstrate the diversity of the ethnic Mexican community in the Northwest. Mexican nationals, Tejanos, and documented and undocumented immigrants from the border states and the interior of Mexico all labored side by side in the fields and the forests, correcting the prevalent image of the Mexican peon fleeing his or her rural village in search of a better life in the United States. These guest workers, citizens, resident aliens, and undocumented aliens came to this region for a variety of reasons, ranging from economic hardship and racial and gender oppression to love and adventure.[10]

MEXICANS IN THE PACIFIC NORTHWEST

In recent years scholars have attempted to reclaim the Mexican heritage of the Pacific Northwest. They have pointed to Spanish explorers and Spanish place-names in the Northwest as evidence of a pre-Anglo presence in the region. In the 1850s, this brief moment of exploration gave way to a more sustained migration of Mexican vaqueros (cowboys), who played a substantial role in the early cattle ranching industry in Oregon and Idaho. Alongside the vaqueros, the *arrieros* (mule packers) earned a reputation in the region for their skill and knowledge. The mining booms in eastern Oregon and Idaho brought the arrieros up from California in the 1860s, seeking fortunes in gold mining.[11]

A combination of factors contributed to the rise of Mexican emigration at the turn of the century. The Mexican Revolution displaced large numbers of people who found refuge on the US side of the border, while labor shortages during World War I encouraged further migration to the American Southwest. During this period many Mexican immigrants began to venture further away from the Southwest to the Pacific Northwest, the Midwest, and the American South. In the Pacific Northwest, Mexican immigrants worked on the railroad, in the forests, and most prolifically in the sugar beet industry. The exact number of Mexicans remains difficult to pin down; the 1930 census enumerated 562 Mexicans in Washington, 1,278 in Idaho, and 1,568 in Oregon. The number of migrant workers who were on the move or otherwise invisible to census takers is impossible to know. Anecdotal evidence suggests that the number might have been much higher; a letter from the Mexican Consul in 1918, for example, claimed that 1,500 workers, including 500 women, were laboring in the sugar beet fields in Twin Falls, Idaho alone. The Mexican anthropologist Manuel Gamio recorded Oregon, Idaho, and Washington as the point of origin for hundreds of money orders sent to Mexico by workers.[12] Regardless of the exact number, the population remained relatively small and was eclipsed in the postwar era.[13]

The Second World War ushered in a new era in Mexican immigration to the Pacific Northwest. During the war years, the number of braceros in the region was over 40,000. The number who skipped out on their contracts and became undocumented is impossible to know. Records for the number of "Hispanic" residents are not available for the 1950 or 1960 census, but according to the Oregon Bureau of Labor and Industries, the number of interstate migrants from Texas was as high as 85,000 during the 1950s. Many of these families remained in the Northwest and made it their home. Mexican businesses, radio stations, and cultural celebrations began to take hold during this era of settlement. By the mid-1960s Tejanos no longer made up the bulk of the migrant workforce—they numbered only 15,000 by 1965—and had transitioned into other industries. The 1970 census reported that almost 70 percent of 105,000 "Hispanic origin" residents in Washington and Oregon lived in urban areas, defined as areas with a population over 2,500.[14] Almost 85 percent of Mexicans lived in only twenty-five counties in the Northwest, and the majority of those were located along the Interstate-5 corridor. The remaining counties were agricultural and had a larger proportion of Mexican residents in comparison to their urban counterparts. Malheur County in Oregon, for example, had the highest percentage of Mexicans in the state. Still, in the case of Oregon these numbers are misleading. The "urban" counties that line the I-5 corridor are the heart of the region's niche agricultural economy, the Willamette Valley, and are the main focus of this book.[15]

The 1980 census was the most complete census to date and recorded the number of Mexicans in the Pacific Northwest. The overall population of Mexicans in Oregon and Washington grew from 105,311 to 185,863, an increase of over 76 percent. Meanwhile in Idaho, the Mexican population was recorded as 36,560, the first time that Mexicans were enumerated in the state. Between 1980 and 1990 the population grew by 70 percent in Washington, 67 percent in Oregon, and 41 percent in Idaho. By the 1990s the total number of Mexicans in the Pacific Northwest was over 410,000, the product of an explosive growth that saw the number of undocumented immigrants in the area rise exponentially.

One day while doing research for this book, I was in the Malheur County Library looking through 50-year-old newspapers. I ran across a story about a 23-year-old migrant worker who died on August 13, 1951. The details of his death were sketchy; the only thing certain was that he suffered a head injury and that he left his wife and three small children behind. The man's name was Remijio Sifuentez, whom I later discovered was my grandfather's younger brother. The news came as a shock to me. I had never heard of this man or any stories about losing a family member. When I spoke to my dad, he confirmed that his uncle had died before my father was born. My great uncle's family moved away and my dad's family never heard from them again. Shortly after Remijio's death my grandfather named his newborn son after his deceased brother. Until I read that newspaper article in the Malheur County Library, my Uncle Remi was the only Remijio Sifuentez I knew. What follows in these pages is a testament to those who labored and died in the fields, canneries, sugar refineries, packing sheds, nurseries, and forests so that their children, grandchildren, and great-grandchildren whom they had never met could live a better life. I wrote this book in the hope that my great-uncle's life was not in vain and would not be forgotten.

1 ❧ MANY MILES FROM HOME
The Bracero Program in the Pacific Northwest

On August 4, 1942, the United States and Mexico entered into a bilateral agreement to bring temporary guest workers from Mexico to the United States. Despite claims that the bracero program sought only to alleviate the wartime labor shortage, the program lasted until 1964 and issued 4.6 million contracts to guest workers. The term *bracero* literally means those who work with their arms, and the program regarded them as such: they were merely physical labor. Between 1942 and 1947, growers in the Pacific Northwest imported over 40,000 braceros. Only men were allowed to participate in the program, and those who were married were not allowed to bring their families with them.

Growers' fear of labor shortages in agriculture reached a fever pitch during World War II. Hundreds of thousands of able-bodied men left their homes to fight in the war, while others left the farm for the cities. Before the Second World War, growers customarily sought to keep labor costs down by ensuring an oversupply of labor.[1] As the defense industry boomed, Los Angeles, San Francisco, Seattle, and Portland became centers of war production. In the Northwest, Seattle and Portland attracted thousands of workers from within and beyond the region.[2] Those jobs, however, were distributed unevenly according to race. Unlike Mexican Americans, African Americans found some protection from discrimination through the Fair Employment Practices Committee (FEPC) established by President Franklin D. Roosevelt. The FEPC failed to address the grievances of Mexican American workers because officials feared that documenting abuses of Mexican Americans would reflect poorly on the United States and jeopardize the newly established bracero program.[3] Mexico had worked diligently to secure an accord that would ensure the safety of its nationals.

The arrangement between the two countries guaranteed certain rights and conditions that were intended to protect Mexican workers from exploitation. Employers could not use braceros for military service, as strikebreakers, or in industries other than agriculture. The contract required employers to pay workers' transportation costs to and from Mexico, promise employment for three-quarters of the contracted period, provide adequate housing, and pay the same wage that prevailed in the industry and the area. These provisions were meant to alleviate the fear that growers would use guest workers to undercut the wages and working standards of native-born workers. Finally, and most importantly to Mexico, discrimination of any kind was prohibited. The Mexican government held the right to refuse to send braceros to any state that discriminated against Mexicans. Making good on that promise, Mexico barred Texas from participating in the program.[4]

While many scholarly works on the bracero program rightfully focus on the exploitative nature of the program and the dehumanizing conditions, they also consistently portray the helplessness and powerlessness of its participants. These portrayals often victimize the braceros and limit the agency they exercised in the face of oppression and dehumanizing conditions. The bracero experience in the Northwest demonstrates that conditions were often ripe for challenging the status quo and that those challenges sometimes won the braceros concessions, while at the same time acknowledging the fact that these challenges just as often failed. Nevertheless, there were challenges. From the moment that braceros came to the Northwest in large numbers they began to lay the foundation not only for a future migration but also for an oppositional politics. The oppositional politics originated in three main factors. First, labor shortages in the Northwest were more acute than elsewhere, and evidence suggests that employers truly struggled with finding agricultural laborers. This was unlike the Southwest, where growers often complained about labor shortages but had armies of Mexican American farmworkers in reserve. In the Northwest, those communities existed on a much smaller scale. Second, the distance from the border made transportation of replacement braceros costly and timely, particularly in the Northwest, where many of the niche crops, like strawberries, ripened quickly. Finally, many of the initial braceros came from urban backgrounds that ill-suited them for agricultural work. Many were small businessmen, young adventurers, and others who sought to escape family strife, but almost none of them came from rural peasant backgrounds. The wave of braceros to the Northwest was young, enterprising, and often urban.

Braceros were supposed to fill the demand for short-term labor and then return home, but they permanently changed the face of the Pacific Northwest. Eventually the braceros brought or formed families and settled in the area, becoming the backbone of the region's rapidly expanding agricultural economy in the postwar era. This chapter explores the experiences of braceros in the Northwest. It demonstrates that braceros not only made a substantial contribution to the economy but also were different from braceros in other regions because of their militancy on the job, the range of occupations in which they engaged, the wages they demanded, and the migration patterns they established.[5]

The Pacific Northwest needed braceros because defense industries in the region attracted most of the labor available locally. This was unlike the Southwest, where most of this labor was white. The Mexican American community in the Northwest during the prewar era was generously estimated at 11,000 in Oregon, Idaho, and Washington combined. Oregon, for instance, had an estimated 3,000 Mexican Americans and foreign-born Mexicans.[6] The shortage of agricultural workers hit eastern Oregon, eastern Washington, and southwestern Idaho particularly hard. The federal government had recently made a significant investment in developing the land for agriculture, completing several Columbia River dam projects that brought nearly three million acres under irrigation. Growers called out for laborers to tend the crops on land that had just been cleared of sagebrush.[7] Additionally, as historian Erasmo Gamboa notes, agriculture in the Pacific Northwest fluctuated between intense periods of work and relative quiet throughout the year. As a result, large numbers of workers were needed for short periods of time. In the Pacific Northwest, typical harvests required large crews for short periods of time of about 180 days.[8] The type of crops also contributed to this pressing need. For instance, hop cultivation required 130 "man-days" of labor for 5,500 acres, while fruit orchards required the same amount of labor for ten times as many acres.[9]

State and local officials went into a panic, trying out a myriad of schemes to put bodies in the fields. Historian Erasmo Gamboa details the great length to which many rural communities in the Northwest went to alleviate the shortage.[10] In Yakima, Washington, the mayor ordered sheriff's deputies on the nearby Indian reservation to look for loitering "Mexicans and Negroes" so that they could be put to work. Apparently, the mayor believed that "Mexicans and Negroes" avoided work by passing themselves off as Indians and hiding out on the reservation.[11] In towns across the Northwest, stores limited their hours of operation during the harvest, police rounded up the indigent, schools let children out early so they could aid in the harvest, and local newspapers urged all hale and hearty people to get out into the fields and work.[12]

In Idaho, despite Governor Clark's vehement opposition to the Japanese presence in the state, he nevertheless acquiesced to using them as a temporary solution to its labor problems. In May 1942, the War Relocation Authority approved the use of 3,714 internees to harvest beets. The Amalgamated Sugar Company hired 235 Japanese laborers from the Tule Lake camp, and Minidoka internees worked on farms in Buhl, Filer, and Paul.[13] Japanese internees had to pass a "loyalty test" and remained under surveillance, their movements being restricted while they labored in the fields. By 1943, the program had grown large enough to merit three district offices in Idaho Falls, Twin Falls, and Boise to assist farmers who wished to hire internee laborers from the camp, around 4,000, but this could not satisfy the labor needs of the state.[14]

Growers even experimented with the Farm Security Administration's domestic migrant program. The program brought migrants from the South to work in the fields, but once they arrived they almost immediately left for the greener pastures of Portland's and Seattle's defense plants and shipyards. Growers had to look elsewhere for labor, but they hesitated to import Mexican workers. Growers attempted to corral patriotic sentiment, asking women's clubs, schoolchildren, labor unions, and other civic organizations to make up for the labor shortage. In Idaho, Governor Clark and his daughter led "white collar" workers into the fields and by all accounts saved the sugar beet harvest to the tune of a reported $16 million.[15] Rural newspapers reiterated their opposition to imported Mexicans and their belief that whites were "patriotic enough and anxious to lend assistance to the great task facing us this season."[16] Industry newspapers like *Northwest Farm News* echoed this belief disparaged the Mexicans as "ne'er-do-wells and hobos,"[17] and expressed doubt that the Mexicans who were being imported were sufficiently skilled to work in the fields.[18]

While growers voiced concerns over the braceros' lack of farming experience, their primary concerns pertained to the terms of bracero contracts. They complained that their wages were set too high and that it cost too much to bring them to and from the border. "They [the US government] arranged to have a contract which would deal with each laborer as a free agent and put all sorts of conditions which the farmer who had to hire him had to agree to."[19] Farm Bureaus across the Northwest proposed a system by which they would handpick braceros in Mexico using the contractors they had used in the past, but officials scoffed at the suggestion. Despite all the bravado, local Anglos could not keep up with the labor needs. At the very moment they were celebrating their performance in the fields, plans were already underway to secure thousands of Mexican laborers.[20]

BECOMING A BRACERO

The resistance to importing Mexicans, while strong, quickly gave way to necessity. As the labor shortage grew desperate, opposition to the importation of foreign labor faded. In the first year of the program, growers in Washington, Oregon, and Idaho hired over 5,000 braceros to save their crops.[21] Many of the men on the other side of the border waited expectantly to board a train and help participate in the war effort to the best of their abilities. What awaited them was a mix of cautious gratefulness and unexpected difficulties.

Braceros were contracted through a fairly standardized set of procedures. Responsibility for recruiting workers in Mexico fell to the Mexican government's Bureau of Migratory Farm Labor Affairs. Candidates had to bring a recommendation attesting to their good character and must be landless, a condition that was intended to alleviate Mexican officials' worry that small farmers would abandon their land and leave for the United States. If a candidate met these requirements, he would travel to a sprawling complex known as an assembly center, usually in a major Mexican city.

When the men arrived at the center they answered a series of questions about their background to assess their suitability for the program. The most telling part of the examination was the "hand check." Inspectors at the assembly centers inspected the men's hands for signs of wear; rough and calloused hands indicated that the applicant was accustomed to a life of hard work. The tougher the hand, the more likely the applicant was a suitable farmworker.

After approval, the men boarded trains for the trip north and stopped at the border. Employee agents from the Farm Bureau, the government-sponsored agencies that served growers, anxiously awaited their arrival and subjected the men to a round of examinations that was even more thorough and more demeaning than the last. Hundreds of braceros waited in line in the hot and dusty air. When their turn came, a female receptionist fingerprinted the men, collected information, and asked them to strip down to their underwear, the first of many indignities they suffered that day. The medical evaluation that followed forced the men to strip naked, often in the presence of onlookers and the female nursing staff. Assumptions that Mexicans were prone to contagious diseases dictated that the medical staff screen them for tuberculosis and VD; a positive test for either one meant automatic disqualification. But negative results on both tests did not allay Americans' suppositions about "dirty Mexicans." Candidates who passed both tests suffered the humiliation of being "disinfected" with dichloro-diphenyltrichloroethane, commonly called DDT, a powerful pesticide that was used on many crops at that time but is now known to be a carcinogen.

The employee agents waited in the corral-like structure for the braceros who passed their immigration and medical examinations. In the pen the agents poked and prodded the men to ascertain their musculature. The braceros had no choice but to endure further embarrassment. The supply of workers at the reception center far outstripped the demand, and if a bracero failed to be contracted within five days he had to return home. Workers took whatever offers the agents made. Once contracted braceros traveled by train or truck to their destination. Most went to work in the US Southwest, but many were taken as far as the state of Washington, Florida, or Delaware. Bracero contracts lasted thirty, sixty, or ninety days. Upon completion employers returned the bracero to the reception center to wait to be contracted again or to return home. Contractors held a considerable amount of power at this stage. At the reception center, officials issued an identification card to braceros in good standing. If their employer gave them a good recommendation, the bracero could expect to receive his card quickly and get a new contract without going through the formal process he had initially endured. The more a bracero complained about his wages, living conditions, or treatment, the less likely he was to receive a positive recommendation. Workers had no choice but to bite their tongues and tolerate harsh conditions. This system worked well for employers near the border. Proximity made it inexpensive to return unruly braceros and exchange them for new ones. On the other hand, if a worker found himself in a tolerable or even decent situation he could continue to be recontracted with the same grower and develop a relationship that guaranteed him work. Recontracting occurred often, and some men completed numerous work contracts in a year.[22]

Juan Contreras was one of the thousands of men who were heralded as the saviors of the Northwest's agricultural economy. When the train loaded with farmworkers arrived in Portland, Oregon, a band playing American music and a throng of intrigued spectators greeted them. As the men left the train carrying the flags of both the United States and Mexico, a rush of excitement ran through Contreras's body. Braceros received an equally warm welcome in small towns and major cities across the region. Describing the scene, the *Yakima Daily News* commented, "many of them wore their native brimmed hats, which will stand them in good stead later on."[23] For the Anglo readers of the *Yakima Daily News*, this caricature of the Mexicans arriving in their town aligned perfectly with their expectations. Contreras, however, painted a slightly different picture: "A lot of them thought we were going to walk off with a huge sombrero and a serape . . . but that was a lie, because most of us were from Mexico City, we didn't dress like that! They must have been thinking, 'What are these *cabrones* (bastards) wearing?!' "[24] His attire and background belied the image that most Americans had of braceros.

Contreras was born in Tuxtla Gutierrez, Chiapas, a state with a predominantly indigenous population in southern Mexico. His father was a soldier stationed there, and at an early age Contreras felt out of place and restless. He left home for Jiquilpan, Michoacán, in search of work and eventually moved to the capital. In Mexico City, a friend relayed rumors about a program that would take guest workers to the United States. Contreras was accustomed to moving and was excited by the prospect of traveling to the United States, but the procedures for recruiting men had not yet been codified. His friend had already preregistered for the program and urged him to do the same. So Contreras visited the secretary of external relations and preenrolled. Then he returned home to Michoacán and waited.

After fifteen days he received a telegram informing him that he should report to the Buena Vista station in Mexico City if he was still interested in joining the program. Possession of the telegram entitled him to a free train ride from anywhere in Mexico to the station. There Contreras signed a contract and received his identification number: "That is where I got my number, 76. . . . We were the first to leave."[25] US officials contracted the workers and handed out jackets, blankets, and shoes to those who needed them. "There were some with huaraches. . . . They [the Americans] gave them shoes, these little shoes . . . made of plastic."[26] As the men boarded the train a mariachi band bid them farewell by playing "Las Golondrinas," a song often associated with the funerals of Mexicans who die far away from home, and a Catholic priest came to bless the railcar and the men. The mood quickly changed, and the men began to speculate that they were being taken off to fight in the war. "Once you were on the train you had officially immigrated," Contreras explained. "There were Mexican soldiers guarding us. So that no one would jump off. . . . That is when people came up with the idea that we were going to war. That is when a lot of people jumped off the train. They didn't want to go to war."[27] Fearing conscription, men left the train at Tlalnepantha, a small town just north of Mexico City. "The train stopped there for a little while . . . and then I saw the first ones running with their blankets as fast as they could [laughs]. Yea, it was a strange thing."[28] For his part, Contreras fatalistically accepted the possibility that he might be going off to war: "My friends that came with me, we all stayed. 'Let's go. If they take us [to war] they take us!' That is it."[29] This sense of reckless abandon served Contreras well in the struggles he faced in the United States.

Contreras began the trip north with seven railcars full of braceros, but by the time they reached El Paso, Texas, only three or four carloads remained; the other men had lost their nerve and jumped off the train. When Contreras arrived at the border, the infamous screening practices had not yet been implemented, and he traveled straight through to Portland. After receiving a warm welcome, a hundred braceros boarded another train to the countryside.

Libby's fruit company contracted the braceros to work in its cherry orchards and later in its canneries. Contreras recalled that they had comfortable accommodations and their sheets were changed every three days. "In each room there were about four or five workers. We had everything; there was a place to wash up, bathrooms. Everything was well arranged over there in Oregon."[30] The braceros' lack of experience with the crop confirmed the suspicions of many growers but also led to some amusing situations. Contreras recalled the astonishment the braceros felt upon seeing the size of the cherries. Capulins, colloquially known as Mexican black cherries, are much smaller than the Bing cherries grown in the United States "The paisanos would say 'Chingado (Fuck) these bastards [Americans] even have big capulins!' But they were cherries [laughs]. They were cherries! [laughs]."[31] Contreras struggled to acclimate himself to the life of a farmworker. He joked that at first "I think we ate about as much as we picked! For my part I never filled a bucket."[32] The men were paid a dollar per bucket, but he never really got the hang of picking cherries. Cherry picking required climbing a 15- to 20-foot ladder that leaned against a tree. Contreras did not care much for the heights and was relieved when the harvest was over. Yet one of the state's major newspapers, the

Oregon Statesman, perhaps trying to put a good face on the importation of labor, insisted that "reports from all over the state where the Mexicans are employed are uniformly good. The men are chosen from the farming region of Mexico, are friendly and cooperative, and their work is very satisfactory."[33]

From there the company shipped the men all over the region; eventually Contreras even lost track of his location. After three months the fruit harvest ended and the company handed Contreras over to the Utah-Idaho Sugar Company instead of transporting him back to the border to be recontracted. Strictly speaking, this type of handoff violated the provisions of the contract, but companies and growers in the Northwest consistently violated the clause because it saved them time and money.[34] According to historian Johanna Ogden, this type of arrangement proliferated throughout the Northwest.[35]

Juan Contreras enjoyed working in the sugar beet fields; he felt more comfortable closer to the ground. Sugar beets require a tremendous amount of attention and constant thinning. Contreras explained, "Sugar beets grow at different times in different areas, they grew in zones, so we would thin one zone, harvest another, and then come back to harvest the zone we had thinned earlier."[36] While he enjoyed the work, he found that it paid even less than the cherry harvest. According to Contreras, the growers "had all kinds of excuses: the sugar beets weren't packed right, they were too green. They never left us with much money."[37] In addition to the poor pay, he experienced varying degrees of poor treatment depending on his location. "In those days, well, no one knew how much one was supposed to be paid."[38] Contreras moved from contract to contract struggling to find better-paying work. He spent most of his time in the Northwest working in the fruit harvest, which he grew to master and eventually enjoy. The workers eventually became adept at harvesting, thinning, and picking and built a reputation as skilled farmhands across the Northwest.

Atanacio "Nacho" Jimenez Lopez, liker Contreras, wanted to leave Mexico, but he was propelled not by restlessness but by his desire to escape an extremely abusive family. Like Contreras, Jimenez had little experience working in agriculture and had worked mostly in an urban setting.[39] Jimenez was orphaned at the age of five and taken in by his uncle, who was also his godfather. The man treated him very poorly, and often physically abused him. One particular beating stood out in Nacho's mind. "The only time I was allowed out was for church," he explained.[40] His uncle ordered him home immediately after church to finish his daily chores. Instead of heading directly home, Jimenez got sidetracked by a game of marbles. When he arrived two hours late, his uncle beat the young boy viciously. "He hit me so hard I got dizzy. . . . The next day I got up to milk the cows. I can't do it. I'm all bruised. I refused to work and to eat for a few days."[41] After the beating Jimenez decided to run away. He borrowed money from his older brother and headed out for Guadalajara.

Although Jimenez enjoyed being free from the beatings, he faced low wages and poor living conditions. "I found work right away," he recalled. "I helped bricklayers. They only paid one peso" per day. "I paid three centavos for a place to sleep . . . in the same place where the donkeys slept."[42] After working for a number of years as a bricklayer's assistant, in the wheat harvest, and as a cowman, he left for Queretaro in search of a bracero contract. No sooner had he arrived there than thieves robbed him of his entire savings. Being robbed represented a significant setback. Although the bracero program did not require applicants to pay a fee, the multitude of people seeking to enroll provided corrupt officials with the opportunity to take *mordidas* (bribes, literally bites) for processing individuals' applications. Without the money for the bribe and alone in Queretaro, Jimenez looked elsewhere for work. An owner of a local restaurant answered his pleas for work coldly. "She told me, your kind are everywhere." Hungry, desperate, and perhaps a touch resentful of his treatment, Jimenez attempted to steal a handful of tortillas. The owner caught him and he was arrested. The police brought Jimenez before the court, where the judge, peering down at him over his glasses, questioned him. "The judge asked me why I was stealing. I told him, 'I was hungry. I asked for work. I asked for food. I was robbed last night. I had no choice.' "[43] Witnesses corroborated Jimenez's version of events, and the judge ordered the restaurant owner to give Jimenez a job as a dishwasher. He worked there for eight days until a friend of his happened to come into the restaurant. He borrowed money from his friend and used it to pay the bribe and enroll in the bracero program.

"Nacho" Jimenez boarded a train in Queretaro to the border at Ciudad Juarez. Like Contreras, he participated in the program before the dehumanizing examination process was instituted. (In later years, however, US officials subjected Jimenez to examination and disinfection when he reentered the country as a bracero.) At Ciudad Juarez he boarded a train headed for Portland, Oregon. Upon his arrival, farmers and contractors separated the braceros like "a herd of cattle, fifty this way, ten this way; they took us off one train and put us on another, headed to different places."[44] Unlike most other braceros, Jimenez did not end up working in agriculture but went to work on the railroad. The railroad industry successfully established that it had a labor shortage during World War II and was therefore eligible to employ braceros, the only industry besides agriculture to do so. Ethnic Mexicans had a long history of working on the railroads in the Southwest as track hands and section men, so the railroads were confident they would make good workers. Sociologist Paul Taylor also recorded the presence of Mexicans working on the railroad in the Northwest.[45] By 1945, thirty-five railroad companies employed 69,000 braceros across the country.[46]

Jimenez began laying tracks in Tangent, Oregon, for the Southern Pacific railroad and enjoyed higher wages and better living conditions than braceros employed in agriculture. Railroad work required an immense amount of skill, and braceros went through an extensive training period. Their wages reflected the amount of training they received. Railroad braceros made up to a dollar or more an hour, far above the 30 cents an hour that was the prevailing wage for farmworkers in Oregon. In most instances growers failed to meet the minimum threshold. Those lucky enough to work on the railroads had significantly higher earnings and a profoundly different experience than braceros in agriculture.

The work was divided into three jobs: laying railroad ties, laying new track, and flagging. Newcomers were assigned to the physically demanding task of removing and replacing railroad ties. Using a jack, they tore out dilapidated railroad ties and replaced them with new ones. After setting the new ties, they drove railroad spikes into them with a sledgehammer. Workers had to prove their mettle and endurance before they could be promoted to jobs that required more skill and responsibility.

As tedious as replacing railroad ties could be, laying and adjusting track required even more endurance and skill. Every pass of a train caused a minuscule shift in the ballasts and ties that held the tracks together. Over time the shift could become substantial enough to derail a train. The men had to inspect sections of track to determine if there had been any slippage and mark the tracks that needed to be adjusted. They also used a mirror to inspect underneath the rails to look for cracks or other signs of damage and marked damaged track with yellow chalk. Behind them another group of braceros pried the tracks back into place or replaced them. Jimenez described the work: "We would put in a mile, two miles, depending on the job. . . . It was very rhythmic, like we were trying to make music. Teams of two, usually the best guys, stand on each side of the rail and use this tool here [shows the tool to the interviewer] and we would work our way up the track, ting, ting, ting."[47] Every four ties, a bracero drove a spike into the rail to secure it, while another team inspected the spikes to ensure they were secure.

The flagger had the most envied job in the railroad camp. It required less manual labor and offered better pay, but also carried a tremendous amount of responsibility. A flagger had to warn conductors when a train was approaching a section where maintenance was being performed. Flaggers strapped "torpedoes" on the track that, when a train passed, exploded and caused a loud bang, indicating to the conductor to stop the train. Simultaneously, the bracero flagged the train down, but in fog, snow, or darkness the conductor could have trouble seeing the flagger. If the bracero failed to set the torpedo properly, the train could derail at the worksite, with disastrous results for the workers as well as the people on the train. When the train stopped, the flagger, having few English skills, handed the conductor written instructions for how to proceed.

Initially Jimenez had no idea what railroad work entailed, but he quickly grew fond of the work and his colleagues. He worked hard and earned the respect of his boss. "He was a big white guy from Texas, his name was Bill. He liked me a lot. I really worked hard. I never stood still."[48] Eventually Jimenez earned the opportunity to be trained as a flagger: "If the boss trusted you enough you could be a flagger. I was a flagger."[49] His experience had its rough patches as well. Jimenez recalled the poor treatment he received at the hands of his crew boss, Modesto, a Mexican national from Guanajuato. "The old man was a despot and an ugly, ugly man."[50] Having a common heritage did not necessarily mean fair treatment.

Agustin Bautista, like Jimenez, came to Oregon in the early years of the program and worked on the railroads. Bautista was born in the small village of Los Laureles in Jiquilpan, Michoacán, one of ten children, and first entered the United States with one of his brothers in 1943. His initial contract was with the Western Union railway that operated between Sacramento and Las Vegas. After six months he returned to the border to reenlist in the program. He enjoyed railroad work so much that he sought another contract. His second stint brought him to the forests near Klamath Falls, Oregon, an isolated place near the border with California. Bautista, who executed the work with great care, recalled it in vivid detail. Like Jimenez he quickly moved up the ranks and became a flagger. "My bosses trusted me. Sometimes they even left me in charge. I was young and single but I understood the kind of responsibility I had."[51] Just three days after his arrival Bautista had an experience that illustrated the importance of being responsible and the dangers inherent in railroad work. To get from job to job, railroad workers rode and transported their tools on flatcars. While riding to the next job, Bautista and the rest of the crew were eating lunch atop the flatcar when it suddenly derailed. Tools went flying every which way. Some crewmembers fell off the flatcar, while others hung on for dear life. "My brother landed in the snow but he hit his head on a rock but it was only a minor injury. Absolutely nothing happened to me." A compatriot was not so lucky: "We lost one that day. He was in the front. . . . He fell right onto the middle of the tracks [and was run over by the car]. His name was Juan Luis Vargas; he was from Puebla. I will never forget that. We used to sleep in the same room."[52] Although he was shaken by the death of his coworker, Bautista said, "we were tough, we were young. I was 21."[53] The accident caused Bautista to take his work very seriously. No one knew what had caused the derailment, but Bautista was determined to never see one again.

The memories of these men paint a picture of what life was like for many braceros in the Pacific Northwest. Newspapers typically expressed joy and gratefulness upon the arrival of braceros. Most of them were paid at much higher rates than in other places in the Southwest and experienced decent living conditions. Nevertheless, the work was difficult and many of the braceros had to adjust to the life of a farmworker. Working conditions, while better than in many places in the Southwest, still left a lot to be desired. But life as a bracero also meant finding diversions from work life, and the braceros were adept at that as well.

BRACERO SOCIAL LIFE

Braceros labored diligently and sent money home to take care of their families. Sometimes they lived in squalid conditions, did not receive adequate compensation, suffered abuses at the hands of their employers, and had to cope with the death of friends on the job site. Yet these men found ways to deal with the difficult lives they led. They had fun, even though growers only saw them as laborers. They went to dances, flirted with girls, and celebrated patriotic holidays. Braceros found joy in their lives and made themselves visible, despite Anglo attempts to make them invisible. Braceros' recollections of their social lives should not be read simply as nostalgia or an effort to mask the exploitation of the past, but as an expression of their resistance. Throughout the course of my interviews with braceros, they often initially denied having any free time and echoed the sentiment that all they did was work. When this happened, I would tell them about newspaper articles I had found describing the dances and patriotic festivals. A wide grin appeared on their faces and without exception they told me some story of escapades they enjoyed while working as braceros. These stories paint a more complete picture of the braceros and restore a humanity that their employers and the communities that benefited from their presence so often failed to acknowledge.

Surprisingly, braceros found enough time to partake in local entertainment on a fairly regular basis. Jimenez recalled, "Every Thursday and Saturday they had dances in Albany [Oregon]. . . . Those places were packed with women! All their boyfriends had gone off to war!"[54] According to the *Oregon Statesman*, the Portland office of the War Food Administration sent young women to dance with the braceros.[55] When asked if this interaction created any tensions in the community, Jimenez responded, "No way! They were all over us. . . . As long as you had a nice *tacuche* [suit] on they were all over you!"[56] While some Anglo women were undoubtedly paid, others were attracted to the Mexican men. Aware of that fact, Anglo men, and growers in particular, constantly policed the boundary between braceros and local women.

In the Southwest, established Mexican American communities offered braceros the opportunity to court and marry Mexican American women, but in Oregon the lack of a substantial Mexican American enclave meant that braceros often sought out Anglo women.[57] Fear of miscegenation led camp officials to admonish arriving braceros. Contreras recalled, "We were warned about socializing and flirting with gringas. He [the camp manager] told us that if we flirt with gringas they would call the police and take us to jail!"[58] Despite the warnings, braceros continued to socialize with Anglo women and faced few repercussions. Threats to call the police rarely came to fruition. "It wasn't true. The gringas looked for us!"[59] Contreras remembered an incident that demonstrated some women's forwardness. "One time three or four of them came looking for us and took us to a creek. Before I knew it they got naked and jumped in the water! We followed them in . . . and they were Mormon!"[60] Jimenez and Contreras found that the absence of rival men created a unique situation that blurred the lines of race and ethnicity while validating their masculinity. The women's approval demonstrated their masculinity at a time when it might have been called into question because of their subordination at work. Camp managers and growers tried to reiterate and reinforce the lines, but braceros and local women constantly transgressed those boundaries.

Other men found that isolation made it difficult to experience the same kind of freedom. Bautista, who worked in a remote rural area, "almost never went into town." Instead, "we bought beer at the little store and drank in our cabin." "Every now and then," however, "they would put us on a train to Portland. We wouldn't ride on a regular train; we rode in one of those passenger cars, *puro* first class! Sometimes we had no idea where we were going. We just got off wherever the train stopped."[61] If by chance they ended their week's work in the vicinity of a town, they often went exploring. On one occasion their work brought them to the Native American town of Chiloquin, Oregon, home to the Klamath nation. Bautista found that he was attracted to many of the women in Chiloquin and confessed to his boss "Tex" that he believed they were interested in him too: "So he tells me 'Go talk to them,' but what was I going to say? I didn't speak English. But man! They were beautiful; they looked just like Mexican women."[62] The language barrier kept Bautista from pursuing one of the Native American women, but the sense of connection he felt left a strong impression on his mind many years later.

Despite the small size of the Mexican American community in Oregon, it provided a sense of escape and a taste of home for braceros. Some of the men traveled to Salem, Eugene, Portland, and Corvallis for patriotic festivals and to see Mexican movies. The city of Salem, Oregon's state capital, held a Mexican Independence Day celebration on September 16th beginning in 1943. Camp managers vacillated between promoting and forbidding Mexican national holidays. Growers' attempts to entertain the braceros bordered on the comical; on one occasion camp managers planned a party, but according to Contreras the men were disappointed because "Instead of having beer . . . they gave us ice cream!"[63] Contreras recalled some workers voicing their displeasure, but most found it amusing. Growers sought to divert the braceros' attention from their working conditions and wages by occasionally bringing in entertainment. In Contreras's camp, the managers brought in a Latina dance instructor. "Since we were Latinos they wanted to teach us a Latin dance. But she was from Argentina or Brazil or somewhere." Her style of dancing left the men dumfounded. Although most came from urban areas, they had not seen anything like it. "What is with this *zancona*?' (laughs) What an odd thing. She kept jumping and jumping around!"[64] She encouraged anyone who could perform the steps she was trying to teach them to dance with her, but no one obliged. Finally, one of the men stood up and informed her that "We can't dance that way. We are from Mexico."[65] Undaunted, the woman asked for the names of performers and songs that they liked to dance to, and a week later returned with the music in hand. She brought *danzones*, a Cuban musical style popular in Mexico, Agustin Lara records, and other Mexican music. "I don't know how she did it but she found them. She brought one danzon, I remember it well, 'Long Distance Telephone' . . . Cantinflas danced to that danzon."[66] Before Contreras could jump up to dance with her a line of men eager to take their turn had formed. The men began to teach the instructor how to dance like they did. She returned week after week, admitting to the men that she learned more from them than she taught.

Taken collectively, these stories should remind us that while the braceros labored and toiled in difficult jobs, they maintained their humanity. The dances, the visits to town, and the flirting all added to the men's confidence and sense of self-respect. I contend that these small acts of reclaiming space and making themselves visible often led directly to more organized forms of resistance, and in the case of the braceros it appeared to do just that.

RESISTANCE

Initially, employers were pleased with the bracero workforce, praising the workers' pliable nature and their ability to learn quickly. *Northwest Farm News*, a weekly periodical based in Bellingham, Washington, consistently published positive pieces about braceros. One grower stated, "The men are good workers. They want to work and they do the work."[67] But this positive opinion of braceros depended on their compliance. According to one grower's wife, the men acquiesced, saying, "We sure like these new Mexicans, they want to work all the time. . . . They are eager to get their money and send it back to Mexico."[68] In the first few years of the program the *Oregonian* repeatedly published stories of crops being "saved" by Mexicans. In Independence, Forest Grove, and Corvallis, the braceros saved the hop, wheat, and flax industry respectively.[69] Their hard-earned reputation, however, did not last long. Soon braceros began to resist their oppression. Employers in the Northwest met the conditions of the contracts haphazardly and inconsistently at best, and braceros responded to violations with strikes and slowdowns and by skipping out.

One practice called "loading sacks" became so commonplace that camp managers wrote about it extensively in their reports.[70] In the bean harvest, braceros weighted their bags with rocks in order to make their pick heavier and get paid more. Depending on the means available and the type of work being done, braceros adopted a variety of methods to challenge exploitation. Their complaints revolved around three major grievances: housing, food, and wages. Over two dozen strikes broke out within the first three years of the program, and many resulted in improved housing and higher earnings.

Monitoring living conditions at the bracero camps proved to be a particularly difficult task. In 1943, the bracero program had only two inspectors in Portland, Oregon, to oversee all the labor camps in Utah, Idaho, Oregon, Washington, and Montana. Jimenez recalled, "We saw them [inspectors] every now and then to check on the camps."[71] Depending on the worksite, housing varied from comfortable to barely tolerable. At base camps, railroad braceros slept in "house[s] made of railroad ties; we had heaters and a wood stove for cooking."[72] But most of the time braceros worked in remote locations. Railroad crews slept in railroad cars and endured crowded conditions. "You could fit about 10–12 men on the bunk beds. . . . Man, it was cold out there! Snow would come down like you wouldn't believe."[73] Jimenez himself never complained to his bosses about his living conditions and never became involved in direct labor actions. Instead he chose a far more commonplace practice, skipping out.

In Texas and California, braceros easily skipped out on their contracts and could blend in to nearby Mexican American communities or return across the border. The Northwest did not provide those options, yet the competition for braceros in the region drove wages up and allowed braceros to leave unsuitable situations for better pay. Although historian Johanna Ogden argues that braceros were preferable to Mexican American workers in the Northwest because of their inability to leave, camp managers complained more frequently of desertion than anything else.[74] The Work Force Administration (WFA) in Portland estimated that close to 20 percent of braceros had abandoned their contracts in 1945. The WFA categorized this act as "desertion," but the braceros did not desert the Northwest; they simply skipped out on the contract. Jimenez recalled that "people would leave all the time. . . . you could always make more money somewhere else."[75] In a practice that came to be known as bootlegging, growers spread rumors about paying better wages and where their pickup locations were. Intrepid workers followed the rumors and went to pick on neighboring farms. Contreras remembered, "Most of the guys didn't believe it, but a few of us were willing to try anything."[76] A farmer picked them up at the edge of the field and they went to work for him instead. The man who encouraged Contreras to skip out on his contract needed help for just a few months on his small farm because his sons were in the military. The bracero program required growers to ascertain their labor needs, and the larger the request the more likely it would be approved by the Department of Labor. This process put small farmers at a distinct disadvantage. To get around it, they formed growers' associations and made requests collectively; alternatively, they bootlegged.

Bootlegging provided some measure of relief for braceros looking to escape labor camps. During their time on the small farm, Contreras and his friends received a great deal of instruction about how to thin and harvest sugar beets. He received better pay, developed new skills, and bought better tools. Indeed, he never went back to work as an official bracero. Instead, he continued to be bootlegged by local farmers and made significantly better wages: "We made between eighteen and twenty dollars a day! Before that we made three or four!"[77] Eventually Contreras and four of his friends earned enough money to buy an automobile, which enabled them to chase higher wages. The downside of skipping out on their contracts was that without contracts they were undocumented immigrants, which carried the risk of arrest and deportation. For Contreras and others the prospect of making more money overshadowed potential drawbacks. Staying in the program meant receiving unpredictable wages and moving constantly. The reality on the ground was that most braceros were only temporarily braceros. Efforts to distinguish between braceros and undocumented immigrants disregard the fact that often, one person can embody both identities throughout the course of their working life, sometimes even changing from month to month and location to location.

Newspaper reports indicate that companies transported braceros to various locales throughout the three states. The growers associations requested large numbers of braceros and passed them from one member to another. In the Hood River Valley, for instance, six hundred braceros worked in an array of jobs being handed from one farmer to the next, even going as far as being employed as laborers in private homes.[78] Historian Johanna Ogden noted that braceros were "digging basements or doing construction, lay[ing] roads for the county or work[ing] in the lumber industry."[79] Across the region growers used braceros in jobs that fell outside of the purview of their original contracts. Stipulations in the bilateral agreement limited the employment of braceros to agricultural work. Farm Labor Associations began to interpret the stipulations broadly as allowing braceros to work in canneries and other processing facilities. Since many of the growers also owned canneries, they began placing braceros there. While growers could easily justify the need for agricultural laborers by claiming that locals could not or would not work in the fields, cannery work was an entirely different manner. Considered a good job with good wages, cannery employment was long reserved for whites, but cannery owners began to feel stiff competition from the defense industry. Faced with paying white workers higher wages to keep them from leaving for more lucrative jobs, growers instead sought to replace them with a cheaper option, braceros.

The treatment of braceros varied greatly depending on the circumstances, changing on a week-to-week basis. In eastern Oregon and western Idaho, associations that formed near the border included growers from both states. Even though they belonged to the same association, growers often paid different wages. On the whole, braceros in Oregon tended to receive better wages and housing than their counterparts in Idaho. The braceros noticed the difference, particularly when they worked in Idaho one week and in Oregon the next.

Well before the braceros arrived, the Idaho legislature took steps to quash any potential labor activism. The Idaho Sugar Company had imported foreign laborers as early as 1904, and foreign workers made up most of the laboring class in the mining and lumbering industry. The large number of foreign workers attracted the organizing efforts of the Industrial Workers of the World. The IWW's efforts proved successful enough in the mining industry that they briefly turned their attention to the farms. According to one author, the threat to organize the fields was enough to force Governor Moses Alexander to send in the National Guard to break the IWW hold on mining and lumbering lest they organize the whole state.[80] Strife in the fields continued during the 1930s with the rush of migrant workers coming into the state during the Depression. Work stoppages and strikes were common occurrences, and by the time braceros arrived, the anti-worker culture permeated Idaho's power structure.[81] In 1943, the state passed a draconian antiunion law in anticipation of union leaders flooding the state to organize braceros. The law criminalized picketing, prohibited boycotts of agricultural products, and denied union organizers the right to set foot on a farm without the owner's permission.

The rush of labor organizers that lawmakers feared never came, but it did not prevent the braceros from taking up their own fight against unfair labor practices. In the first year of the program, few newspapers reported strikes in the labor camps, but in the second year evidence of braceros' discontent appeared regularly. In Twin Falls, Idaho, 285 braceros went on strike against the Amalgamated Sugar Company for two days in June 1945. They won a raise to 50 cents an hour for harvesting beets, 20 cents above the prevailing wage set by Mexico and the United States. In most of the country employers failed to pay prevailing wages steadily, so these wages were better than expected. Nonetheless, the braceros voiced their displeasure with the way their wages were computed, demanding an hourly rate rather than a piece rate. The more skilled work, thinning and hoeing, paid on a piece rate of eleven dollars an acre; an efficient worker could thin and hoe an average of two acres a day.

Braceros working in the harvest felt underpaid and underappreciated, so they also went on strike. Bracero representative Ruben Gomez called a meeting with the Farm Labor Association of Twin Falls and demanded a wage increase to 80 cents an hour, almost three times the prevailing wage. The employers' association deliberated and offered the braceros 70 cents an hour. The very notion of an employers' association negotiating a pay increase with braceros flies in the face of conventional notions about the powerlessness of braceros. Ruben Gomez accepted the offer on behalf of the men and promised the association no further labor trouble: "If we are paid seventy cents per hour, there will be no more difficulties from now on."[82] County agent Albert Mylroie assured the public that "the agreement will be strictly enforced on both sides . . . and the first worker violating it will be sent back to Mexico."[83] Yet the threat seems to have been empty bravado. If the labor association and the Amalgamated Sugar Company had the desire or the wherewithal to deport braceros, it would have been prudent to do so at the first sign of trouble. Instead, they chose to negotiate with the braceros and came to a settlement.

While labor peace reigned at that labor camp, the braceros' militancy appears to have infected nearby camps. Only two months later on Wednesday, August 7, 1945, a separate group of 170 braceros working at the Lincoln labor camp in Twin Falls staged a strike. The arrival of fifty new braceros from northern Idaho seems to have been at least partially responsible. Stanley Boyle, the placement officer, informed the newspaper, "upon their [the braceros'] arrival they had advised camp officials they would not work at the current sixty cents per hour for common farm labor." Boyle added that the other workers "went to work as usual." The newly arrived braceros had been paid 75 cents an hour at their previous worksite and demanded the same at the Lincoln camp. Contrary to Boyle's claim, the additional 120 braceros stayed out of the fields and refused to go to work. According to Boyle, the other braceros felt threatened by the strike leaders and acquiesced to their demands. What seems more likely is that those in favor of the strike pointed to the success of the earlier Twin Falls strike to convince the other men to take collective action.

The next day 170 braceros lined the fields and ignored camp officials' demands to go back to work. The conflict escalated when three braceros attempted to enter the field. A chorus of boos rained down on them and they backtracked almost immediately. Fearing for their safety, they jumped into a contractor's car and left without delay, presumably for another worksite. Still believing that the strike leaders were pressuring braceros to stay away from work, Boyle and other camp officials called in the sheriff's office. They told the sheriff and his deputies that a riot was developing and that strike leaders were forcibly preventing braceros from working. When confronted by the police, the braceros maintained a strict discipline and remained calm. The sheriff informed the men that officers would offer them protection if they decided to return to work. No one took them up on their offer. Camp officials were stunned and had no other choice but to negotiate with the striking braceros. They raised the men's wages to 70 cents an hour. The strike committee promptly accepted the offer, and the men returned to work the following Monday. The fact that the braceros stood up not only to their employer but also to law enforcement officers is astonishing. Typically, sheriffs landed squarely on the side of employers and often resorted to violence to force striking workers back into the fields. The ability to force growers to negotiate is indicative of the strong bargaining position that braceros held.[84]

As braceros won victory after victory—disturbances, strikes, work stoppages, and walkouts occurred monthly. Growers tried desperately to maintain some sort of leverage over the men, but the more time the braceros spent in the Northwest the more astute they became and the more opportunities for resistance they created for themselves. As workers like Contreras and Jimenez took advantage of these situations, growers began to take notice. One Anglo camp manager summed up the common belief that workers should be constantly recycled through the bracero program: "In the first year they are very cooperative, in the second year they are too smart for their own good, the third they begin to think they are running things, and by the fourth they expect to take over."[85] Some took the advice to heart; an unidentified camp manager told a Farm Extension employee that at his camp he tried to replace braceros who had returned for three straight seasons. When he arrived with replacements, the old braceros staged a sit-in at one of the barracks. The manager then returned with law enforcement officers who attempted to remove the braceros. The scene so disturbed the replacement braceros that they too began to sit in and refused to work. Scenes like these were repeated in Yakima and Walla Walla, Washington; Notus, Idaho; and elsewhere across the Northwest.[86]

The sentiment that braceros grew more militant the longer they were in the country, appeared regularly in local newspapers. One camp manager told the *Northwest Farm News*, "I conscientiously believe, we would have a better working condition if we had a yearly change"[87] of braceros. Although the managers' statements about the potential power of braceros indicate obvious apprehension and a degree of paranoia, it is clear that the more time that workers spent in the United States, the more aggressively they asserted their rights. The number of bracero contracts issued each year in the Northwest tailed off over the five-year period that the program operated in the region while labor demand stayed virtually the same, indicating that thousands of braceros continued to work in the region after their contracts had expired or skipped out on their contracts altogether.

Despite growers' hard-line stance toward labor militancy, in many instances their hands were tied. In the Southwest a steady flow of braceros and undocumented workers forced wages down and provided a plentiful reserve of potential replacement workers, but the relatively small numbers of braceros in the Northwest made that very difficult. Small numbers, however, did not mean small impact. According to Ogden and Gamboa, the number of "placements" far outstripped the number of braceros. In other words, the braceros continued to be recontracted and had a tremendous impact on the harvest.[88]

The remoteness of the border contributed to both the small number of braceros and their militancy in the Northwest; it was difficult and expensive for the federal government to continuously recycle braceros through the program. The long distance between the contracting center and the farms meant that valuable time would be lost if growers tried to import new braceros. Time was the one thing that growers with perishable crops to harvest did not have. Growers had to give in to some of the demands in order to get the men back to work. These conditions made the Northwest a hotbed of labor unrest as braceros took advantage of the situation. When the braceros recognized the same faces at camps and noticed the managers' willingness to negotiate, the groundwork was laid for successful acts of resistance.

COMMUNITY CONFLICTS AND CONSULAR MEDIATION

The level of resistance in the fields sets the Northwest apart from the history of the bracero program in other parts of the country, and one major contributing factor was the advocacy of the Mexican consulate. The presence of a vociferous Mexican consulate in the area emboldened braceros. Mexican consuls have played varied roles in the Mexican community in the United States. The consulate has vacillated between having no interest in the plight of Mexican immigrants, and being a crucial defender of the rights of Mexican workers.[89] For the most part, the consulate has operated on a conservative and nationalistic premise that has proven ineffective in mobilizing working-class support. In Southern California, the consuls acted against the interests of braceros. Critics such as Ernesto Galarza charged that the Mexican consulate was an impediment to labor organizing and failed to take contract violations seriously. Galarza's National Farm Workers Union drew the ire of the Mexican consulate when it pointed out growers' use of braceros as strikebreakers despite the provisions of the bilateral agreement. In the Northwest the consulate took on a decidedly different role, going to great lengths to protect braceros from abuses and to negotiate on their behalf during strikes.

The consulates in Salt Lake City and Portland stood out as staunch defenders of braceros. The small numbers of other Mexican immigrants in the region and the consulates' locations appear to have given the Northwest consulate's staff slightly more autonomy than their counterparts in Southern California. One incident is particularly telling. In an inspection of labor camps, Alfonso Guerra, assistant secretary of Mexican foreign affairs, noticed Jim Crow–style segregation signs directed at Mexicans in various Idaho towns. Just outside of Boise, Idaho, establishments in Nampa and Caldwell had signs that read "No Mexicano Aqui" and "We Cater to White Trade Only" hung in their windows. The official responded to the problem by threatening to remove all braceros from Idaho. The agreement prohibited discrimination, and if Idaho did not stop the open exclusion of Mexicans it could be barred from the program, as Texas had been. When

Idaho farmers did not respond to the allegations, Ignacio Pesqueira, the Mexican consul in Portland, banned Idaho from importing braceros. On October 12, 1945, Pesqueira wrote to the Idaho Employment Service: "I have been directed to inform you that employers in Idaho are hereby suspended from importation of nationals from my country . . . this suspension is prompted by discrimination against our nationals on social and economic grounds."[90]

The Notus Farm Labor Committee, which represented growers, acted quickly to meet with Caldwell business owners and had the signs removed from restaurants and bars. The committee clearly understood the importance of the braceros to members' operations: "We have worked hard to get labor in here and it is doing us a service. . . . If by our discriminating signs we are to lose the labor it will be a blow to the farmers of this area."[91] Twenty miles east in Nampa, the Franklin Farm Association met with the Nampa Chamber of Commerce to protest the placement of crudely written "Trafico Blanco Solo" signs from stores. In a letter sent to the business group, grower Arthur L. Wittenberger stated: "The signs are irritating to the workers and to their government, whose cooperation is necessary to the continuation of the laborers."[92] As in Caldwell, the chamber of commerce capitulated to the request of the farm labor association. These conflicts underline the tensions generated among whites in Idaho by the presence of Mexicans. Eliminating Jim Crow signs and yielding to labor pressures are indications of the braceros' determination and the Mexican consuls' resolve. It also reveals the relatively weak bargaining position of Northwest growers when faced with organized workers and their nation's representatives, as well as the pressure they could bring to bear on local businesses.

The consul also had to intervene on the behalf of braceros when many white workers began to complain of being displaced from nonagricultural jobs. The displacement of white workers by braceros caused a stir, but growers continued to use braceros in the canneries despite protests from the Anglo community. The local extension service, which was responsible for placing braceros on worksites, refused to certify workers in these new jobs and warned growers not to assign them to nonagricultural tasks. Farmers ignored the threats and countered that cannery work was a form of agricultural labor. Growers came to rely heavily on braceros in a range of jobs that violated their contracts. Eventually the extension service's fears came to fruition. In Washington, towns like, Kennewick, Mt. Vernon, Prosser, Puyallup, Seattle, Walla Walla, and Wenatchee all saw instances of white workers protesting and picketing canneries.[93] These confrontations frequently erupted into violence against braceros. As the tension spilled over, it generated friction between canneries run by association members and independent canneries, whose owners felt that employing bracero labor provided association canneries with an unfair advantage. The division yielded an unexpected benefit for the braceros. When the association canneries refused to give up bracero labor, independent canneries responded by "bootlegging" the bracero workforce. Braceros jumped ship and went to work for the better-paying canneries. Employers eager to acquire the labor of braceros paid the braceros more than they could earn by working in the fields. Soon this situation was replicated in other industries, such as nurseries and packing sheds.[94] By the end of 1946, the Work Force Administration had issued an official statement informing canneries and other employers that hiring braceros without a contract violated the law and would incur sanctions. The practice, however, did not end, and there is little evidence that employers ever were punished. The main result was that competition for bracero labor grew more intense, increasing the upward pressure on wages and putting braceros in a better bargaining position.[95]

Braceros were at the center of tensions between growers and canners and faced hostility from white workers and local residents. They also faced confrontations with other groups of racialized workers. The *Idaho Statesman* reported that in Emmett a "colorful harvest" began with "Mexican nationals . . . Gypsies and transient Filipinos."[96] Farmer Louis Mort commented, "It is quite a sight, probably the most picturesque aspect of the scene being the colorful costumes of the Gypsies."[97] Tom Hicks of the United States Employment Service added that he saw "imported Mexicans, Japanese-Americans, Southern Negroes, somber Indians, Southern Whites . . . and colorfully garbed Armenian Gypsies all working together." But this exuberance about the "colorful" workers in the fields was soon replaced by stories about rising tensions and eruptions of violence.

Twin Falls, Idaho, was the scene of a violent confrontation between Jamaican guest workers and southern whites over the use of laundry facilities. The disturbance began when a white southerner, James Visser, struck a Jamaican camp supervisor who was attempting to quell an argument between Visser and an unnamed Jamaican. The half-hour-long brawl ended without serious injury but landed Visser in the county jail. Perhaps, accustomed to the racial order in the South, Visser's father was irate that his son was being held for striking a black man. The elder Visser threatened more violence if his son was not released. When pressed, he backed off and declared that he was moving his family out of the labor camp and that "several other white workers are doing the same thing."[98]

In Weiser, Idaho, a "near riot" broke out between Mexicans and Jamaicans after the Mexicans complained about the food they were served by the Jamaican cooks. Braceros told the sheriff who arrived on the scene that the Jamaican cooks gave the best food to other Jamaican guest workers. The Mexican guest workers dumped their food on the mess hall floor in protest. The men refused to go back to work until they received assurances that Mexicans would also be allowed to cook. The favorable resolution of these flare-ups for the braceros indicates that they occupied a position of relative strength. They leveraged the need for their labor into better treatment that extended beyond wages to living conditions.[99]

At the same time, it also made them prime targets for recruitment whenever any labor shortage appeared. Uncertified farmers, rogue contractors, and canneries all vied for the labor of the braceros, which contributed to their assertiveness. Soon an unexpected player threw its hat into the ring. In 1944, the National Forest Service (NFS) began to recruit braceros to work on fire crews and in reforestation in an attempt to keep them in the region. J. R. Beck, state supervisor of the emergency farm labor program, announced in the *Oregonian*: "now that the canning pea and cherry harvest are completed . . . there will be about 600 Mexicans in excess of farm demands until the middle of August. . . . If not employed they may be moved to the Middle West."[100] Fearing the loss of the braceros to Midwest farmers, state officials put them to work in the forest. Soon they moved from reforestation work into firefighting.

During the summer of 1945, numerous fires broke out near the Coeur d'Alene National Forest and the Nez Perce National Forest in Idaho. The shortage of available firefighters prompted the National Forest Service to bring in braceros from nearby labor camps. The blazes destroyed more than 20,000 acres and required an intense amount of labor to put out. Department of Agriculture official Jose Romero reassigned 210 braceros from labor camps in eastern Oregon and western Idaho to major fires. Braceros who worked in the forests performed a wide range of tasks, including digging fire lines, planting trees, and spraying for pests. Unlike working in cannery or packing jobs, braceros often had no choice when it came to working for the NFS. Despite the WFA's insistence that the men go voluntarily, the NFS rarely complied. Rounded up and put into trucks, braceros did not know their destination until they reached the forest. In the spring of 1945 braceros replanted 400,000 white pine seedling trees in the Coeur d'Alene national forest and also worked in Blister Rust control and insect control programs.[101] Although initially regarded as an emergency measure, the practice became routine.[102]

While job competition created higher wages in other sectors, the NFS paid considerably lower wages. Francisco Murillo Almaraz was contracted as a reforestation worker in Oregon. He made slightly better wages than he did in California, but that was not enough to keep him in Oregon. Almaraz complained, "It was too cold . . . and too many snakes."[103] Skipping out on his contract proved decidedly more difficult; Almaraz had to spend three months in the forest before he could finally come back into town and abandon his contract. He returned to Enpalme, Sonora, and then found a new contract that kept him in California. We know very little about the braceros who worked in the forests. Almaraz's short story is indicative of the high turnover rate for braceros in the industry. Newspaper accounts consistently mention the presence of braceros fighting forest fires, digging fire lines, thinning trees, and replanting trees.[104] The braceros were the forerunner of undocumented workers who toiled in the forests during the coming decades.

The end of the war brought administrative changes in the bracero program that put power back into the growers' hands. Mexico held a strategic bargaining position during the war that forced the United States to make an effort to protect the rights of braceros in the country, but the need for a food surplus no longer existed when the war ended. With soldiers returning from the war and looking for jobs, growers felt they no longer had to bend to the will of braceros. Strikes occurred with less frequency, and braceros' advocates felt the repercussions. Ignacio Pesquiera, the Mexican consul, had often encouraged workers to go on strike and assert their rights as workers under the arrangements made in their contracts. He mediated various strikes throughout the region and, more often than not, the outcomes favored the braceros.[105] However, his policy of defending the braceros came to an end with the end of the war. He was transferred to New Orleans and replaced by Carlos Grimm.

Despite the end of the war and the removal of their staunchest advocate, the braceros continued to take militant action. In June 1946, over 1,000 braceros and non-braceros walked out of the Nampa labor camp, along with surrounding camps, to protest working conditions as well as wages. The strike lasted from June 17 until June 26, when Consul Carlos Grimm intervened. At its peak the strike involved five hundred braceros in four different labor camps. The existence of cooperation between braceros and non-braceros belies the notion that braceros were always in competition with non-braceros. In this case the braceros made up half the striking workers and called in the Mexican consul to mediate. The strikers agreed to return to work for ten days until a meeting could be held between local farm officials and the Mexican consul. Ten days later, Carlos Grimm still had not shown up and the men went back on strike.

Grimm responded by sending a telegram urging the braceros to return to work. For two consecutive nights farm labor officials met with representatives of the workers who promised that the men would return to work the following morning, but the workers continued the strike. The walkout continued for eight days, forcing Grimm to appear in person. Farm labor officials met with the Mexican consul and refused to give in to the strikers' demands. The hourly rate was set at 60 cents, a dime less than the workers had demanded. For years the braceros had been able to count on the Mexican consulate to represent them in labor negotiations and keep their best interests in mind. The end of the war brought not only the end of the relationship between braceros and the consulate but also the demise of their bargaining position based on the severe shortage of labor.[106]

CONCLUSION

As the war ended, so did the bracero program in the Northwest. The story of the braceros in the region is a story of resourceful resistance. Braceros pushed the limits of power beyond what most historians have given them credit for.[107] They understood the pressures on growers and took advantage of them to gain whatever benefits they could. Despite Mexico's privileged negotiating position, the men still risked a great deal to stand up for their rights. Braceros in the Northwest succeeded more often than their counterparts in other regions. Unfortunately for braceros, postwar changes to the program took much of the power out of the Mexican government's hand, a shift that could be seen in the growing ineffectiveness of the consul. It was during the postwar period that many of the most heinous abuses against braceros occurred. The demise of the bracero program in the Northwest was not a foregone conclusion. Although the wartime emergency that had served as the major rationale for importing Mexican nationals ended, employers sought to continue utilizing this source of cheap labor and successfully lobbied for the program's continuation. In April 1947, Public Law 40 extended the bracero program until 1964. But the legislation included provisions that made it too costly for growers in the Northwest to participate. The most important among those provisions stipulated that the federal government would no longer pay the cost of recruiting, screening, and transporting Mexican workers. All future contracts would be negotiated between employers and the braceros themselves. Growers in the Southwest had long advocated for this system because they felt that the original version of the program placed unnecessary burdens on them. In reality, growers were resentful of the stipulations put in place by the federal governments of both Mexico and the United States, and they were delighted to be able to negotiate contracts without government "meddling." For those in the Southwest, the power it gave them was well worth incurring the extra costs it entailed. But for growers in the Northwest, the expense of transporting Mexican nationals was prohibitive.

Oregon growers and their political allies argued that the new policy discriminated against growers so far from the border and threatened their productivity and livelihood. They claimed that the round trip from a labor-recruiting center in Mexico City to Oregon took seven days and cost close to $160 per worker. The fact that braceros earned on average of around $200 after deductions for an entire season made the new arrangement unprofitable for them. According to one report, Medford was the only county that continued to import braceros after the changes.[108] The report stated that the need for braceros stemmed from a lack of family housing that attracted migrant families in other parts of the state. The Oregon Bureau of Labor reported that between 1947 and 1957, Oregon imported an average of less than 700 braceros a year, down from the wartime high of nearly 5,000.[109]

Even before the end of the war, growers in the Northwest grew weary of the militant braceros and began exploring alternative sources of labor. The Oregon State College Extension Service, which provided advice to farmers, voiced serious concern: "It is reasonable to expect that the transported labor program will not continue long and unless local arrangements are made to maintain an adequate supply of labor . . . farmers will be forced to change the type of agriculture drastically or suffer enormous financial losses because of lack of necessary help to harvest crops."[110] The *Northwest Farm News* warned its readers that "no industry can long afford to remain [dependent] on the seasonal importation of foreign labor."[111] Growers heeded their advice, and the number of braceros rapidly dwindled.

The presence of braceros in the Northwest has had a lasting impact. Workers suffered hardships and trying times like their counterparts in other parts of the country, but the program also afforded many of these men an opportunity to better their lives and, simply, to enjoy an adventure. The braceros triggered a large-scale migration of Mexican Americans and Mexican immigrants to the Northwest. Many of the men returned as undocumented immigrants after their contracts expired; some made the region their home and brought family and friends.

From the beginning of the recruitment of braceros, local Anglos worried about the possibility that the braceros would stay. The *Hood River News, Oregonian, Oregon Statesman*, and a host of others continually reassured their readers that the Mexicans were not staying.[112] The *Farm Labor News* promised its readers that "just as fast as men and women from the war plants show a desire to take over the jobs the Mexicans are now doing, the Mexicans will be repatriated."[113] On January 11, 1948, the *Oregonian* proclaimed the return to normalcy on Oregon's farms and announced, "The farmer can again get his cherries picked without wondering how to say it in Spanish."[114] The newspaper echoed the sentiments of the majority of the white population; they believed that the presence of Mexicans in the Northwest had been an aberration, a temporary evil brought about by wartime conditions. Local whites believed that "the Mexican nationals are gone and won't be coming back."[115]

The *Oregonian* was partially right: the braceros did not come back as braceros, but the flow of ethnic Mexicans and Mexican nationals into the Northwest had just begun. In spite of the troubles that braceros caused them, the growers persisted in the belief that Mexicans were suited for fieldwork. In their never-ending pursuit of cheap labor, growers continued to seek out Mexican farmworkers. An unidentified grower quoted by the newspaper indicated his intention: "In eastern Oregon we will still be recruiting Mexicans, this time from Texas and California, to work in the sugar beets."[116] The Texas-Mexicans (Tejanos) whom the grower mentioned came to dominate ethnic Mexican migration to the Northwest for the next twenty years.

2 ⇥ LOS TEJANOS

The Texas-Mexican Diaspora in Oregon

After the war, when returning veterans did not fill the ranks of farm-workers in the Pacific Northwest, growers once again looked south for labor. Many Anglo growers in the Northwest grew accustomed to the cheap and reliable labor of the braceros, but the costs of employing braceros under the terms of the postwar program were prohibitive. Braceros had also grown increasingly militant, and growers consequently grew tired of them. Since braceros were no longer a reliable or cheap option, growers found an ample supply of ethnic Mexican workers in Texas.[1] Recruited by small-scale growers, labor contractors, and large corporations such as the Amalgamated Sugar Company, Tejanos—ethnic Mexicans from Texas—began migrating to the Northwest in the early 1950s and continued to do so well into the 1980s. Unlike the braceros, the Tejanos rarely attempted to organize work stoppages or strikes. Instead, they resisted in more indirect ways, forging a vibrant cultural community and claiming space in a predominantly Anglo society. Tejanos sank roots in the Northwest, challenging preconceived notions of their migratory nature. Women in particular played a crucial role in settling migrant families.[2] They carved out a social space through music, dance halls, and businesses, and fought over public space.[3] Three major factors contributed to the Tejanos' ability to settle in the Northwest. First, their status as American citizens and their English language proficiency emboldened them to challenge a much milder form of racism than they experienced in Texas. Second, Tejanos found work opportunities in food processing and other arenas that allowed them to stay year round. And third, Nisei farm owners provided the space, in terms of housing and recreation, for Tejano culture to flourish.

The postwar expansion of the bracero program in the Southwest had significant, although indirect, effects on the Northwest. The recruitment and use of undocumented labor and the continued use of bracero labor near the border pushed ethnic Mexicans on the US side north. In 1957 Oregon received the sixth-most migrants of any state in the country, behind California, Texas, Michigan,

New York, and Florida.[4] Contractors serving large growers in California and other states near the border recruited not only legal braceros but also unprecedented numbers of undocumented workers. Employers used the deliberate oversupply of labor to lower wages, and the influx of new immigrants displaced residents of the Rio Grande Valley and other border communities. Tejanos whose wages and living standards were being undermined by the intense competition for employment and the mechanization of Texas agriculture began trekking north to the Midwest and the Pacific Northwest.[5] They worked and eventually settled in many different agricultural communities and became a diasporic presence across the country, a fact that Oregonians were acutely aware of.[6] In 1958, the *Oregon Journal* called for an end to the bracero program and a stop to undocumented immigration because of the growing im/migrant population in Oregon: "while Oregon does not use large numbers of bracero workers, they are extensively used in Texas . . . and therefore push many migrants working in the South into Oregon . . . these workers [undocumented] also push many 'Texican' migrant families into Oregon."[7]

JAPANESE AMERICAN FARMERS IN MALHEUR COUNTY

The opportunities that ethnic Mexicans from Texas found in the Northwest resulted in part from the expansion of cultivation made possible by the completion of two dams that brought water to arid regions of eastern Washington and Oregon, as well as Idaho. The Owyhee Dam, completed in 1932, irrigated 192,000 acres of land in Oregon and Idaho. Its success provided the impetus for an even larger project. The Bonneville Dam on the Columbia River, completed in 1937, irrigated nearly three million acres of previously unusable, sagebrush-covered land and ushered in a mass migration of farmers. Malheur County, in the southeastern corner of Oregon, was among the places that benefited immensely from immigration; between 1930 and 1940, the population of the nearly 10,000 square-mile county nearly doubled from 11,269 to 19,767.[8]

Japanese Americans were among those who flocked to eastern Oregon for the opportunity to farm. In 1940, Oregon's ethnic Japanese population of 4,958 was concentrated in the Hood River Valley, the Willamette Valley, and Portland, with only 137 living in Malheur County, 25 of whom were classified as "farm operators."[9] The public eviction notice that was handed down in the wake of Pearl Harbor divided Oregon awkwardly into military zones to include pockets of large Japanese communities. According to historian Janet Nishihara, "Nikkei were allowed to remain in Oregon as long as they were outside Zone 1 and 2, those already living in Zone 3, and in particular the eastern part of the state, were allowed to stay. This area came to be known as the 'Free Zone.'" The "voluntary relocation" required proof of private employment or sponsorship by friends or relatives. Many of those who had earned a living as farmworkers and truck farmers before they were forcibly relocated saw eastern Oregon as offering them a chance to reestablish family farms and provided the prospect of recovery from the displacement.[10]

The Japanese who moved to eastern Oregon were mainly Nisei—that is, they had been born in the United States and, unlike their parents who were forbidden by law from becoming naturalized, were citizens. Joe Saito Sr., a truck farmer in Clackamas County, Oregon, had fallen on hard times during the Depression and struggled to recover. Fortunately, his family and a few other Japanese farmers moved to eastern Oregon before they faced forced relocation. Joe Saito Jr. recalled, "My dad came up here [Ontario] and saw that onions were growing everywhere and he knew some Japanese people who lived here that were from the same area of Japan that his folks came from. . . . They helped us out and we got started."[11] Shigeo "Sig" and Mitzuko "Mitzi" Murakami, who were both born in Washington, came to eastern Oregon after a short stay in Los Angeles in order to avoid relocation. In an oral history conducted by the Snake River Valley chapter of the Japanese American Citizens League, Mitzi Murakami recalled her impressions when the couple arrived in Ontario: "When we first came here it was so desolate and so cold that I wasn't happy at all. The population I think was less than a thousand."[12] The Murakamis eventually turned that barren land into one of the biggest onion farms in the state.

Other Japanese Americans who came to Ontario, especially the American-born children of Japanese immigrants, were well-educated, middle-class professionals but were forced to relocate to the rural area in order to avoid internment. Joe Komoto was born in Los Angeles and spent most of his childhood in the Willamette Valley. His father Gaichiro owned a small farm and was able to afford to send his son to college. Joe earned a degree in pharmacy from Oregon State College in Corvallis but barely had a chance to use it. Less than a year after he graduated, the war began and the presidential order removing people of Japanese descent from the West Coast was issued. The Komotos scrambled to find an alternative to the dire prospect of internment. A classmate from Oregon State, Roy Hashitani, came to the aid of the Komotos. Hashitani lived in Ontario and sponsored Joe so that he could move his family there. Robert Komoto, Joe's son, recalled, "The Hashitanis had been farming this area for quite some time. So he gave my dad a job as a crew boss."[13] Because of the requirements for "voluntary relocation," many Japanese Americans came to work in the fields as farmworkers and contractors for the small Japanese farmers already there.

With wartime hysteria and racism rampant across the western states, Ontario proved to be a safe haven. Japanese Americans owned land and businesses and even had the backing of Elmo Smith, Ontario's mayor and the future governor of Oregon. Smith owned and operated the local newspaper, the *Ontario Observer*, where he often editorialized against racial prejudice and poor treatment of the Japanese. By 1920, the thriving Japanese American community had built a Japanese Hall to serve as their social center. After the United States and Japan went to war the Japanese community, out of necessity but also as a sign of trust, signed over the deed to their hall to the city. The Nisei anticipated that putting their hall into the hands of the city would give whites a vested interest in protecting it from vandals and hoped that the city would return it to them after the war. True to its reputation, the city returned ownership of the hall to the Nisei at war's end. The Japanese Hall would later serve as an important cultural space for Mexican immigrants as well.[14]

The presence of Japanese Americans in the area prior to World War II made Ontario's whites more receptive to the new arrivals. The Commercial Club of Weiser, Idaho, in a letter to Oregon governor Sprague, expressed a desire to continue employing the Japanese after the war. An anecdote from Gaichiro Komoto's life illustrates the extent to which white residents had adjusted to dealing with the Japanese. Gaichiro's daughter-in-law remembered, "Joe's father [Gaichiro] says in Japanese 'oh these pants do not have the quality I want' and the Caucasian clerk comes over and says in Japanese, 'oh this is the highest quality of material you can get.' In Japanese! We were shocked."[15] This was in stark contrast to Idaho, where many towns passed ordinances prohibiting the speaking of "languages of countries with which the United States is at war," by which they meant Japanese.[16] The hostility in Idaho no doubt influenced them to settle instead in eastern Oregon, for example, across the border in Idaho towns like Weiser, which implemented a curfew on Japanese Americans, while Ontario did not.

Continuing to advocate on behalf of Japanese Americans even after the federal order mandating the internment of Japanese—including U.S. citizens—who lived in the military exclusion zone on the West Coast, and mindful of local farmers' need for labor, Elmo Smith used his newspaper to lobby the War Relocation Authority for the release of seventeen Japanese internees from the nearby camp in Minidoka, Idaho, to work in the fields of Malheur County. The Amalgamated Sugar Company took this one step further and convinced President Roosevelt to allow evacuees to work in Malheur County.[17] Several hundred Japanese families moved into the labor camp across from the sugar refinery in Nyssa, Oregon. Smith and his ilk were so persuasive that by war's end the number of former internees working in Malheur County numbered 5,000, the largest number of free Japanese anywhere in the country.[18]

The War Relocation Authority quickly realized that Japanese Americans' agricultural skills could enable the feeding of camp inmates. Still, those who were released often headed to Malheur County. Komoto played a role in recruiting workers from the nearby camp in Minidoka, Idaho. Japanese American labor contractors became an essential component of the growing Nisei farming community. Many of these contractors had access to the internment camps, where they actively sought out internees and convinced them to leave the camps and work in the fields. The internees approached the possibility of nominal freedom with caution. Despite the promises of employers and the assurances of Mayor Smith, many internees were reluctant to leave the camps at first. Anti-Japanese rhetoric and violence permeated Idaho, and the internees had no reason to believe that Ontario was any better.[19] In fact the vehement racism of Idaho governor Clark forced the Japanese already in Idaho to resist the relocation of the "free zoners."[20] Japanese American Citizens League leaders often voiced opposition to the new arrivals and consistently criticized their behavior and use of the Japanese language instead of English.[21]

Free Japanese continued to travel to the camps to recruit workers. In the end the Minidoka camp led the way, with the most internees out on working assignments. Joe Komoto urged his friends in Minidoka to come to Ontario, reassuring them that it was friendly and safe. One of the first people he persuaded was his future brother-in-law. Joe's wife, Nelly Komoto, recalled, "Well, first he convinced my brother to come out of the camps and later my parents; they were a little more [fearful] about leaving."[22] When they left, they worked in the fields and lived in nearby Adrian, Oregon. Many families initially went to work for Joe and other Nisei contractors, but the ex-internees quickly found other work. Joe's son Bob Komoto recalled, "At first my dad had a lot of Japanese working for him, but after a few years they all went on to other jobs. All of 2nd Avenue became Japanese business[es]."[23]

Malheur County became a popular destination for "free zoners." Many anticipated a day when they could return to their homes, and the proximity of Malheur County to the West Coast would facilitate the move when the time came. After the war, however, anti-Japanese forces in Hood River, Gresham, and Forest Grove, led by the American Legion, created the Japanese Exclusion League in an effort to prevent the West Coast evacuees from returning. Few of the displaced farmers had been able to retain the deeds to their lands, and they had nothing to go home to. In reality few returned; close to half of the wartime "free zoners" remained in Ontario. Those who did return to their former lands faced harassment, exclusion, and violence to such an extent that FBI agents often provided protection to the returnees. The prewar population dropped by as much as 50 percent in those areas.[24] The new arrivals to Malheur County joined the longer-term residents to establish a vibrant community complete with a Buddhist temple, tofu factory, appliance stores, insurance agencies, grocery stores, and restaurants. The fields proved to be a temporary station for the Japanese as they moved into professional roles after the war. Soon the Japanese exodus from the fields left Japanese farmers in need of workers. The influx of Tejanos filled their labor needs.[25]

TEJANO FAMILIES

Before the bracero era only large corporations and growers experimented with importing Mexican labor. The Utah-Idaho Sugar Company had been recruiting Mexicans since the 1920s; Mexican nationals as well as Mexican Americans migrated to toil in its sugar beet fields in Oregon, Minnesota, and Delaware.[26] Sugar beets are an extremely labor-intensive crop that requires up to eight months of thinning and weeding, and the company's profits depended on having a reliable workforce. Sugar beet workers were paid piece rates, with wives and children being paid separately, and 51 percent of beet growers used an end of the harvest bonus in an attempt to keep workers on the farm. In places like Nyssa, Oregon, the company took advantage of its beet fields and built a sugar refinery plant that had to be staffed. During the war, as white farmworkers steadily left the fields in search of better wages in the defense industry or were drafted, the Utah-Idaho company initially imported braceros in large numbers. The sugar refinery's promise of year-round work attracted Tejano migrants to fill the void left by the braceros.

By the 1950s an estimated 40,000 migrants came to Oregon every year, and newspapers consistently reported on the growing number of Tejano families.[27] A Bureau of Labor survey revealed that the average age of the head of a household was 36 years old, with more than half having more than five children. Most had been coming to Oregon for less than three years, coinciding with the end of the bracero program, and an overwhelming 78 percent of the families considered Texas their home residence but worked in Oregon an average of six months. The average pay per person ranged from $0.70 an hour to $1.12 an hour, but these numbers depended heavily on weather and crop conditions, with weekly earnings varying anywhere from $19.28 to $41.80.[28] A profile written by Joe Bianco of the *Oregonian* followed a typical migrant family consisting of Pedro Sanchez Martinez, his wife, and their five children, through the fields of Oregon. The Sanchez's, originally from Texas, earned $25 a day working in strawberries, beans, beets, and potatoes, and told the reporter that they could make more money in Oregon than in Texas. Two of the five children, ages 12 and 9, worked with their parents and lived in a wooden shack next to a junkyard; according to Bianco it was difficult to distinguish between the shack and the junkyard.[29] The *Ontario Argus* observed that some Mexican Americans returned each season: "Concerning the domestic [migrant] Mexicans, there seems to be a trend for certain families to return to the areas and neighborhoods where they found employment a year ago. In fact, one family near Vale is here for the third time and brought their neighbors with them this year."[30]

Previous migrants played a key role in bringing new migrants with them on return trips. Although the news report suggests that the process was organic, those migrants often contracted their own family members at the behest of the companies, essentially acting and being compensated as labor contractors. The experiences of the Rivera sisters, Mercedes, Juanita, and Josefa, exemplify this process. The sisters were second-generation Tejanas born in El Indio, Texas. Their father operated a cotton gin but did not earn enough money to provide for his family, so he looked for another occupation. Their maternal uncle, Diego Martinez, was employed by the Utah-Idaho Sugar Company as a contractor and urged them to go to the Treasure Valley to work. Like many migrants, the Rivera sisters worked in Payette, Idaho, but lived in a nearby labor camp in Ontario, Oregon. Josefa was shocked by the poor living conditions. "We had just one room with a bunch of cots. Each house did not have its own bathroom. You had two in the middle [of the labor camp] where the washrooms were, one for the women and one for the men. And the toilets were a hole outside."[31] More often than not the labor camps were leftovers from the bracero era, with nearly 85 percent being built before 1952.

The Oregon Bureau of Labor and the Oregon Migrant Health Project conducted surveys of the camps in 1958, 1962, 1966, and 1968.[32] Staff members went into the fields and collected information on 242 contractors and crew leaders and visited hundreds of labor camps throughout the state, with a majority of them located in Malheur County.[33] During the bracero era, when the federal government operated and managed the housing units, it maintained a decent level of sanitation, but after the war the camps fell into disrepair and growers bought many units cheaply. The owners raised the cost for farmworkers without paying for upkeep, so conditions worsened. The living conditions were not suitable for single men, let alone entire families, yet 75 percent of migrant families lived in one-room units.[34] The 1958 survey found that migrant families paid over 50 percent of their wages for housing; 63 percent lived in a single room with no plumbing, heating, cooking appliances, or refrigeration, while at the same time reporting that the cost to growers averaged about $2.00 a square foot. A little more than 50 percent of the camps had water-drinking facilities, and 20 percent of those were judged to be unsatisfactory. There were flush toilets reported in 80 percent of the camps, but upon inspection only half of those passed muster with the Oregon State Board of Health.[35] The camps got worse over time. The initial survey led to public outcry in the media, with one newspaper urging its readers "to visit a migrant camp. The migrant problem in Oregon is your problem too, and it may grow bigger."[36]

Despite these findings, the state government did little about the horrendous living conditions, which often continued to deteriorate. A decade later, in the 1968 survey, 88 percent of the camps had no running water and 89 percent had no refrigeration. Camp owners occasionally received fines and warnings but were rarely forced to close down; between 1958 and 1965, only four labor camps closed down permanently.[37] Typically, it was labor contractors who faced discipline and not the growers themselves. In 1962, near Hillsboro, Oregon, the Oregon Bureau of Labor charged labor contractor James Gray with "general irresponsibility" for the conditions in his camp. Al Heffner, the bureau inspector, said he found the camps with "dirty privies, unrepaired cabins, and no facilities for showers or hot water."[38] Heffner found another camp on the property of berry farmer Frank Tankersley in similar disrepair. Heffner testified at Gray's hearing that workers "jumped into [his] car" begging to be taken away from the camp. The charges against Gray were dismissed. Even when camps were closed after inspection, they often reopened when new migrants arrived.[39]

The survey, which laid the conditions of migrant life bare, led to a five-hour-long hearing before the Oregon Interim Committee on Migratory Labor in Portland. Thomas G. Current, the assistant commissioner of labor, testified that "All through the main recruiting area in Texas, the word was that the Texas exodus to Oregon was to begin early this year, the contractors and recruiters moved the migrants to Malheur County area as much as seven weeks early."[40] When the migrants arrived they found there was no work and were forced to run up bills at local grocery stores that would later be deducted from their pay. Contractors often had lucrative side contracts with grocers that paid them as much as twenty-five cents on the dollar for every dollar a migrant spent in the store. One grocer testified that he "lost 30 percent of his trade" when he refused to cooperate with the scheme.[41] Ultimately, the report indicted the labor contractors for "cheating workers out of their pay, collecting duplicate fees from workers and farmers for a single service or expense, getting kickbacks from merchants and tavern operators patronized by the contractor' laborers, and trafficking in marijuana and prostitution."[42]

According to Current, growers also took advantage of the migrants' desperation. They started work in the fields as late as possible without causing damage to the crops and offered even lower wages than before. The extortionate cost of housing, the lack of work, poor wages, and deductions made it difficult for workers to save money. The typical Texas family left Oregon with an average of $235 after expenses. After the harvest, many families had to work elsewhere before they could afford to return home. The Rivera family, for example, traveled to the west Texas communities of Lubbock, Plainview, and Post to pick cotton. Josefa recalled, "We had to stop in west Texas to make enough money to finish our trip home."[43] The meager wages forced the family to buy food on credit when they returned to Eagle Pass. Mercedes recalled the hardship: "We would buy flour, milk, and *fideo* in bulk and we would use the money we made in Oregon to pay it back."[44] Many migrants constantly juggled credit, loans, and favors to survive until the next paycheck. The Rivera family did the same until their situation became so difficult that they could no longer return to their Texas home. Mercedes recalled the hardship: "It was too much . . . with my sister's wedding and the money we owed in Eagle Pass. So we stayed [in Oregon]; we stopped moving."[45]

The Rivera family was fortunate to find year-round employment with Nisei farmers. Unlike large corporate growers, these small-scale farmers did not have the resources to recruit labor in south Texas; instead, they chose to offer higher wages to those who would work in their onion fields. The strategy paid off, as many Tejanos left the sugar beet industry and went to work in the onion fields. In essence they "bootlegged" farmworkers in the same manner that small growers had during the bracero program. Nisei farmers struggled to remain competitive as agriculture in Oregon was consolidating into large corporate farms. By the late 1950s, capitalist agribusiness had changed the rural landscape. Mechanization, pesticides, and fertilizers benefited large-scale farms that could afford these investments. Between 1950 and 1966 the number of farms in the state fell from 63,000 to 43,000, while their average size increased by 150 acres. The Nisei's small-scale farms survived because they never posed a real threat to large corporations like the Utah-Idaho Sugar Company.[46]

Nisei farmers responded to corporate consolidation by devoting their resources to onions, because the crop's labor needs did not coincide with the height of sugar beet season and they were slowly being pushed out of potato production by cooperatives of white farmers. As the size of sugar beet farms grew, onions became a niche crop. Between 1947 and 1956, the acreage of sugar beets in Malheur County rose steadily from 14,478 to 19,496, and the crop's value rose from $3 million to $5 million. In contrast, Nisei-owned farms held steady, growing onions on 3,000 acres and producing a crop worth just under $1 million.[47] Aware of the advantages that cooperation brought but excluded from the white-controlled co-ops, Nisei farmers formed the Onion Growers Association of Malheur County. The association helped them branch out from growing onions to packing, shipping, and selling them, which extended their control over their product and increased their profit margin. The Nisei's domination of onion farming can be seen in the association's leadership: its vice presidents included Joe Saito, Aye Nagaki, Harry Fukiage, Kay Teramura, Sig Murakami, Roy Hirai, and Joe Komoto.[48] Through the association, Nisei farmers cooperatively bought packing sheds. They freed themselves from their previous dependence on white packinghouse owners, who did not always offer them a fair price; instead, they could package and ship onions directly to buyers. Nisei farmers had familiarized themselves with the packing shed industry and saw the potential to expand their own businesses. Joe Komoto began working as a plant supervisor at Ontario Produce and learned the intricacies of the operation. After many years as a labor contractor, farmer, and plant supervisor, Komoto and the Nagaki brothers bought Ontario Produce packing shed in 1953. The change of ownership brought about a dramatic shift in the makeup of the workforce.

Many of the "free zoners" not only had experienced "voluntary relocation," but upon their arrival in Idaho and other states they faced oppression. They were constantly under surveillance, faced language bans, were denied housing, and were refused service at commercial establishments. In some cases, as discussed above, some of the criticism of this treatment even came from fellow Japanese in the form of the leadership of the JACL. When they arrived in Oregon they found a more hospitable terrain that lacked curfews and other insults to their integrity. As a result the Nisei treated Tejanos with the respect that they were denied. Under white ownership, the sheds employed primarily white and Japanese workers, but the transfer to Nisei owners meant year-round work for Tejanos. Bob Komoto explained their rationale: "During the summertime we employed Mexicans, [and] by the time the farming wound down we tried to use the same people to move the onions into the sheds and keep them busy until spring."[49] By offering the Tejanos employment in the sheds, Komoto effectively ensured that the same people would be available for the next spring planting season. In addition to providing work, the Nisei took other steps to ensure the stability of their workforce. They arranged for work permits for Mexican nationals, rented homes to Tejanos, and provided loans to employees. Bob Komoto speculated that the internment experience made his father and other Nisei sympathetic to Tejano migrants: "I think my dad and his friends saw a little bit of themselves in the Mexicans."[50] Perhaps motivated by past experience, their treatment of the Tejanos also provided them a formidable and loyal workforce.

Like the farms, the packing sheds began as small operations employing twenty or thirty people and gradually expanded to employ hundreds of people over the following decades. Eventually the Nisei came to own and operate all the onion-packing sheds in the area. The need for labor grew as the industry expanded. The previous practice of "bootlegging" farmworkers from the sugar beet fields was no longer adequate; instead, Nisei farmers began to hire their own contractors and recruiters.

The process of recruiting workers from Texas was well established by the time the Nisei became involved. The Oregon Bureau of Labor reported that by 1957, over 12,000 migrant workers traveled to the state every year to labor in the fields. Only a handful of contractors were responsible for bringing over half of them. At the time of the report the average contractor was forty years old and had been a contractor for over five years. More than 80 percent of contractors were second-generation from Mexico, 5 percent were third-generation, and 15 percent were from Mexico but had been in the United States for more than ten years. All were bilingual and did not labor in the fields, as opposed to "crew leaders" who worked alongside the crew.[51] The report identified Isabel (Chabelo) Ruvacables as the largest-scale contractor. Located in Romansville, Texas, Ruvacables handled 3,000 farm workers, 8 subcontractors, and 40 crew leaders. According to the report, contractors like Ruvacables typically charged each worker five to eleven cents for every dollar earned. The average farmworker made a little over a dollar an hour. Out of this charge the contractor paid subcontractors anywhere from three to eight cents per hour per worker. Under this arrangement contractors could reap significant profits. Assuming that the farmworkers contracted by Ruvacables worked at least eight hours a day, Ruvacables stood to make $3,600 a week. In contrast, the average single worker in Oregon made $84 a week.[52]

Tejano migrants typically worked in family units, and the division of labor in the onion fields lent itself to cooperative work. The harvesting of onions began with a machine that uprooted the onions and left them lying on the ground. The next step was called *tapeo*, or topping. Mixed gender crews worked in teams of two, one cutting the top off of the onions and the other bagging them. The filled bags were then left on the ground for a few days to cure. Then a team of men loaded the sacks onto a flatbed truck and took them to the packing shed. Another team of men unloaded the bags and emptied them onto a conveyor belt. Inside the shed, a team of women sorted the onions by size and quality and repackaged them into burlap bags and loaded them onto pallets. Men driving forklifts put the pallets on a truck. From there the onions were shipped to wholesalers, processors, and retailers.

Initially the Nisei operated as their own contractors on a much smaller scale but were no less crucial to the success of their operations. According to many reports, the Nisei treated their workers more fairly than other contractors operating at the time. The report insisted that "they function in a paternalistic manner, act in and defend the interests of their workers. They operate differently and apart form the Spanish-American [Tejano] group of contractors although their crews are also largely Spanish-American."[53] Despite the reports of fair treatment by Japanese contractors, the system as a whole came under scrutiny thanks to the report. The committee's suggestions resulted in the State of Oregon passing legislation requiring contractors to register with the state, disclose financial backers, and pay liability insurance for their workers.[54] Additionally, the states could revoke the license of a labor contractor if they were found to have misled workers about the terms, conditions, or existence of employment. In order to avoid incurring the extra costs and to negate the risk involved in such a seasonal industry, growers left the contracting to people like Osvaldo Gonzalez.

Like many other contractors, Osvaldo Gonzalez first came to the Northwest as a migrant laborer. Although he was born in Allende, Coahuila, Mexico, in 1936, his mother was born in Pearsall, Texas. His Tejano grandparents owned land in Texas but were forced to sell their land and go to Mexico during the Depression. His family was among the millions of Mexican Americans forced out of the country by zealous, well-organized groups of Anglos who placed the blame for Depression-era unemployment on Mexicans' shoulders. The fact that many ethnic Mexicans, like Gonzalez's grandparents and mother, were US citizens meant nothing to those looking for a scapegoat. When Osvaldo was a young boy his father moved the family back to Texas and adapted to the cultural life of Tejanos, including the pattern of labor migration. In 1949, Osvaldo's family was contracted in Eagle Pass, Texas, to work in the west Texas cotton fields. That was only the first stop in a long migratory road. They picked cherries and corn in Wisconsin and Illinois and ended up in Weiser, Idaho, just across the Snake River from Malheur County.

The Utah-Idaho Sugar Company contracted Osvaldo's father. He recalled, "A friend of my dad's asked him if he wanted to come to this area to work, and he said yes, and the Amalgamated Sugar Company contracted us. They paid for our expenses and life insurance in case something happened."[55] Gonzalez remembered that the company sent recruiters to south Texas: "They used to come to Eagle Pass, Laredo, McAllen, offering people jobs and offering to pay their expenses."[56] For Tejanos who could not afford to travel, the offer was compelling. Gonzalez worked for a short time for the sugar company but, like so many before him, he left to work for Nisei farmers in the onion fields.

Gonzalez was a farmworker for ten years before becoming a contractor. He explained the emergence of his new role: "Farmers didn't want to do this so they started paying me one large sum and had me find the workers. Farmers didn't want that responsibility."[57] He continued, "The first contractor I ever worked for was Frank Jokoda; he chose me to be a supervisor and he paid me a little more than the others. But when he got sick another Japanese man took over, and when that contractor couldn't continue, that is when they chose me to contract."[58] His transition to contracting might have been connected to new laws regulating farm employment. "At first I started to gather people in Texas to work and I would get a percentage of the work they completed, say about $2.00 an acre."[59] Then as Gonzalez's reputation spread, he hired more and more workers: "I started out with maybe fifteen workers and by the seventies I had around 250 people working in the onion fields." The network of migrant workers became so steady and routine that eventually Gonzalez did not even have to travel to Texas to find and contract them. "They would come up here on their own. People talked and heard that I was a contractor and came looking for me."[60]

Nisei farmers provided Gonzalez with an opportunity that Anglo growers did not extend to Tejanos. Gonzales recalled, "In those days only the Japanese would hire me to contract workers. I worked with a lot of Japanese farmers who heard about me. It wasn't until much later that I finally started getting contracts from Americans [Anglos], but only about two or three."[61] Gonzalez continued contracting mostly for Nisei onion growers. Like other contractors in the region, he focused primarily on recruiting families, whom he saw as more dependable and more efficient than unaccompanied men.

SETTLING OUT IN OREGON

After a decade of migrating across the country, Tejano migrants began to settle in Oregon. In 1957, almost 50,000 or 85 percent of the farmworker population were interstate migrants, but by 1965 that number had fallen to 12,000 or 20 percent of the total farmworkers.[62] The Nisei played a crucial role in helping Tejanos find housing and settle in Malheur County. Although racial-ethnic segregation was not codified in local laws, it was common practice, and Tejanos found it difficult to secure housing. Because of the squalid conditions of the labor camps, many families searched for alternatives, even if that meant leaving the sugar beet fields. Gonzalez and his family decided to leave the labor camp when he went to work for Frank Jokoda; they rented a house from the contractor. Gonzalez recalled, "We lived on the Eastside; back then it was a Japanese neighborhood and a few Mexican families. We paid about $20 a month."[63] Gonzalez had the impression that all the Tejanos who lived there had Japanese landlords. Although Ontario had earned a reputation among Nisei residents as a welcoming, or at least an open and tolerant place, the reception that Mexicans received was mixed at best.

Tejanos fought back against the discrimination they encountered. In newspaper editorials, local Anglos repeatedly denigrated Mexicans as shiftless, violence-prone gamblers and drunks, while praising the Japanese as industrious, clean, and sober. Despite the hostility they felt from local whites, however, the new arrivals were relieved that Oregon was not Texas. Adela Menchaca recalled her initial impression of Ontario and nearby Nyssa: "There was a lot of discrimination, you know, they didn't want you in the nightclubs, they used to have signs up. It wasn't as bad as Texas but you could feel it. It was worse in Nyssa than in Ontario."[64] The difference between the Northwest and south Texas was evident in the contestation over public space. Benito Menchaca recalled an incident at the Polar Bear drive-in in Nyssa that shook his previous conception of the racial order. His friend, Marcos Ayala, was leaning on a 1957 Ford that belonged to a white police officer, Ron Ruckstall. Benito retold the story: "He [Ron] was a mean guy. He said to Marcos, 'Hey! Don't put any grease on my car!' "[65] Ayala responded by physically confronting the police officer, and the two began to fight. "Marcos used to hit pretty hard. They exchanged punches and Ron got beat."[66] The ability to survive an altercation with a law enforcement officer that was precipitated by a racist slight was a far cry from the often-deadly violence that Benito and other Tejanos had faced from police in south Texas.[67]

Benito and Adela Menchaca's experiences in their hometown are typical. Both were born in San Benito, Texas, and both came from landed families. Benito's father owned a ranch outside of San Benito but passed away when Benito was just two years old. After her husband's death, Benito's mother could no longer afford to maintain the ranch and was forced to sell it for much less than its market value. Adela's grandmother owned a substantial amount of land but, like Benito's family and so many other Tejanos, lost it to Anglos in a land grab. Adela recounted, "Back in those years they would intimidate you and make you sell for very cheap. . . . My dad used to tell us stories about men that would offer to buy your land. If you said no, they would threaten your family."[68] Adela's grandmother eventually sold most of the land except the small plot that they lived on. Benito's brothers moved into town and then went to work on the cotton circuit throughout Texas. When Benito was in seventh grade he dropped out of school and joined them. Adela's family managed to maintain a privileged position in San Benito. Her father became a bracero contractor in south Texas and earned a comfortable living. He sent his children to school, although it was segregated. Adela explained, "There was a Mexican side of town and a white side of town, a Mexican school and a white school."[69]

Historically, Mexican American women often sought employment as a means to avoid close familial supervision as well as to attain financial independence. For Adela, paid work enabled her to escape the surveillance of her father, her dependence on his money, and the familial obligations imposed on her because of her gender. Her father was not an abusive man, but Adela felt trapped by the confines of a traditional Mexican family. She recalled, "I had to cook and clean for my brothers, you know, the typical stuff. I had to get away from it."[70] But having a job and making her own money did not provide the freedom she sought; she needed to leave south Texas altogether.

Adela's path to Oregon sprang from her desire for liberation, not simple economic necessity. Her marriage to Benito offered her a chance to escape south Texas and experience new things. She met her husband when she was seventeen and married him shortly after. Joining him on the migrant trail, she soon discovered she was ill-equipped for the difficulties it entailed. She found fieldwork much more challenging than factory work. At first, she said, "I thought it was such an adventure! Then I thought, 'Oh my God! What did I get myself into?' I had to learn the hard way . . . it was a rude awakening."[71] Eventually she became an adept farmworker. Adela still felt confined by her new family life, but her economic contribution made her feel like an equal partner. The Amalgamated Sugar Company contracted Adela along with Benito and his family, and they traveled across the United States to work in sugar beet fields. But the Midwestern weather discouraged them from returning. Benito remembered that his mother "didn't like those tornados!"[72] They started coming to Oregon in 1958, contracted by Ambrosio Juarez of Pharr, Texas.

Tejanos often saw their sojourn north as a temporary solution to their financial woes, but as time went on more and more Tejanos found reasons to stay. Year-round employment was among the most important. After seven years of working in the fields and living in labor camps, Benito Menchaca secured a job at the sugar refinery and settled in Nyssa: "The sugar factory paid better than anyone else at the time."[73] Wages were still inadequate to support the family, though, so Benito and other Tejanos supplemented their wages with fieldwork. "When I had my vacation I would go work in the fields. We used to buck onions [throw bags of onions onto a loading truck]. We would get paid two and a half cents a bag."[74]

Although Tejanos predominated in the fields, Mexican nationals also made their way to the Northwest. Many of the Mexican nationals had previous ties to the Northwest through the bracero program. Fathers or grandfathers who had come as braceros in the 1940s returned to the region to work, often for the same growers who had employed them as braceros. According to reports by the Oregon Bureau of Labor, 30 percent of the migrant stream to the state came from Mexico. The bureau estimated that half of the Mexican nationals came without proper documentation. Sisters Micaela Rodriguez Guijarro and Aurora Rodriguez Banda both came to Oregon from Mexico. Micaela explained her family's immigration status: "Back then no one talked about it. If you did have papers no one knew. My older brothers and sisters did not have papers. I always did."[75] Mexican immigrants did their best to fit in with the Tejanos and go unnoticed. In families like the Rodriguez', the fact that some family members had legal status made it easier for those who did not.

Mica and Aurora Rodriguez's experience is representative. Their father, Feliciano, had worked in Oregon as a bracero. The sisters were born in Fresnillo, Zacatecas, one of the richest silver-producing states in Mexico. Despite its silver mines and thriving agricultural economy, Fresnillo was a major source of braceros because of the poor pay in the mines.[76] Feliciano came to Oregon to work as a bracero for the Nagaki brothers in the 1940s and sent the money he earned back to his wife to open a small corner store in Zacatecas. When the program ended, the Nagaki brothers helped Feliciano arrange for temporary residency cards for himself and some of his relatives. The family returned to Zacatecas every October and came back to Oregon every March.

The Rodriguez family was among the first wave of migrants to arrive in Oregon after the bracero program ended. Aurora recalled the Nisei farmers' reactions when her family came to Ontario in 1950: "When we first got here, there were very few Mexicans here; you could count them on one hand. The farmers were so grateful that we were here that they used to bring us sodas and doughnuts in the fields!"[77] When one of the Nagaki brothers saw that Feliciano had come with his entire family, he offered them a house on the farm with a wood stove. "In California, we always lived in the camps, we never had a house or apartment,"[78] Aurora lamented. She had a favorable impression of the Nisei: "They were very good people, very good bosses. Sometimes they ate with us in our little house. They started to like chile!"[79] Yet the relationship remained one-sided: "We never ate with them. They never invited us. They never brought anything with them either. They were like an *azadon* [hoe], everything in and nothing out [making the motion]."[80]

For the Rodriguez family, living conditions in Oregon represented an improvement, but being one of the only families on the migrant trail entailed other dangers. Feliciano was an overprotective father and often met his daughter's suitors with violence. He did not allow the girls to look up from the ground when they were working, and he scolded them for making eye contact with men. He generally did whatever he could to keep the girls in line. He was especially vigilant regarding Aurora, the eldest daughter, who was fifteen years old at the time: "I remember one time he smashed up my boyfriend's bicycle so that he would not ride out to the house to see me."[81] Despite his efforts at controlling access to his daughters, Feliciano often acted irresponsibly and left the house for the weekend to gamble and drink in town, leaving his wife and daughters alone in the house. One weekend when Aurora's father was away, another worker sneaked into the house and raped her. "I was so ignorant. . . . My stomach began to grow and I didn't know why, until one day my mom noticed. She began to ask me questions and I was so afraid. . . . In those days people didn't talk about sex. I had no idea what happened to me."[82] No one reported the rape, and Aurora could not recall what happened to the man.

Women in migrant families faced the risk of sexual assault in labor camps as well. Young migrant women were often paid to perform household tasks for groups of single men. They washed clothes, cooked meals, and cleaned dormitories, which took them away from the surveillance of their families. The Oregon Bureau of Labor recorded one such incident as typical in the labor camps. The sixteen-year-old daughter of one of the men in the labor camps performed housekeeping duties for five single men, and her father received $25 a week for his daughter's labor. Over the course of time it became apparent that various sexual encounters had taken place. The report does not specify whether these encounters were consensual or were sexual assaults. When her father heard of the rumors he violently confronted the men and ultimately resolved the situation by raising the fee to $50 a week. The report does not specify the issues involved. Perhaps she had been assaulted and he demanded monetary compensation for the violation of his daughter, but he continued to put her in harm's way. Perhaps the relationship was consensual, and the payment was for the privilege of courting his daughter. Maybe he accepted the extra money on his daughter's behalf in exchange for sexual favors. In any case, the young woman's opinion was not mentioned in the report and, apparently, did not factor into the negotiations over her body.[83]

The tendency to disregard women's opinions often extended to decision-making and the responsibilities of the head of the household. This pattern is clear in Aurora and Micaela's family. In 1959, Aurora and Micaela's mother and their youngest sister died in a bus accident in Mexico. Shortly after her death Feliciano remarried and decided to stop migrating to Oregon. The sisters did not get along with their father's new bride and decided to carry on their migratory labor without Feliciano. In her father's absence, despite being the oldest child, Aurora had to concede head of household status to her younger brother, Feliciano Jr. The shift in responsibilities did provide some relief for the younger siblings. While the elder Feliciano never valued education, especially not for girls, Feliciano Jr. encouraged all his younger siblings to go to school. Aurora was no longer of school age and had a child, but Micaela began attending school. The break from her father gave Aurora a new sense of agency. When her father convinced several of her siblings to return to Mexico, she refused and chose instead to stay in Oregon with her child: "Why would I go back? To what? The yelling and to be treated badly? No, I won't go back!"[84] She told her brother that she preferred to stay in Oregon by herself rather than return to an abusive family.

For women like Aurora, breaking away from traditional kinship networks represented a bold step toward personal freedom and presented a new set of challenges. Expanded employment opportunities made the decision to leave an abusive husband, father, or family easier. As a single mother with no relatives remaining in Oregon, Aurora needed to find year-round employment. She found it at Ontario Produce: "The Nagakis also owned Ontario Produce and I worked for them."[85] Aurora worked with other women as a sorter. She found the experience refreshing: "It was nice and there was so much respect from your boss and your coworkers."[86]

Working in the packing sheds and canneries proved to be a liberating experience for many women. Adela Menchaca made the transition to cannery work during the winter in an effort to supplement the family income. Adela performed double duty, taking care of the children during the day while her husband worked at the sugar refinery, and working in the cannery at night. As in the packing sheds, the cannery workforce was made up entirely of women. As more of the men got jobs in the sugar refinery, the field-workers, too, became predominantly female. "It was kind of fun being out in the fields without the men," Adela said. "We could talk about them and there would be no one to shush us!"[87] Adela found the experience more enjoyable without the men around, and she formed a bond with other women in the fields and canneries. The women were not able to talk while working in the sheds because the noise made it difficult to hear one another, but the lunch hour offered a chance to gossip and get caught up on the latest movies and music.

Graciela Olvera Machuca and her husband Jose arrived in Ontario as undocumented immigrants from Jalisco. Neither Graciela nor Jose had experience in fieldwork before coming to the United States. In Mexico, Jose drove a beer delivery truck and Graciela worked for her aunt in a corner store. Like many of the Mexican nationals who came to Oregon, Graciela already had a family connection there. Her oldest brother came to the United States as a bracero, worked in California and Oregon, and decided to stay in Oregon after the program was phased out. He encouraged his sister and her husband to join him. He helped them find work in the fields for Joe Nagano and at Ontario Produce with Joe Komoto.

The lunchroom at Ontario Produce not only created a sense of community but also provided an opportunity for entrepreneurial activities. Since Graciela was one of the few Mexican nationals in the workforce, the food she brought for lunch was a frequent topic of conversation: "In the lunch [room] we would offer each other food. After a while they [her coworkers] would tell me, 'Oye Chela, why don't you bring tacos and tortas to sell during break?' I did it. I started and they sold! Then later they started again, 'Oye Chela, why don't you start selling dinner at your house?'"[88] Graciela was skeptical about the venture but eventually started to sell food on Sundays: "I started making tacos, pozole, tamales; I made everything and people started showing up!"[89] Graciela and Jose rented a small house on the bank of the Snake River. One summer a flood destroyed most of the house and with it their source of supplemental income. Discouraged and afraid that the river had contaminated the house, the Machucas began to dream about opening a restaurant. Graciela and Jose pooled their money and even took out a loan from Joe Komoto. Once again the Nisei farmers provided ethnic Mexicans with a resource that would otherwise be unavailable to them. Two undocumented immigrants obviously would not be eligible to receive a loan from a bank, but the Machucas used kinship networks and their relationship with the Nisei to borrow money. The Machucas featured authentic Mexican cuisine: "There was only one other [Mexican] restaurant in Ontario . . . but the food was very different. Their food was very American. We cooked food from Mexico."[90] The Machucas believed that the Tejanos would appreciate the opportunity to buy more traditional fare. Her Tejana coworkers were right; the Machucas have since retired but their children still own and operate the restaurant today.

Like the Machucas, other Mexican immigrants came to Oregon with little experience in agricultural work but some connection to former braceros. Ernesto Guijarro came from a city and had never done farmwork. Born in Fresnillo, Zacatecas, Ernesto was the son of a taxi driver who made a comfortable living. When he was seventeen, Ernesto learned welding from his uncle; eventually he opened a successful shop in Fresnillo. For ten years, Ernesto operated his own shop and had no plans to leave—until love came calling. Every winter, Micaela Rodriguez and her family returned to Fresnillo from Oregon, and every winter Ernesto and "Mica" grew closer. After they married, Mica continued to migrate to Oregon with her family, but after two years Ernesto got tired of waiting. He closed down his shop and followed Mica to labor in the onion fields of Oregon. Joe Komoto once again proved invaluable as he helped arrange for a work visa for Ernesto and hired him as a favor to the Rodriguez family. His initial foray was short-lived, because having to work in the fields discouraged him. "I was really sad. In Mexico I had a profession and I was competent. I had my own shop and here I was just an onion picker."[91]

Ernesto loved the countryside but grew frustrated with the work and took his family back to Mexico. But Mica grew increasingly ill during her pregnancy, and the doctors could not provide any answers. She left Zacatecas to rejoin her brother in Oregon and received medical treatment, and her health immediately improved. She gave birth to her first son, Ernesto "Netito" Guijarro Jr. Shortly afterwards Ernesto joined her in Oregon, immigrating with a work visa that the Komotos had helped arrange. After Ernesto had spent six months working in the fields and the sheds, Joe Komoto encouraged him to look for work elsewhere as a welder. Ernesto found a job at Rotary Corrugated Company as a welder. The supervisor was a Tejano: "He spoke Spanish, which is the only reason I got the job. I didn't speak any English and it was hard for me to learn."[92] For Mexican immigrants, having previous connections in the area proved invaluable for surviving and adapting to their new home.

The immigration status of ethnic Mexicans was a tightly guarded secret. Most Tejanos did not know and did not ask. Mica recalled, "I didn't know any [undocumented immigrants]. At least they didn't say."[93] Despite the secrecy, the Immigration and Naturalization Service (INS) made regular stops in Oregon. News reports in the *Argus Observer* revealed that immigration raids were commonplace in the Pacific Northwest. In 1948, shortly after the bracero program ended, the INS deported sixty-five undocumented Mexicans found in the Ontario area.[94] In fact, from 1948 to 1954 the INS consistently raided once a year during harvest season. On average, INS deported about one hundred undocumented Mexicans per year, a relatively small proportion of the total number of ethnic Mexicans working in the agricultural sector.[95]

Even when the raids took place, they had a seemingly inconsequential effect on the workforce. Jose Machuca recalled one incident that provides a glimpse into one of these raids: "Immigration showed up and started asking everyone for their papers. My brother was working with me at the time and they got him. I got really nervous but I was driving the forklift. So I just kept driving past them and pretending like I didn't hear them!"[96] Ontario Produce employed nearly one hundred people at the time, and the INS apprehended only two people. A few weeks later Jose's brother and the other coworker were back on the job.

CREATING AN ETHNIC COMMUNITY

The Nisei played a crucial role in the lives of ethnic Mexicans; they offered year-round employment, provided housing, and even offered loans. In addition, Nisei provided a social space for Tejano migrants. Social spaces, like residential neighborhoods, were customarily segregated. Tejano migrants fought for access to public parks but had a much harder time finding Anglo business owners who were willing to rent them a space for dances, *quinceñeras* (fifteenth birthday celebrations), and weddings. Fortunately the Nisei offered the Tejanos a place in their Japanese Hall. The multipurpose building on the outskirts of Ontario near the Oregon Slope was used for a variety of events including judo tournaments, Christmas bazaars, and dances. The Nisei had also built a baseball field on the grounds of the hall in order to host Japanese League baseball games.

The Tejanos created a cultural and social space at the Japanese Hall that gave them a sense of community. On the weekends Tejanos held dances and played Sunday afternoon baseball games against teams composed of Tejanos from other places, Japanese Americans, and even African Americans. Jesus Garcia, a member of the Nyssa team, recalled, "We used to have a team that would travel around and play other labor camps. . . . There was a black team and a Japanese team too."[97] The ball games were free of charge, but spectators would pass a hat for a collection to defray the cost of travel and equipment. The games, which women watched even though they could not play, became an important diversion from the workweek. Josefa Rivera said, "It was a lot of fun. The Mexicans from Ontario would go play against the Mexicans in Payette or Weiser. The contractor would take us in buses to go watch our players."[98] Josefa remembered that pride was at stake in these games: "Sometimes when teams would lose they would pelt the other team's bus with rocks!"[99] These outbreaks of violence were rare, and the environment was tense but fun.

Baseball games were a popular pastime for workers but paled in comparison to the dances. The weekly dances held at the Japanese Hall were another sign of the cultural space that Tejanos increasingly occupied. According to Mercedes, "Everyone used to go there. People would come from as far as Weiser for those dances."[100] Wealthy individuals like Donacio Gonzalez sponsored the dances. Gonzalez and others brought in popular bands from Texas as well as featuring local artists to play conjunto music. Conjunto music is an accordion-driven ensemble music that is strongly associated with the Tejano working class.[101] Gonzalez and other entrepreneurs witnessed the trend of Tejanos remaining in Oregon year-round and recognized an opportunity to make money. He opened a *tortilleria* and a *carneceria* on Highway 26 between Ontario and Nyssa. The growing number of businesses that catered to the Tejano migrants demonstrated the desire to meet the needs of a more sedentary population.

The dances were a reprieve from work and a reminder of home for both Tejanos and Mexican immigrants, despite the cultural differences. But Ernesto Guijarro found the music a strain: "The first time I went to a dance here, man! I thought it was a carnival from Brazil. It was like a stampede, people running around in circles."[102] Ernesto was accustomed to more "refined" musical tastes: "It was the first time I had ever seen an accordion. At home we danced to orchestra music. Huge beautiful orchestras that played *piezas*, all kinds of music, and they were elegant. You had to come dressed up, long dresses, and sometimes you even needed an invitation."[103] The Tejano dances were more of a working-class affair. Mica saw the dances as a way to escape the stress of work: "I was fine with it, and to me it was just a way to relax after working out in the fields. It was about having something to do on the weekends."[104] The Guijarros' experience demonstrates a distinct regional difference between Mexicans from the interior and the Tejanos who made up a substantial portion of the ethnic Mexican population.

The cultural differences between Mexican nationals and Tejanos occasionally flared up at the dances and in the fields. This tension often arose around access to women. Mexican immigrants tended to come as bachelors, while the Tejanos usually lived in family units. As a result, the only single women in the community were the daughters of Tejano patriarchs, and competition for them often escalated to violence. Mica Guijarro recalled, "It [the violence] is one of the reasons we did not like going to dances as newlyweds. We would rather wait for quinceñeras or weddings where the crowd was more selective."[105]

Although many residents downplayed the tension between Tejanos and Mexican nationals, various instances of animosity appeared in the public record. The Oregon Bureau of Labor reported on the conflicts in a subsection entitled "Other Important Problems": "The imported labor and Spanish-speaking laborer working in the same area frequently create a general feeling of antagonism and jealousy."[106] The report gave various reasons for this sentiment, including differences in wages and living conditions as well as romantic competition. The bureau also reported, "There is frequent criticism of the Spanish spoken by the domestic to imported laborer."[107] Workers called each other "*pochos*" (Americanized) and "*surumatos*" (pejorative for recent immigrants from Mexico), and the teasing occasionally escalated into violence.

For women, the dances became a place to express their growing independence. Despite familial supervision, many found the freedom they desired on the weekends. The Rivera sisters frequented the dances despite their father's disapproval. Family honor and the reputation of their daughters were fiercely intertwined in the Tejano community. Young Mexican American women could expect to see their mothers or older brothers closely monitoring their actions at dances, at church activities, and in the streets. Mercedes remembered, "At first my dad did not like us going to the dances. We were already fifteen or sixteen years old and he still wouldn't let us go but we would convince our brother to ask for us."[108] Over time young women challenged their parents' rules through an array of tactics. In the case of the Rivera sisters, work proved to be the liberating factor. Their father reluctantly allowed them to go chaperoned for a few hours. Eventually the sisters decided to attend without their father's permission. Juanita recalled, "We had to go walking to the dances because neither my dad or my brother would take us."[109] Juanita remembered being envious at the sight of women driving to the dances: "Some of the women had their own cars! They went in groups and drove themselves! I did not even learn to drive until I was married."[110] The women Juanita Rivera admired attended dances on their own and even drove themselves in cars they had bought to get to work. Eventually the Rivera sisters became friends with other young Tejanas with cars. Having a vehicle opened up a whole new world of possibilities. Mercedes and Josefa typically spent Sunday with their friends: "Every Sunday was ours. In the morning we would go to church. After we got out of church we would go eat at Bluebird [Drive-In], it was right across the street. After we ate we would go to the movies in Payette [Idaho]. After the movie we would go to the park."[111]

Beck-Kiwanis Park in Ontario served as a meeting place for Tejano youth. On Sunday it was filled with Tejanos and their cars playing conjunto music and drinking beer. Mercedes recalled, "We felt like we had a place. We belonged there. It was a nice place to gossip!"[112] Despite the drudgery of work, the sisters looked forward to Sunday and went out no matter how tired they were. The weekend became a crucial component in building a Tejano youth culture in Oregon. As the Tejanos carved their social space, they also became more integrated in other kinds of work. They became schoolteachers, counselors, receptionists, construction workers, firefighters, truck drivers, and contractors, once again leaving a void of cheap labor for area growers, who moved to fill it with undocumented workers. The citizenship status of the workforce led to greater exploitation and abuse; this time, however, an organization would emerge to challenge grower power.

3 ❧ THE GENESIS OF THE WILLAMETTE VALLEY IMMIGRATION PROJECT

In the 1940s braceros had succeeded in challenging the power of growers by using work stoppages and strikes in the fields, and winning concessions on a fairly regular basis. While the Tejanos used less direct means, they too defied Anglo expectations by insisting on establishing a community and later utilizing reform programs to their advantage. By the 1970s, however, there had still been no organized grassroots effort to improve the lives of farmworkers. But in the Willamette Valley, three hundred miles west of Malheur County, the largest farmworkers' union in the Pacific Northwest was beginning to form. This chapter traces the growth of the Willamette Valley Immigration Project and the emergence of organized resistance to the power of growers in the Pacific Northwest. Three activists from outside the Pacific Northwest converged in Oregon and brought with them a social justice lens acquired through other Chicano/a, worker, and civil rights organizations to formulate a new strategy that was informed by their prior experience. The activists borrowed tactics and applied theories from their organizing with the United Farm Workers (UFW), the Centro de Acción Social Autónoma, and the National Lawyers Guild (NLG), while at the same time not being bound to them. Instead they innovated and adjusted to their surroundings and laid the groundwork for one of the most successful farmworker unions in the country.

In September 1976, Larry Kleinman drove along the damp roads of Mt. Angel, Oregon, on his way to Colegio Cesar Chavez. Three years earlier, two Chicano administrators at Mt. Angel College took over the operation of the failing institution and rechristened it Colegio Cesar Chavez, after the charismatic leader of the United Farm Workers.[1] The college was the first of its kind, a four-year institution aimed at providing Chicanos/as with a new kind of academic experience. The "college without walls" awarded college credit for life experiences and required all graduates to have a working knowledge of both Spanish and English.[2] The Colegio was determined to ensure that academic programs served the Mexican community in Oregon. Notable faculty included Raza Unida Party founder Jose Angel Gutierrez, celebrated Chicano artist Alurista, and basketball player for the Portland Trailblazers Bill Walton.[3] The college eventually closed due to financial difficulties it had inherited, but during its ten-year run, the Colegio served as a meeting point for local activists. That fall, Kleinman drove to campus to meet one leader in particular, Cipriano Ferrel.[4]

Cipriano Ferrel was born in Delano, California, in 1949 and labored in the grape harvest alongside his parents and ten siblings. Ferrel grew up close to the Chavez family and attended school with Cesar's daughters Linda and Sylvia. His activist spirit manifested itself early in his life. At the age of sixteen he started his own newsletter, La Fuerza (Power), and later he founded a chapter of the militant Chicano nationalist group known as the Brown Berets.[5] The militant stance of the Berets suited him, as he rarely backed down from a confrontation. After high school, Ferrel joined the United Farm Workers and worked on the impending grape boycott. At the time Cesar Chavez and the UFW were engaged in what would turn out to be one of the most successful farmworker organizing efforts in history. A crucial component of their success was the table grape boycott. After facing grower intransigence in the fields and at the negotiating table, Chavez launched a consumer boycott of all table grapes and a secondary boycott against all stores carrying grapes. In the typical, haphazard UFW fashion, Chavez sent his daughters Linda and Sylvia as well as Ferrel to Detroit with nothing more than some buttons and a list of phone numbers to initiate the boycott. After returning from Detroit, Ferrel served for a short time as Cesar's bodyguard and then was sent by Gil Padilla into the lettuce fields of Salinas as an organizer, but Ferrel's adventurous spirit limited his time as a UFW organizer. He left California and traveled to Eugene to enroll at the University of Oregon. But after a few days following his arrival, he heard about the radical mission of Colegio Cesar Chavez. So Ferrel promptly moved to Mt. Angel. The Colegio became a hub of radical activity and attracted activists from all walks of life. Ferrel became involved with a number of movement organizations, including the American Indian Movement (AIM), Puerto Rican nationalists, and the Black Panther Party.[6]

Larry Kleinman took a more wayward path to the Colegio. Kleinman was born in Chicago in 1953 to second-generation working-class Jewish parents. Larry's father, a World War II veteran, attended college and law school on the GI Bill. Like hundreds of thousands of other white families, they took advantage of the low-interest mortgages the GI Bill provided to move to the suburbs.[7] Kleinman attended the predominantly Jewish Highland Park High School and, like Ferrel, demonstrated a precocious political consciousness. Despite his affluent surroundings, Kleinman maintained a close affinity with his Russian immigrant grandparents. They lived in the Jane Addams housing projects on the west side of Chicago, where they had been active community organizers, and they imbued him with a strong sense of social justice. Because of his relationship with them, he felt deeply connected to the Civil Rights and antiwar movements. Upon hearing of the assassination of Dr. Martin Luther King Jr., Kleinman sat on the floor of his English classroom as an expression of his personal grief.[8] As the cochair of the Congregation Solel[9] youth group's Social Action Committee, Kleinman led antiwar demonstrations and counseled young Jewish men seeking conscientious objector status. He continued his antiwar activism at Oberlin College, and after graduation he joined the federal antipoverty program, Volunteers in Service to America (VISTA). In the state of Washington, he worked as a paralegal, first aiding low-income families to fight eviction and then serving as a criminal defense team member. During that time, Kleinman met and befriended Rocky Barilla, who was working at Marion-Polk Legal Services as an attorney. After a short time Barilla insisted that Kleinman meet his old friend Cipriano Ferrel, who was doing an internship with Rocky as a paralegal. In addition to his paralegal work, Kleinman was a freelance journalist. Barilla convinced Kleinman to write a story about the Colegio and its financial troubles. Kleinman agreed to meet Ferrel at the school.

That day in September 1976, Ferrel gave Kleinman a tour of the campus and explained the college's predicament. Kleinman's subsequent story in the *Portland Scribe* did nothing to avert its closure, but Kleinman and Ferrel's long, impassioned conversation about the predicament of the state's Mexican farmworkers proved much more consequential.[10] Ferrel described the recent rash of Immigration and Naturalization Service (INS) raids in the area. The INS raided labor camps, laundromats, and restaurants, sowing panic in the immigrant community. Cipriano declared, "We've got to do something . . . a few of us are talking about exactly that."[11] Cipriano's description of "La Migra" (as the notorious federal agency was known in Spanish) resonated with Larry's family experience of anti-Semitic persecution. Moved by the correlation, Larry joined Cipriano and other volunteers the following month and founded the Willamette Valley Immigration Project (WVIP).

The Willamette Valley follows the river for 120 miles from the Portland metropolitan area south along the Interstate 5 corridor to Eugene. It is home to the majority of Oregon's population, including most of the state's ethnic Mexicans. The valley is Oregon's most diversified and productive agricultural region, contributing nearly half of the state's agricultural output. It ranks among the nation's leading producers of hops, grass seed, hazelnuts, berries, and vegetables, and it has large nurseries, Christmas tree farms, and stands of timber. The conditions in the field remained unchanged into the 1970s, but what had changed were the faces in the field. The overwhelming presence of Tejanos gave way to that of undocumented immigrants. Just as suddenly the INS began to make its presence felt with continuous immigration raids.[12]

On May 2, 1977, a year after Ferrel and Kleinman met, the WVIP opened an office in downtown Portland. A press release announced its goals: "to conduct community education on immigration law and policy, and provide legal representation on immigration matters, particularly deportation."[13] In an interview with the *Oregonian*, WVIP cofounder and volunteer staff attorney Ann Witte articulated this message: "We want to let undocumented aliens know that they do not have to incriminate themselves if they are approached by immigration officers. They do not have to answer questions . . . we will provide legal services to them."[14] Unofficially, the WVIP sought to slow down the deportation process and raise the INS's operating costs, thereby resulting in fewer arrests.

Equally important, the project sought to change the terms of the debate about undocumented immigration. In press conferences, official statements, and media interviews, the INS and its agents repeatedly voiced the belief that the raids "freed up" jobs for "real" Americans. Yet after raids, US citizens rarely showed up to fill those jobs. The Tejanos who previously held those jobs had moved on to other forms of manual labor in canneries, packing sheds, and construction. The project's early meetings focused on developing the message that immigrants did jobs that other people did not want. Additionally, people like Cipriano Ferrel brought a decidedly internationalist perspective to the immigrant debate. They believed that the organization ought to expand the debate about undocumented immigration to include discussions of the American empire. The project felt compelled to force Americans to think about economic exploitation and recognized that US foreign policy created the economic disparities that led to undocumented immigration. The varied backgrounds of project members contributed to this analysis, which developed within an environment of intellectual as well as political engagement.

The WVIP volunteers all contributed to the direction, structure, and vision of the project and laid the foundation for a democratic organization. Loosely organized working groups set out to develop an immigrant rights project and an immigrant defense project; the first focused on outreach and education, while the second focused on developing a legal strategy. The project decided against forming a farmworkers union, despite the large number of farmworkers among the undocumented. Project members attributed the decision to the influence of the left-leaning National Lawyers Guild and the Centro de Acción Social Autónoma (CASA).[15] Members who were also active in the NLG believed that a legalistic approach would best serve the growing undocumented community in Oregon, while those with ties to CASA were apprehensive about the anti-immigrant stance taken by labor unions. Two of the founders had a formidable effect on the shape of the project: Cipriano Ferrel and Ramon Ramirez.

Ramon Ramirez was born in East Los Angeles and, like Ferrel, became politically active in his youth. A speech Cesar Chavez had given at Ramirez's high school motivated him to get involved in grassroots politics. He remembered, "People used to tell us all the time . . . go to school, get an education, and come back and help your community. Cesar told us we could help now. That really resonated with me."[16] Ramirez responded by joining the National Chicano Moratorium Committee, which held antiwar demonstrations across the country. The largest demonstration took place in Laguna Park in East Los Angeles near Ramirez's home. On August 29, 1970, an estimated 30,000 protestors gathered peacefully in the park. The crowd listened to speakers, shared food, and danced until the police in full riot gear shattered the gathering with tear gas and batons. Under the pretense of searching for a robbery suspect who had supposedly escaped into the park, the police brutalized and injured a multitude of protestors and killed *Los Angeles Times* reporter Ruben Salazar.[17]

The incident remains etched into the collective memory of Chicano/a activists and historians, but the repression that followed is less well known. The police continued to harass the residents of East Los Angeles long after the activists had left.[18] Ramirez recalled, "The police stepped up the repression after everything died down. . . . I got harassed and beat up by the police. I grew up in a place where police violated people's rights. Police brutality ran rampant. I wanted to get out of East L.A."[19] Before leaving, Ramirez participated in community organizing on behalf of immigrants. His commitment to the rights of undocumented immigrants developed from his own experience with the INS. Although he was a citizen, he was continually stopped and questioned. He also observed the destruction that the INS wrought on communities. Ramirez remembered, "My sister's husband was deported when she was six months pregnant. . . . the feeling of frustration . . . that feeling of hopelessness. That is where [my stance on immigration] comes from."[20] His brother-in-law's deportation motivated Ramirez to participate in an immigration march in downtown Los Angeles sponsored by CASA. The politics of the organization shaped Ramirez's growing political consciousness.

CASA, founded by Bert Corona in 1969, originally functioned as a mutual aid society but soon expanded its efforts to defending the rights of all workers regardless of immigration status. In CASA's view, undocumented workers faced the greatest exploitation because of their vulnerability and needed to be defended. For CASA the plight of Mexican people could only be improved through workplace organizing. Heavily influenced by Marxist-Leninist theories, CASA members often clashed with Chicano nationalists. CASA believed that Chicano nationalism acted as a divisive force between Mexican immigrants and Chicanos.[21] After Ramirez joined the rally for immigrant rights he began attending CASA meetings and "picking up around the office, distribut[ing] leaflets, things like that."[22] A short time later Ramirez met Bert Corona and became a more active member. His time at CASA later informed the direction the WVIP took.

In 1972, Ramirez received a scholarship to St. Martin's College in the state of Washington; a year later he transferred to the University of Washington. There he became the president of the Chicano/a student organization, el Movimiento Estudiantil Chicano de Aztlan (MEChA), and coordinated the United Farm Workers grape boycott in Seattle. Despite his admiration for Chavez and his support of the boycott, Ramirez soon grew irritated by the UFW. He heard rumors that the UFW had called the INS to report undocumented workers in the fields during the strikes in the Coachella Valley. Given his history with CASA, Ramirez was greatly disturbed and he promptly quit working on the boycott and founded a chapter of CASA in Seattle. A few years later Ramirez led a delegation of nearly one hundred people to Mount Angel, Oregon, to protest the proposed closure of Colegio Cesar Chavez. There he met Cipriano Ferrel and was deeply impressed by the number of farmworkers on campus. Mesmerized by the atmosphere, he moved to Oregon to enroll in the college. Ramirez brought his good friend Juan Mendoza along with him. They found an engaging and spirited environment where arguments over the direction of the Chicano movement flourished. Ramirez recalled, "At the time politically we were more aligned with CASA and the Hermandad General de Trabajadores. We wanted more than what the movement could offer."[23] Specifically, Ramirez and his friends looked beyond Chicano nationalism and developed an internationalist critique of militarism, imperialism, and capitalism as it pertained to Mexican immigration.

Ramirez and Mendoza brought the CASA mantra, "Con o Sin Documentos: Creamos la Riqueza y Tenemos Derechos" (With or Without Documents: We Create Wealth and We Have Rights) to the WVIP. Even though the WVIP did not have workplace organizing on the agenda, members clearly believed that the rights of all immigrants needed to be defended. Project activists considered themselves allies of CASA; they organized community forums in correlation with CASA's national campaigns and distributed its bimonthly newspaper, *Sin Fronteras* (Without Borders). At the same time, the project's early foundation in the immigrant rights movement put CASA at odds with many mainstream Mexican American organizations. Since World War II, the League of United Latin American Citizens (LULAC) had supported deportation efforts such as Operation Wetback and the policy of fining employers who knowingly hired undocumented workers. Similarly, the National Agricultural Workers Union and the United Farm Workers often supported stricter enforcement of immigration laws and thought of undocumented workers as strikebreakers.

Influenced by both Cesar Chavez and Bert Corona, the project incorporated philosophies from these two leaders and experimented with strategies and tactics used by their organizations. Cipriano Ferrel maintained that the UFW was doing good work and refused to abandon the union's approach to organiz-ing workers, but he did not adopt its narrow vision of who those workers were. Ramon Ramirez stayed in contact with Corona and Chavez and a host of other activists across the country and developed a model for building a movement. During their time together at the Colegio, Ramirez and Ferrel sowed the seeds of the Willamette Valley Immigration Project.

COMBATING THE INS

In addition to its impressive analytical work, the WVIP had to develop a con-crete strategy to slow down the deportations. Kleinman's previous connection with the National Lawyers Guild proved invaluable. The NLG had a reputation for its commitment to civil rights and progressive politics. Kleinman had joined the NLG in Spokane, Washington, during his time as a paralegal, so he recruited several members to join him in developing a legal strategy. The nucleus of this group went on to form the Willamette Valley Immigration Project and a separate entity, the Willamette Valley Law Project, the former as an "activist organization" and the latter as a research and educational arm.[24]

Despite their legal backgrounds, project members knew little or nothing about practicing immigration law. Yet they stumbled upon a legal defense that changed the course of history. The lack of recognized expertise among the participants created a "study group" atmosphere that allowed everyone to present and explore a wide range of ideas. Members assigned themselves sections of statutes and legal treatises and presented summaries to the group. After months of study, they concluded that if an immigrant invoked their right against self-incrimination, it might be the key to hampering the INS's efforts to deport them. Since the Supreme Court held that deportation cases are a civil and not a criminal matter and that deportation, no matter how drastic its effect, did not constitute punish-ment, the project could not invoke the Fourth Amendment against illegal search and seizure. Nor could it invoke the rights related to criminal prosecution, such as a speedy trial or trial by jury, that the Sixth Amendment guaranteed. Defining immigration cases as falling outside the realm of criminal law meant that the "respondent" (as distinct from a defendant) had no right to a court-provided lawyer, protection against illegal search and seizure, or even the right to a trial.

The court's stance forced the Law Project to look for other solutions. The answer came in the form of the Fifth Amendment, which provides defendants the right to "due process" in all criminal and civil proceedings conducted by the federal government. Legally, "due process" placed the burden of proof on the INS to demonstrate that the accused was in the country illegally. Since few people carry their birth certificates or a passport with them and the United States has no national identification system, often the only proof that the INS could furnish was the undocumented worker's own admission. Therefore, what workers do or do not say becomes crucial. Kleinman recalled, "Without that evidence, the INS would have no admissible proof . . . and the immigrant respondent would walk free . . . or so we theorized."²⁵ The effectiveness of this strategy depended on everyone at risk of detention understanding those rights. As a result, the project embarked on its first educational campaign.

The project created and distributed a tri-fold, wallet-sized, bilingual "Know Your Rights" card. It had a simple design; the right-hand corner featured a woman holding a child in her left arm and raising her right fist in the air. Opposite her a man held his right hand in the air clutching a strand of barbed wire, with the slogan "Ya Basta Con La Migra" (Enough with the INS) encircling both figures. The powerful visual representation framed this advice: "Even if you don't have papers: (1) You don't have to answer questions asked by immigration. Talk to a lawyer first. (2) Don't let officials into your house without a warrant. (3) Don't sign anything, especially a document for voluntary departure." The second panel continued, "Don't give in to threats or promises. Talk to a lawyer about a locally held hearing before deportation."²⁶ The flyers offered to help immigrants get released from jail with or without bail and to help getting their papers. They could receive free help by calling the Willamette Valley Immigration Project. Members spent the entire spring handing out these cards at grocery stores, parking lots, movie theatres, and dances. They distributed 5,000 additional cards at 100 labor camps in the Willamette Valley, Medford, and Hood River at the beginning of the harvest season. Then they sat back and waited for the phone to ring.

No calls came in, but the raids began. In late June, the project learned of a raid sixty miles east of Portland in The Dalles, Oregon. Just as the cherry harvest was getting started, a team of INS agents arrested and deported forty-six workers. Even more workers fled. When Larry Kleinman went to investigate, he found only one worker remaining. None of the arrested workers called the WVIP, and members felt dejected. On his way home, when Kleinman stopped at a supermarket to get something to eat, he found the store's manager ordering INS agents off his property for harassing ethnic Mexican customers. Kleinman recounted the manager's words: "He told us that the INS even pissed off [District Attorney] Bernie Smith. 'He is a grower too you know.' We just nodded our heads. Of course we had no idea who he was."²⁷ Kleinman headed straight to the county courthouse to investigate further.

To Kleinman's surprise, Smith welcomed him into his office without so much as asking who he was or what he wanted. Smith immediately launched into his version of events. Larry recalled, "[Smith] told us that he told the agents to halt the warrantless searches or that he would have them arrested for criminal trespassing. The INS agent responded by threatening him with arrest for interfering with federal authorities."²⁸ The agent went on to tell Smith that he should call the

US attorney for Oregon, Sid Lezak. Smith promptly did so, and Lezak responded by denying that he gave agents any such leeway and underlined that they had only limited rights to search private property. After returning to Portland, Kleinman decided that the opportunity to tell this story was too good to pass up. He contacted the editor of the *Oregonian*, who told him that he could not run the story unless Smith went on the record. Figuring he had nothing to lose, Kleinman called Smith back: "To my astonishment, he not only repeated his statements, but encouraged me to quote him . . . and he added a new twist. He recommended that the sheriff discontinue the informal agreement with the INS covering the federal use of local jails predicated on an end to the warrantless searches. He added that they should triple their charges for the use of jails. Apparently the INS paid local law enforcement ten dollars a day to house federal prisoners. That was something else we didn't know."[29] The story appeared in the *Oregonian* on July 13, 1977, although the editor removed many of Smith's quotes. Despite these damaging admissions, the antideportation campaign seemed stymied.

LEGAL SHOWDOWN

Two months later another raid set off the first legal showdown between the INS and the project. On August 16, 1977, agents raided Joe Cereghino's truck farm in Gresham, Oregon, fifteen miles east of Portland, and arrested ten Mexican farmworkers, including eighteen-year-old Alfonso Garcia Dominguez, his cousin Toribio, and his uncle Pedro. Alfonso and Toribio had come to the United States from Alvaro Obregon, Michoacán. Pedro, in his forties, had come to the United States several times, starting with a stint as a bracero in the 1950s. Agents handcuffed the three men and took them to gather their possessions. They lived on property owned by their employer, Joe Cereghino. Approaching Joe, Alfonso showed him a number that he had written on his arm and told him to "contact Ann." Before Joe could write the number down, INS agent Travis Martin grabbed Alfonso's arm and rubbed the number off. He then took Alfonso and the rest of the men to a holding facility. Over the next twenty hours Alfonso demanded numerous times to be allowed to call his lawyer, but with no success. By the next morning all three of the men had given up hope and signed voluntary departure forms. Only then was Alfonso allowed to call the WVIP attorney, Ann Witte.[30]

After hearing from Alfonso, Ann immediately went to the detention center just eight blocks from the project office. Agent Casey allowed her to see Alfonso, but only to "say good-bye." Casey informed Witte that the trio had already signed voluntary departure forms. After ten minutes Witte had convinced the men to repudiate their story and demand a hearing. Casey, Witte recalled, "puffed up and grew red and stomped down to the detention facility."[31] Unwilling to take Witte's word for it, Casey demanded that the men tell him face to face that they demanded a hearing. Casey insisted that Witte had "filled them full of bull." He went on a tirade in broken Spanish and grew frustrated with his inability to persuade the men. When Casey left to make a call, Witte was able to speak to her clients. In an internal memo, Witte wrote, "I explained to them that they had the rights I had told them about earlier and that if they wanted me to work for them, to try and get bail for them and tell the judge their side of the story, they should just turn their heads over to Mr. Casey and say 'Si.' So they did."[32] On August 19, three days after their initial detention, Joe Cereghino put up $4,000 bond guaranteeing the court appearances of Alfonso and Pedro. Unfortunately Toribio accepted voluntary departure and faced immediate deportation. Alonso later explained that after Ann left, the guards proceeded to insult and verbally harass them, ridiculing them as "los tres locos." The insult to his dignity proved too much for Toribio to withstand, and he signed the form.[33]

The case of Alfonso Garcia-Dominguez taught the WVIP several important lessons. First, they needed to find a better way to inform farmworkers of their presence. Alfonso had acted on the advice of the WVIP but never even had one of their cards. Luckily, he had met Ann Witte at a party and written her number on his arm. Second, they needed to adjust their tactics so that they did not depend on the benevolence or ignorance of INS agents. Had Agent Casey not allowed Ann Witte to see her clients, she would have had no other recourse. The WVIP had no way of telling whether other workers had been detained and denied legal representation. Ten weeks after the Law Project's formation, they had the first test case of its resistance strategy.

The Law Project was scrambling until the very moment of the hearing. Project researchers had discovered that immigration regulations allowed nonprofits to seek "recognition" to serve as advocates before the court. Recognized organizations could nominate individuals for a three-year renewable term of "accreditation," enabling them to practice at the administrative level before the INS immigration court and the Board of Immigration Appeals. Foreseeing the legal battles on the horizon, the WVIP viewed recognition as a great opportunity to bring more non-lawyers into their fold in an attempt to demystify the legal process and involve more union members. Just one week before the hearing, Larry Kleinman received his certification.[34]

Nervous and feeling woefully unprepared, Kleinman and the WVIP faced their most important battle. With a touch of bravado to conceal his own apprehensions, Kleinman assured Alfonso Garcia Dominguez that everything would turn out fine. The cramped room was packed with the throng of supporters the project brought with them. Kleinman mused, "Nothing about it resembled a courtroom. There was no elevated dais, no bailiff, and no gated area in front of the tables . . . none of that would have fit."[35] Taken aback as he entered the room, Judge Jones immediately ordered all observers to leave. Kleinman retorted that the hearing was public. Before he could finish, Judge Jones fired back that he was wrong. Scrambling for another rationale, Kleinman deftly argued that his client waived all his rights to privacy. Judge Jones relented. As the hearing progressed, the INS entered into the record Garcia's admission of his unlawful status. Garcia then testified and recounted the story of his arrest and his treatment during detention. According to the trial summary, Kleinman then moved to call Cereghino, who was seated in the hallway waiting to testify, as a corroborating witness. Kleinman stated, "The immigration judge advised counsel that another witness would not be permitted unless the Service [INS] contested the respondent's testimony in any way."[36] The courtroom remained silent for several moments before it became clear that Judge Jones had left Alfonso Garcia Dominguez's testimony as unchallenged and, in effect, let it stand as fact.[37] Neither agent Martin nor agent Casey testified. Using the voluntary departure forms he signed as evidence, Judge Jones ruled in favor of the INS on the grounds that Alfonso Garcia Dominguez was in fact deportable. Oddly, the judge argued that no violation of the Fourth Amendment had taken place, even though Kleinman never made a Fourth Amendment argument. The judge remained silent on the Fifth Amendment case that the project was trying to make.

The Board of Immigration Appeals reversed Judge Jones's ruling on January 16, 1980. It found that the Fourth Amendment exclusionary rule did not apply to civil deportation hearings (*Matter of Sandoval*, 1979) and that the court did not believe that Garcia Dominguez's arrest was unlawful. On the Fifth Amendment argument, however, the board found that Garcia Dominguez "did present a prima facie case that the admissions . . . were involuntarily given" and determined that his detention and denial of access to legal counsel violated his Fifth Amendment right to due process.[38] The board's ruling in *Matter of Garcia* set a legal precedent for all immigration courts. The ruling remains in force today. In its first case before the immigration courts, the WVIP had changed federal immigration law.

THE FIGHT FOR WOODBURN

After the Garcia victory, project members recognized a few flaws in their approach to the immigration cases. One liability was their distance from the farmworker community. During their early strategy sessions, project members decided that they needed to be close to the courts, INS offices, and detention centers. Kleinman explained, "We needed to have quick response; if you couldn't get to the detention centers within three or four hours of someone being arrested, they were gone."[39] As the game of cat and mouse continued, however, they discovered the limitations of that location. When someone called the offices to inform them of a raid or a family member who had been picked up by the INS, project members would call the INS to confirm that the individual was in fact being detained, rush to the INS offices and file a "notice of appearance," and hope that the detainee had not already signed a voluntary departure form. If they hadn't, they would raise money to post bond. The staff grew increasingly frustrated by this course of events. Kleinman recalled, "We lost many more races than we won. And in most cases, there was no race to run. The INS had already deported the person by the time we made contact."[40] It was becoming obvious that the Project had to adjust its tactics.

The need to be close to the heart of the Mexican community in the Willamette Valley outweighed the benefits of being in Portland. Woodburn, a small rural town thirty miles south of Portland on Interstate 5, was home to one of the largest Mexican immigrant communities in Oregon. Kleinman explained, "The idea behind the Woodburn offices was to be closer to the community and to be around when the INS was most active."[41] Dubbed the "City of Unity," Woodburn boasted a diverse population of Anglo retirees, Russian Orthodox "Old Believers,"[42] and ethnic Mexicans. The city seal at the time displayed a retiree with a golf club in hand, a bearded Russian, and a sombrero-wearing Mexican and his trusted donkey.[43]

On weekends Woodburn took on a distinctly Mexican feel. Families from as far south as Eugene and as far north as Longview, Washington, flocked to Woodburn to buy pan dulce, clothing, tortillas, and the latest music. The local move theatre, "The Pix," played classics of the Mexican big screen, and its parking lot became a de facto town square. In addition to finding entertainment, families traveled to Woodburn to receive medical care. The clinic, Salud de Familia (Health of the Family Clinic), stood adjacent to the movie theatre parking lot. The clinic primarily served farmworkers and their families and set its fees on a sliding scale. The neighborhood served as the perfect home for the WVIP, which opened its doors in a one-room storefront across from the Pix.[44]

During the few years the WVIP had been on the scene, the INS had ramped up its efforts in the Pacific Northwest, and large-scale raids continued to dominate the headlines. The Border Patrol from Blaine, Washington, conducted monthly raids and rounded up anywhere from 30 to 150 immigrants at a time. The constant raids gave the WVIP little opportunity to concentrate on less immediate issues.[45] Kleinman recalled, "The thinking at the time was, if we couldn't get any traction with the INS . . . where did we think we were going to get with anything else?"[46] The fear of deportation seemed to be the most pressing issue: "People felt a reign of terror. It's one thing to be abused at work . . . it's another thing for your family not to know if you are coming home from work."[47]

On October 15, 1978, the INS swept through Woodburn and detained one hundred people. The phones in the office rang off the hook as raids continued for nearly a week. By the third day, the project had alerted its media contacts and began patrolling the streets hoping to catch INS agents in another act of blatant misconduct. Then the office received a frantic call from a Woodburn daycare center: "They are here," a woman on the line yelled, "they are in the parking lot!" Kleinman knew exactly who "they" were.[48] A staff member alerted the media and they rushed off to the child care center. They encountered a dramatic scene: two agents were arguing with the day care center director, who was holding a baby. The director screamed at anyone who would listen, "He just came in here and wanted the baby!"[49]

The agents had come to get eighteen-month-old Luz Elena Magallanes, a citizen. Her parents, Rodolfo and Cecilia Magallanes, who were already in custody, refused to sign a voluntary departure form until they were reunited with their daughter.[50] When Kleinman arrived, the agents left. As they returned with Cecilia to pick up her daughter, Kleinman intercepted her and informed her that she did not have to accept immediate deportation. Cecilia broke into tears. Furious, the agents stormed out of the center and headed for Kleinman's car, but then a Portland news crew arrived. As they began videotaping, the media-savvy Kleinman positioned himself in front of the cameras and declared, "We are asking this woman to be released on her own recognizance because she has a sick child."[51] When the cameraman panned over to the remaining agent, he stood frozen, mouth agape, and clearly flabbergasted. The other agent returned from his vehicle and told Kleinman, "We are going to bring her husband here and release them both into your custody . . . you better bring them to the [INS] office tomorrow."[52] That evening thousands watched the drama unfold on the local news, and the morning newspapers carried the story on the front page, with a photograph of the tearful Cecilia holding her baby.

The ongoing raids had a devastating effect on the local economy as well as the Mexican immigrant community. As the crops began to rot in the fields, angry growers demanded that Governor Straub intervene. Responding to the governor's calls, INS director Dahlin suspended the raids: "After all, my guys are entitled to a day off," he quipped to the media.[53] When reporters asked Dahlin why the INS had targeted Woodburn, he responded that he had received over fifty complaints from local residents; apparently the city was not as united as its boosters claimed. By the end of that week the INS had deported 156 immigrants. The streets remained deserted for days, as the remaining immigrants had retreated into their homes and those of their friends. Woodburn felt like a ghost town, even on the weekend. The WVIP had won the media battle, but little else.

Nonetheless, an important new strategy developed out of the Woodburn raids. Project members had noticed a peculiar and disturbing degree of cooperation between the police and the INS. During its study sessions, the project had found memos from the US attorney general that delineated the extent to which local authorities could aid federal immigration officers. The memos clearly stated that local law enforcement authorities had no right to initiate action, but in Woodburn officers took a more proactive approach.

In 1976, Rocky Barilla had brought suit against the Polk County sheriff and the police chief in Independence, Oregon, for performing the duties of immigration officials. In *Trevino v. City of Independence Police and Polk County Sheriffs* (1977), Barilla won a federal district court order that barred the town police officers and county deputies from stopping, questioning, or detaining individuals in order to determine their immigration status, and brought the deputies into compliance with federal law.

In the city of Woodburn, thirty miles away from Independence, Police Chief Lyle Henderson disregarded the court order. Woodburn police officers continued to take the initiative to assist the INS. For instance, Woodburn police officers escorted INS agents to apartment complexes and housing projects and pointed out which units were suspected of housing "illegals." Ramon Ramirez, who lived four houses away from one of the housing projects, noticed Woodburn police and INS agents in its parking lot. Well aware of the prohibition against this type of cooperation, Ramirez confronted the officers, who in turn asked him for his papers. He responded by scolding the agents and refusing to leave the scene. With the recent media troubles undoubtedly on their minds, the officers backed down and left the apartments.

As the struggle with the INS continued, the WVIP developed new strategies to combat "La Migra" that took advantage of its structural weaknesses. The INS had a relatively small team of agents in the Portland area, and the continuous large-scale raids began to wear on its resources and infrastructure. The presence of the WVIP also made the INS's operations increasingly difficult and prevented the raids from always yielding satisfactory results. As a result the INS developed a strategy that included local jailers. Typically, individuals arrested for minor criminal or civil violations could post bail or be released on their own recognizance. At the behest of the INS, however, local jailers began to question Spanish-speaking individuals about their immigration status. If jailers suspected an individual of being in the country illegally, the jailers held him or her until INS agents arrived. The INS had developed a circuit of jails that they routinely visited to check for undocumented immigrants. This procedure was more efficient than coordinating raids.

The strategy caught the WVIP off guard, but the research team prepared a challenge. Local jailers had no legal right to question individuals about their immigration status. They could only place an individual under a twenty-four-hour hold if they suspected they were undocumented. If the INS agents failed to appear before the hold expired, the detainee had to be released. The research proved valuable the next summer in the case of Trinidad De La Cerda. The WVIP's ever-expanding network of informants tipped them off to a case 180 miles east of Portland in Umatilla, Oregon. There, local jailers held Trinidad De La Cerda for three days on an INS telephone hold. The project filed a federal suit against Umatilla County for violating De La Cerda's right to due process. The county was forced to pay $1,000 in restitution to De La Cerda for his illegal detention. More important, the court directed the INS to send written notification to all county sheriffs, police departments, and district attorneys informing them of the 24-hour rule and of federal policies limiting local cooperation.

DIFFERENCES IN ORGANIZATION STRATEGY BETWEEN THE UFW AND WVIP

In Oregon, organizing efforts in the 1960s and 1970s failed not only because of concerted attacks from opponents, such as growers and their political allies in Salem and Washington D.C., but also because of financial mismanagement and incompetence that destroyed people's confidence in their leadership. Many of these Community Action Programs originated from President Johnson's War on Poverty. The CAPs followed a fairly predictable script across the country. Despite mandates that the target communities were to have "maximum feasible participation," they instead began as programs run by well-meaning liberals with little or no input from the communities they were trying to help. After some time the communities fought back and took control of the programs, only to see them disintegrate under political pressure and mismanagement.[54]

In Oregon, the Valley Migrant League, a CAP program meant to improve the lives of farmworkers, lived up to the pattern. Originally the program staff consisted of growers, clergy, and social workers who had long invested in migrant betterment programs. It focused on hygiene, English language use, and schooling. For better or worse, these programs often had a patronizing agenda. Anglos disregarded the opinions of the few Mexican Americans in the organization, assigned them to menial posts, and paid them less than their Anglo counterparts.[55] Eventually a group of college-educated Mexican American staff members, along with sympathetic Anglo board members, staged an internal "revolution" and rewrote the bylaws to force inclusions of migrants on the board. Afterwards, the VML came under severe scrutiny from local politicians and federal authorities and slowly began to disappear. In the meantime, however, the VML struggled with balancing the tension between its federal mandate and its desire to aid migrants in meaningful ways. The federal funding required the VML to remain politically neutral, an almost impossible task when trying to get at the heart of the exploitation of migrants. From afar, El Macriado, the official organ of the UFW, criticized the VML for what it saw as its insufficient effort at improving the lives of farmworkers; "while doing some good in education and vocational training, the VML has emphasized that farm workers who get ahead should leave farm work. Its generous salaries tend to buy off the natural leaders of the farm workers, many of whom end up teaching kindergarten or supervising recreation instead of organizing and building a union."[56] For close observers like Kleinman and Ferrel, the lesson was obvious; federal funding meant you could not serve two masters.

Other programs such as Oregon Rural Opportunities disappeared overnight. Offices closed, and cases were left unsettled. Kleinman recalled, "Papers were left in piles, food was in the fridge, and cups of cold coffee were left on the countertops. It was as if a neutron bomb had gone off and killed all the people and left everything else undisturbed."[57]

Even the work of Cesar Chavez and the UFW left an uneasy feeling among farmworkers. Chavez's first serious encounter with Oregon came in 1971 in direct response to Oregon Senate Bill 677, which was proposed by Gordon McPherson (R-Waldport) and drafted in large part by William Lubersky, a longtime labor lawyer for the 8,000-member Oregon Farm Bureau. The bill was part of a larger national strategy by agribusiness in response to the growing organizing efforts of the UFW. The American Farm Bureau Federation initially tried to pass federal legislation but failed. They shifted focus to the state level, introducing bills in Oregon, Arizona, Colorado, Michigan, Florida, Minnesota, New York, Texas, Washington, and Wyoming.

The Oregon bill, with the endorsement of thirty state agricultural organizations, would have banned primary and secondary boycotts, required farmworker union organizers to register with the state, limited picketers to employees of a farm, banned the picketing of grocery stores, banned strikes during the harvest, outlawed secondary boycotts, and specifically prohibited bargaining about pesticides. Additionally, the bill would have established a system of binding arbitration that would have allowed farmers to reject the arbiter's findings but did not offer farmworkers the same opportunity. It aimed ultimately to extend the antiunion provisions of the Taft-Hartley act to agricultural unions. The draconian nature of the "slave bill" forced the UFW to do battle in Oregon lest it become an example for other states.[58]

Local activists, including the UFW boycott house in Portland, the Valley Migrant League, and other Oregon progressives, organized for months to kill the bill in the senate and led a series of vigils in front of the state capital in an attempt to pressure legislators to vote against it. Despite their best efforts the bill passed easily and awaited Governor Tom McCall's signature. Fearing copycat bills in other states, the UFW finally leaped into action. Cesar Chavez, Richard Chavez, Dolores Huerta, and Jerry Cohen headed to Oregon to put pressure on Governor McCall to veto the bill.[59]

Leading the charge was the brash young lawyer Jerry Cohen. At a meeting with Governor McCall, Cohen threatened to call a nationwide boycott of

Oregon products. Cohen compared the oppression the bill would unleash to the oppression African Americans faced in the South and railed, "If you sign this bill, Oregon will become the Mississippi of the West. We're going to put up a picket line around your state and prevent people from coming in."[60] Cohen and Chavez both knew that the UFW did not have the resources or even the desire to initiate a boycott against Oregon, but they believed that making such a threat would be a powerful deterrent. On the other hand, local residents feared the possibility and believed it to be very real.[61] The *Oregonian* wrote several articles, and editorials flooded the pages expressing concern that Chavez and his union could inflict serious damage to the agricultural industry in the state.[62] The phone calls that poured into Governor McCall's office made Cohen's threat feel real. Fred Ross Jr. (son of legendary organizer and Cesar Chavez's mentor Fred Ross Sr.) traveled to Oregon to coordinate a massive call-in campaign that amounted to over 10,000 letters and phone calls. The pressure was unlike anything the governor's office had ever seen.[63]

Eventually McCall vetoed the bill on advice from his attorney general Lee Johnson that it was unconstitutional. Despite its obvious unconstitutionality, the veto of the bill shocked the Oregon Farm Bureau, which accused the governor of caving in to blackmail. Predictably, for months they insisted that the veto would throw the industry into chaos and harm farmworkers.[64] The governor insisted that his decision had nothing to do with public pressure, contending that the threatened boycott "very nearly persuaded me to sign the bill."[65] Activists chose to believe that their actions and the aid of the UFW forced McCall to veto the bill. After this victory, however, the UFW staffers quickly returned to California. Neither the UFW nor the Valley Migrant League and other Chicano/a organizations that had rallied around the effort to stop SB 677 capitalized on the momentum that had been generated. Despite the dire warning of farmers, no labor unrest spread through Oregon, and the mobilization of volunteers against SB 677 dissipated.

For Chavez, the victory rang hollow because of the struggle's inconclusive ending. Other antiunion bills were proposed across the West and passed in Arizona and Idaho. Chavez admitted to biographer Jacques Levy that Oregon was a distraction: "My heart wasn't in those fights. They slowed us down terribly."[66] Additionally, major players like Jerry Cohen saw little of value in the Oregon organizers, calling them, in typical Cohen style, "Raza bullshitters."[67] Chavez and the union had to turn their focus back to California, where expiring grape contracts and a war with the Teamsters threatened its base. Historian Matt Garcia argues that the UFW turned its attention away from organizing not only in other states but in California as well, as Chavez became more and more enamored with the boycott and less with the arduous task of contract negotiations.[68] This had a disastrous effect on nascent organizing efforts in other states, like Arizona, Hawaii, Oregon, and Texas.[69] Chavez forcefully encouraged UFW branches to turn their attention and money away from local organizing concerns and focus on the boycott.

The departure of the UFW and the failure of other organizations left a void that the WVIP moved to fill. The lack of support and oversight allowed the WVIP to forge its own direction independently of the UFW. Not only was the WVIP free from UFW pressure to pursue the boycott, it was also free to ignore the UFW's anti-immigrant stances. Having already been entrenched in a battle with the INS, the WVIP envisioned a movement for the rights of all workers, not just those with papers, while the UFW had taken a number of anti-immigrant stances, including but not limited to calling the INS on undocumented immigrants in the fields.[70] In the Fresno office for example, staff members kept logs of calls they made to the INS and the response of officers.[71] Cipriano Ferrel believed that the UFW's reputation as an anti-immigrant organization was undeserved. He argued that a few rogue organizers took matters into their own hands and were later reprimanded by the union leadership. Ramirez recalled Ferrel's explanation: "When he [Cipriano] heard that some people were snitching to the Migra . . . he confronted them on the picket line. He told them to stop that shit."[72] Ferrel convinced Ramirez that Chavez and the UFW had been misrepresented.

The actions of the UFW and the words of Chavez himself belied Ferrel's interpretation. The union's anti-immigrant actions permeated its history. In Roma, Texas, for example, UFW members blocked buses of workers coming from Miguel Aleman, Mexico, by lying in front of the buses and even closing the international gate at the border. At the same time, the UFW attempted to build a transnational alliance with the Confederacion de Trabajadores Mexicanos (CTM) to discourage Mexican workers with green cards from crossing the border and working as scabs. Chavez and the UFW also picketed the INS for not monitoring Giumarra Farm's usage of Mexicans with green cards as strikebreakers during the grape strike.

The UFW believed that undocumented workers severely hampered efforts to unionize citizen and resident workers in the fields. Historian David Gutierrez writes that the UFW "consistently maintained this position . . . going so far as to report undocumented Mexican farm workers to the INS."[73] Gutierrez argues that Chavez's stance was increasingly out of step with that of the Mexican American and Chicano organizations he relied on for help. In fact, in 1973 a coalition of Chicano groups confronted the union. In a public statement to the UFW, they insisted that all workers, including undocumented workers, had rights. Chavez attempted to deflect the criticism, claiming that his critics knew nothing about farmworkers or about the labor they performed. Chavez was forced to retract his statement a few days later. Keenly aware of the role that urban organizations played in the success of the boycott, Chavez ceased to publicly call for stricter immigration control.[74]

In contrast, the WVIP maintained its initial commitment to organizing and serving undocumented workers. Although few members publicly distanced themselves from the UFW, they nevertheless saw the WVIP as a separate organization committed to immigrant rights. The WVIP aimed to build a broad-based coalition of people in the community by addressing the issues that mattered to them. Kleinman summed up the situation: "Immigration and immigration raids were the issues."[75] The project set out to build its base one visa at a time, often borrowing tactics the UFW used to build the union. Staffers had handled a few visa cases before that fateful afternoon when Juan Gonzalez stormed into their office, so they had some idea of the increased workload. In order to share the burden, they trained volunteers who wanted to help immigrants with their visa cases and set up a visa clinic.

TENSIONS IN THE COMMUNITY

The raids of 1978 had a profound effect on the WVIP's strategies. Initially members had committed themselves to deportation defense work and dismissed the idea of doing immigration and visa casework because they worried that such burdensome, tedious tasks would slow down their response to the INS. Rather than refusing cases entirely, they planned to train community volunteers to help individuals adjust their residency status. Their fight with the INS, however, had delayed the plan. With a few years of experience under their belt, activists had developed innovative solutions to their problems with the federal government.

The new challenge came from within the immigrant community. Two weeks after the raids in October, a disgruntled Juan Gonzalez stormed into the WVIP office clutching a fistful of papers from the INS and handed them to project member Juan Mendoza. Larry Kleinman heard the commotion and wrote in his unpublished memoirs about the exchange:

> Mendoza told him he had a fifth preference case, because his sister was a U.S. citizen. Then Gonzalez asked him straight to the point if he could get a permit for his family, to which Mendoza answered yes. Gonzalez asked him desperately if we could help and Mendoza told him that we don't handle visa cases but that he could refer him to people in the community that could help him. Gonzalez pleaded with him, told him he didn't have any money, could not read or write English, and didn't know what to do. In a frustrated voice he asked Mendoza: "How do you help people?" Mendoza told him about our work resisting La Migra and Gonzalez, with more than a hint of irony, answered: "So I have to be arrested for you to help me?"[76]

Refusing to accept that the WVIP would only help people who had already been picked up by the INS, Gonzalez flung the work that the project had been doing right back in their faces. The WVIP had spent so much time and energy chasing down and confronting the INS, doing battle in the courts, and receiving an enviable amount of media attention that the work of community building had been utterly neglected. This fact, coupled with the failure of previous antipoverty and farmworker programs, created a sense of disillusionment in the immigrant community.

Although participants were unaware of other organizations using the "clinic" model for immigration work, the UFW service centers had organized similar clinics for the purpose of tax preparation. At the WVIP clinic, trained volunteers met with immigrants, aided them in filling out paperwork, and provided counsel. The program was a huge success. By the end of 1979, the clinic had finished one hundred visa cases, compared to only twenty deportation cases.

Unfortunately, a scandal brought this program to an abrupt end. A member of the volunteer team, Maria Ochoa, left the clinic shortly after receiving her training and started her own business as an "immigration consultant" in Salem. She began passing herself off as a *notaria* or notary public. The seemingly innocuous term *notaria* has a very different meaning in Mexico and Latin America from in the United States. In those countries lawyers are often referred to as notarias/os, have significant legal expertise, and exercise considerable power. Over time Ochoa charged exorbitant fees for doing minimal or nonexistent paperwork. She swindled untold numbers of people out of their money and caused a general panic among immigrants in Woodburn.

The fraud that Ochoa committed also reflected poorly on the WVIP. Members shuddered at the idea of creating another Maria Ochoa, and in response to the damage she caused, they closed the clinic and reinstated the policy of only allowing staff to handle visa cases. Over the next thirty years, the WVIP helped over 6,000 families and individuals adjust their status. While the number could have been significantly larger, the WVIP did not want to risk losing the support and trust of the immigrant community.

THE INS GETS SMARTER

Throughout the late 1970s the INS had focused most of its attention on large-scale sweeps through farms, neighborhoods, and public spaces. Teams of four to fifteen INS agents managed to round up and deport as many as 150 people in one week, but the operations were still rather small-scale. The INS escalated the level and scope of its raids in September 1981 when agents appeared at the Castle and Cooke mushroom plant in Salem, Oregon, whose year-round workforce made it a prime target.

The seven-foot-high chain link fence surrounding the factory was designed to keep the workers in and the project staff out. When WVIP members arrived at the plant after hearing about the raid, they were startled to find four vans, seven patrol cars, and a few buses. Project members had to wait outside with the families and friends of those inside. Together they watched helplessly as INS agents chased men from one shed to another on the thirty-acre site. Sheriff's deputies blocked all the exits. No undocumented worker in the plant escaped.

By 3:00 PM, prison buses rolled into the parking lot and were filled by detainees. One man yelled frantically to the crowd, "Tell them my *mica* [green card] is real!"[77] He held his card up to the bus window hoping Kleinman would see it as the bus pulled away. The buses headed for the National Guard Armory in Silverton, just north of Salem. The stopover bought WVIP enough time to secure the release of sixteen workers, but the overwhelming majority either had undocumented family members, could not afford bail, or simply did want to risk separation from their US-born children by fighting deportation.

Outside the armory, families gathered, worried, and wept. As each bus rolled in, the level of tension rose. The crowd continually urged project members to do something. The WVIP scrambled to learn more about the detainees. Many, they ascertained, had Mexican American wives, so they rushed to gather enough evidence to secure their release. Eventually the WVIP gathered enough paperwork to secure the release of several workers, including Armando Garcia. As the buses rolled out carrying seventy-three workers, one defiantly yelled, "I'll be back next week!"[78] Indeed, many of them did return in the weeks following the raid. The work the WVIP did in trying to aid the detainees paid off later, although they did not know it at the time. Twenty years later many of those workers, including Armando Garcia, initiated a strike at Castle and Cooke.

The raid and its repercussions made headlines. On September 3, 1981, the *Statesman Journal* reported that the raid had left close to one hundred jobs open and encouraged people to apply for work at the Castle and Cooke plant. The INS and its allies consistently argued that undocumented immigrants take jobs away from "real" Americans because they are willing to accept substandard wages and working conditions, and contended that giving Americans jobs justified whatever hardship "illegal" immigrants experienced after deportation. The next day over one hundred people applied for jobs at Castle and Cooke. But their tenure was short-lived. The plant had to replace between thirty and forty workers every week for nearly a month. Three-quarters of them had quit or been fired within a week of taking the job. Managers constantly complained that workers did not do what was asked of them or were lazy. The entire episode had blown up in their faces.

Public criticism did not deter the INS. As the WVIP learned lessons and changed tactics, so too did the agency. On April 6, 1982, the INS began employing the checkpoint, a tactic usually reserved for border areas. This time the INS targeted nurseries, the second-largest component of Oregon agriculture. Nurseries offered many immigrants nearly year-round employment. The work is extremely tedious but must be done meticulously. Employees worked ten-hour shifts and earned just above minimum wage. Glen Walter's nursery, thirty miles west of Portland in Forest Grove, spread over eight hundred acres and employed more than six hundred people at the time, making it one of the largest operations in the state. It also made it a prime target for the INS, which set up a mobile checkpoint on a blind curve just outside the nursery. By checking every car that passed through, agents avoided accusations of racial profiling but still ensured a high yield of apprehensions. Fifteen agents arrested 153 workers in just a few hours and devastated Glen Walter's nursery.

Like the mushroom plant before it, Glen Walter received hundreds of applications after the raid. He hired 126 US citizens, but nursery work did not suit them. Walter added, "Within ten days, only eight were left employed.... Some quit within the first hour. Some worked the whole day. A few worked the whole week. Some even walked out without coming up to office for their pay." Walter estimated that he had lost nearly $12 million: "Four hours without water on a hot day and these plants are dead. I might have to close the operation down,"[79] a dejected Walter added.

Dan Barnhart, executive director of the Oregon Association of Nurserymen, voiced his frustration to reporters: "It's tough, in spite of the fact that Oregon's economy is in shambles, to find 16,000 people to work in nurseries."[80] Once again, the rhetoric of undocumented immigrants taking jobs from US citizens was not borne out by events. INS officials went on the offensive by modifying their message. Commenting to newspaper reporters, unidentified INS officials claimed that it was actually Southeast Asian refugees who benefited from the raids. Portland had become one of the resettlement cities for refugees from the Khmer Rouge, the Vietnam War, and the carpet-bombing of Cambodia, Thailand, and Laos. By 1982, 6,000 refugees lived in the city. Richard Hopkins, Portland Community College's refugee employment project coordinator, rejected those claims: "The INS has shown practically zero interest in refugees; there was a minimal presence of refugees in the field, both before and after the raids."

The INS's rhetoric had been discredited, its plan to employ US citizens had failed, and its effort to permanently remove undocumented immigrants had been frustrated. The next month the INS set up another checkpoint outside of Glen Walter's Nursery and rearrested ninety-seven of the men they had arrested on April 6. Despite the INS's efforts to stem the accusation of racism, its tactics came under scrutiny. Although agents stopped every car that passed through the checkpoint, they detained only those who "looked like Mexicans." The dragnet captured several US citizens of Mexican descent. The WVIP collected statements from them and prepared to sue the INS. Oregon Legal Services filed a federal suit and secured a decree limiting the use of checkpoints. The decree required INS agents to document "articulable facts" beyond race to justify detention. That was the end of INS checkpoints in the Willamette Valley.

As the WVIP adopted increasingly effective tactics, it won the confidence of the immigrant community. Farmworkers began to feel empowered. The project's network of immigrant allies expanded, and legal immigrants displayed solidarity with the undocumented. The written reports that the WVIP made about each raid demonstrate a growing solidarity among workers with and without papers. One raid at Coleman farms provides a humorous example. As the INS vans came speeding into the fields, workers began scrambling and running in all directions. One worker hesitated and then quickly darted off as two agents headed towards him. He headed directly into the latrine and locked himself in a stall. Then he bantered with an agent in Spanish:

"We know you are in there so come out now!"
"I got here first!"
"You're coming with us."
"What did I do?"
"You're illegal."
"No I am not!"
"What do you mean?"
"I have my mica."
"So why did you run?"
"I thought you were trying to get to the bathroom before me and I had to go really bad!"[81]

After emerging from the latrine, the worker presented his resident identification card to the agents. They grew red in the face as the worker and onlookers began to laugh uncontrollably. After the raid Kleinman and the other project members went to the INS offices to seek "stays of deportation" for their clients. In the hallway, a visibly upset INS officer, Oliver Stark, reproached and threatened Kleinman: "You know we are getting close to indicting you for aiding and abetting illegal aliens." Kleinman nodded and replied, "Do what you got to do." The exchange indicated that the WVIP was making some inroads but also served as a warning to tread carefully.

CONCLUSION

The WVIP faced an uphill battle against the INS, they had little connection to the community, they lacked legal expertise, and they had fewer resources. Yet through doing hard work, devising innovative strategies, and responding to the needs of the immigrant community, the WVIP successfully limited the INS's capacity to deport people. It halted the cooperation between federal and local authorities in identifying and detaining undocumented immigrants, limited the effectiveness of large-scale raids and voluntary departure, and in general gave immigrants a sense of agency. The battles that the WVIP fought set the precedent for those of today. Their unheralded strategy in immigration courts paved the way for other immigrants rights organizations, but more importantly they gave immigrants the tools to fight their own battle.

The existence of Colegio Cesar Chavez, although a failure as an institution, brought like-minded individuals together to undertake new initiatives that had lasting consequences. Kleinman, Ramirez, and Ferrel would have undoubtedly been activists in any case, but the Colegio gave them an opportunity to build something together that was much more significant than anything they might have done separately. Drawing on the political philosophies that they developed through their relationships with the UFW, Brown Berets, CASA, and the National Lawyers Guild, they established an organization that was responsive to the community. For all the success, however, the WVIP always *reacted* to the federal government and had yet to take the initiative. Yet it had learned a great deal through fighting workplace raids about the working conditions and grievances of immigrants.

Project members made a collective decision to get involved in labor organizing. Battling the INS began to take its toll. They needed to find other forms of resistance and more effective strategies. The project shifted its attention to the most exploited workers in Oregon. Several of the immigration cases that came across the project's desk involved reforestation workers. Members felt an urgent need to shed light on their exploitation. They had found, however, that shedding light was not enough. They needed to organize workers into a union. With the exception of Cipriano Ferrel, members had little experience with union organizing. Their constituency consisted mainly of undocumented workers, and none had the slightest knowledge of reforestation workers. But in some ways that lack of knowledge contributed to their innovative approaches.

4 ❧ WHIP THAT HOEDAD IN THE GROUND

Undocumented Workers in the National Forest

For many Mexican immigrants the Forest Service provided work during the winter months. Farmworkers spent the rainy season thinning, replanting, and digging fire lines in the remote mountains of the Northwest. The work was arduous and dangerous but typically paid well and negated the risk of traveling south to look for work or having no work. Conditions in the forest, however, were far worse than anything farmworkers faced in the fields. Project members soon began hearing whispered reports about the horrible working conditions in the reforestation industry. Reforestation workers complained about sixteen-hour days without a rest break, low wages, or even no wages at all. Contractors charged them exorbitant fees for equipment and supplies. Workers were isolated and faced harsh weather. Worst of all, they had to fear being entirely abandoned in the mountains. Like the nurseries and mushroom plants, reforestation provided farmworkers with employment during the winter. But reforestation workers encountered extremely difficult conditions and rampant exploitation, as well as nativist attacks by white reforestation workers.

After the initial confrontations with the Immigration and Naturalization Service, the Willamette Valley Immigration Project decided to become involved in labor organizing. Kleinman recalled, "It is kind of a guerilla war that is pretty marginal. It is righteous but we can see this thing going on ad infinitum. It was Cip [Ferrel] that said 'we really need to dig into labor organizing.' "[1] Chasing immigration agents across the state, a tedious task punctuated by dramatic moments, did not develop a community base for the organization or stimulate the growth of a movement. The WVIP responded to the INS raids as an immigrant rights organization, but came to see the shortcomings of that approach. WVIP staff eventually became convinced that even if they adjusted the status of every worker, working conditions would not improve without a union. The project started organizing the most vulnerable group of workers in Oregon agriculture, undocumented reforestation workers. The WVIP chose to organize reforestation for three reasons. First, the level of exploitation in the forests, where the workers' isolation made the exploitation more systematic and common, was more severe than in the fields; second, organizers believed that since most of the work was being done on federal and state land, the federal and state government would be more responsive to the level of abuse; and finally, they knew that most of the reforestation workers were also farmworkers, and they believed that if they could organize the forests, the fields would easily follow.[2]

Americans often romanticize the forest, imagining it as a pristine wilderness. The labor that goes into maintaining the forest, however, is often invisible. Tree planting is amazingly labor-intensive and hazardous. Replanting is done primarily from November to May. Depending on the altitude, workers encounter heavy rain or deep snow, and only the vigorous physical effort that tree planting requires keeps them warm. Workers trudge up the steep slopes of the mountainsides for as many as fifteen hours a day while carrying a forty to sixty-pound sack of seedlings.[3] The seedlings that they carry in their bags average about three feet from root to tip and are planted in the ground with the aid of a hoedad, a specialized tree-planting hoe.

The hoedad handle is around thirty-six inches in length and has a blade between fifteen and eighteen inches long.[4] Workers whip the hoedad blade into the ground and pull up on the handle to break up the soil. If they lift the handle more than a few inches, the hole will fill with topsoil and the seedling will die. After making the hole, the planter rolls the seedling into it with his free hand and simultaneously removes the hoedad. He or she then whips the hoedad into the ground a few inches behind the seedling and pushes the soil back towards the seedling to add stability. The worker can use their feet to firm up the soil around the seedling while being careful not to bruise or damage it in any way. Spacing is also very important: seedlings cannot be too close together or too far apart. Workers have to have specialized knowledge of the needs of different species of trees in order to plant properly. Douglas fir, for instance, cannot tolerate shade, so the seedlings must not be planted too closely together. Tree planters, like their counterparts in the fields, work in rows followed closely from behind by a whistle-blowing foreman who keeps the crew working at a constant rhythm. In each long day, a good worker can plant as many as 1,500 trees.

As early as the 1940s, Mexican immigrants worked in Oregon's forest as planters, seeders, thinners, and even firefighters. Braceros planted trees, thinned mountainsides, and dug fire lines in the national forest and on private timber holdings. By the 1970s, environmental concerns led to massive campaigns to replant areas that had been clear-cut. Environmentalists objected to clear-cutting in particular because it denuded large swathes of land, which resulted not only in the loss of trees but in severe erosion and loss of wildlife habitat. Initially much of the replanting was done quite badly by amateurs. According to veteran tree planter Hal Hartzell, there was very little oversight of tree-planting operations, which led to every imaginable shortcut. Planters were paid by the tree, which encouraged workers to burn, stash, and bury saplings.[5]

As word of the shoddy efforts came out, many environmentalists based out of Eugene, Oregon, felt compelled to go to the forests and do the work. They regarded working in reforestation as politically righteous. The nature of the work appealed to them and their anticapitalist leanings. Replanting required being independent, having a good work ethic, and being far from society for long periods of time. Most importantly, the environmentalists could form a crew without a contractor and be their own boss. What began as a small experiment with a handful of tree planter crews, exploded into a full-fledged cooperative. Over the course of the 1970s the cooperatives planted "millions of trees on thousands of acres in ten western states."[6] These white environmental activists dominated the tree-planting industry for much of the decade until the advent of an unexpected competitor, undocumented immigrants. Contractors attempting to undermine the foothold that environmental cooperatives established in tree planting began to hire undocumented workers and pay them poor wages in order to win reforestation contracts.

TREEPLANTERS, REFORESTATION, AND THE HOEDADS

In Oregon, the creation of sustainable forests required repairing the damage done by decades of clear cutting. In the late nineteenth century most commentators saw the lush forest of the Pacific Northwest as inexhaustible. This attitude persisted well into the twentieth century until the nation witnessed numerous devastating forest fires, which forced loggers and politicians to reexamine their practices.[7] Sustained-yield practices and legislation requiring reforestation began to make headway before the Second World War, but the postwar building boom generated a huge demand for lumber, and builders delayed any effort to reforest. By the late 1970s, nearly three million of Oregon's fifteen million acres lay bare. Despite the creation of a "super" trust fund in 1985, the US Forest Service fell behind in its ambitious plan to reduce the one million–acre backlog on federally owned land. Despite a sharp decline in logging, the amount of clear-cut land in need of reforestation continued to increase by 55,000 acres a year.[8] The backlog pushed the timber industry to reevaluate its approach to tree planting. Efforts in the 1970s were inefficient, ineffective, amateurish, and sometimes fraudulent. According to one former forestry worker, "tree planters were considered the lowest of the low. . . . Contractors hired skid row bums to stuff, kill, and bury seedlings."[9] The 1985 law and government benchmark required skilled and efficient workers. The answer to the Department of Forestry's need for proficient laborers came in the form of the Hoedads.

Named after the tree-planting tool, the Eugene, Oregon–based collective of white male and a handful of female workers began as a group of like-minded leftists. The three founders, Jerry Rust, John Sundquist, and John Corbin, had all graduated from college. According to the Hoedads' biographer, Hal Hartzell Jr., "most of the members were well-educated. Money wasn't the attraction."[10] What attracted them was the opportunity to create a work environment consistent with the political ideas they had adopted in the 1960s. Only a few had any experience in reforestation. Those who did sought out other left-wing activists in the community to join with them in their cooperative effort. They trained others not only in the skills of tree planting but also in the practice of running a cooperative. Former member Roscoe Caron recalled the important role played by a "Wobbly" (a member of the International Workers of the World, an anarcho-syndicalist labor union that had included many lumber and dock workers in the 1910s), who in typical Eugene fashion was known as "Stupid." Caron stated, "Stupid taught us how to run meetings."[11]

The social experiment seemed to be working for the Hoedads. Within a few years of their founding they had expanded to fourteen crews and received a majority of the lucrative tree-planting contracts on both federal and private lands. They had quickly grown to dominate the industry. The original Hoedads created a coordinating committee, the Northwest Forest Workers Association (NFWA), to link all of the crews together and discourage competition between them. Contracts for reforestation work from the federal government were handled through a bidding process; whoever placed the lowest bid secured the contract to reforest acreage. The formation of the NFWA maintained minimum standards among member crews.

Competition for contracts came, instead, from unscrupulous contractors who employed undocumented laborers, whom they either underpaid or did not pay at all. The terms of the contract required the company to pay State Industrial Accident Insurance premiums, which cost as much as $29 for every $100 in payroll.[12] Contractors who hired undocumented workers rarely if ever paid the insurance premiums. These companies undercut the leverage that the Hoedads had once held. By the winter of 1979 the presence of undocumented workers in the forest had a drastic effect on the NFWA's bottom line. Speaking to reporters, one member asserted, "Last year we did three spring contracts worth $150,000. . . . This year we were prepared to do up to $200,000 worth of planting. Instead we've got $36,000 in contracts."[13] The severe decline in employment contracts created discord within the NFWA.

The membership became embroiled in a debate over what to do about the undocumented workers. Rick Koven, an official spokesman for the NFWA,

articulated the conflicting feelings of the cooperative's members: "We are owners of our business and we want to get a fair price for our work. . . . On the other
hand, we are workers and we are sympathetic to Mexican workers. We feel they
are in this country because they haven't got good jobs at home, and we don't
want to go around and try to get them arrested and deported. If we believed
they were getting full wages and benefits, we wouldn't feel that they are unfair
competitors." Koven told a group convened by the Clergy and Laity Concerned
that his co-op had lost forty straight bids in the previous year.[14] The NFWA
demanded that the Forest Service investigate the suspiciously low bids of certain
contractors, but their request fell on deaf ears. Forest Service officials implied
that low bidders were simply making bad business decisions. One quipped, "The
government does not have the right to tell a contractor he can't lose money."[15]
Officials refused to investigate allegations of labor law violations.

Although many of the NFWA members were ambivalent about the surge of
undocumented workers into the industry, NFWA president Gerry Mackie held
a definite opinion. In fact, Mackie had articulated a protectionist ideology even
before companies exploiting undocumented workers began to compete with
the Hoedads. After the first meeting of the NFWA, Mackie expressed concerns
about the group's desire to incorporate other cooperatives by ensuring that
local cooperatives were awarded contracts for work in their vicinity. According
to the minutes of meetings printed in the NFWA newsletter *Together*, Mackie
explained, "Again, I would like to refer to the law of supply and demand. There
is only so much tree planting. The more people who want it, the less they'll get
out of it."[16] Mackie voiced the contradiction at the heart of the NFWA: they
wanted to be a cooperative but functioned within a capitalist economy. Mackie
asked rhetorically, "The concern for local workers is admirable, but where does
our altruism end and our self-interest begin? Are we to sit idle for two months
because we refuse to take work from 'local' people? People we in the meantime
have helped to organize? And what does 'local' mean? Someone who moved
here three years ago? What is our locality? I just don't want to starve because of
its [NFWA's] noble attitude. As far as we can go to help other people is good,
as long as we don't endanger our own existence."[17] Mackie and the contractors
he later demonized shared similar concerns; the contractors who undercut
"local" workers were also acting in their own self-interest. Other members of
the co-op followed Mackie's contention and began holding small protests at
various government agencies. Dean Pihlstrom told the *Eugene-Register Guard*
that about "7,000 tree planters have their jobs in jeopardy" because 57 percent
of the contracts were awarded to "known employers of illegals." Pihlstrom
blamed the problem on the US attorney general, who had directed the INS not
to arrest any undocumented immigrants so that they could be counted in the
1980 census.[18]

Despites Mackie's leadership, the NFWA's course regarding undocumented immigrant workers was still up for grabs. The NFWA newsletter published a letter from one cooperative member, Laurie, suggesting a more measured response to the growing number of Mexican immigrants in the forests: "I'm hoping we can deal constructively with the fact that Mexican tree planters are doing, I'll bet[,] at least a third of the reforestation work here." Laurie pointed out that the NFWA had included Los Broncos, a team of local Mexican American tree planters: "Everyone seems to be avoiding the subject these days, but I think we had a good direction with Los Broncos." Nevertheless, Laurie's letter indicates that the membership was at a loss about how to deal with Mexicans: "Unions are obviously not the answer for these folks and if we start thinking in terms of 'alien competition' we are not going to help them either." The NFWA believed that undocumented workers were not organizable and that unions provided no hope of recourse.

The rift within the NFWA prompted a three-day conference aimed at clarifying the organization's future direction.[19] The organization adopted a resolution stating that their fight was not with the Mexican workers but with the contractors:

The Northwest Forest Workers Association affirms that undocumented workers should be accorded full Civil Rights that are guaranteed to all workers in our country. We recognize that they help produce the wealth that all of us enjoy.

We reject the underlying racism that focus[es] on the undocumented workers as the cause of unemployment and lower reforestation prices. We understand that those problems are the direct result of unscrupulous contractors that exploit and use Mexican workers for their own gain. Corporations that knowingly contract their reforestation work to contractors that employ undocumented workers in order to keep their own labor costs down, also play a part in this exploitation.

There has been a specific history of immigration from Mexico to the United States. Mexicans workers have historically been used to undercut existing labor markets in the United States.

The NFWA opposes a national work card system or any system that attempts to curtail Civil Rights of workers in our country.

We acknowledge that several of our companies in NFWA have been economically hurt by lowered contract prices due to the use of undocumented workers. We support moves that get to the root of the problem and do not penalize undocumented workers for trying to feed themselves.

NFWA supports the right of undocumented workers to organize themselves. Workers in this country have a basic right of job protection from corrupt employers that try to undercut existing labor relations.[20]

The strongly worded resolution demonstrated a sophisticated understanding of immigration reforms and proposals. Few if any workers' groups at the time understood immigration rights in the same context as civil rights. Like CASA, the NFWA acknowledged that immigrant workers created wealth that the rest of the nation enjoys. They explicitly rejected nativist[21] and racist attitudes towards Mexicans and underscored the historical forces that precipitated Mexican immigration to the United States. The NFWA also expressed an understanding of the exploitative nature of guest worker programs. Finally, despite Laurie's belief that unions would be of no use to Mexicans, the statement admitted that they had a right to unionize. Few organizations had worked with undocumented Mexican workers or made any effort to understand their plight. The resolution demonstrated that the NFWA could potentially be an ally.

In the end, however, the resolution might have been the final wedge that broke the NFWA apart. It passed by a narrow margin and caused an even greater rift among the members. The idealism on which the organization was founded gave way to self-interest. Headed by Mackie, some members on the losing side of the vote felt that the group no longer represented them and sought help from congressional representative Jim Weaver. Mackie and other members of the NFWA failed to see the connection between themselves and the undocumented reforestation workers. Both labored under difficult working conditions and both sought to improve those conditions, but instead of seeing a potential partnership, many members of the NFWA saw only "unfair" competition. The other injustice, however, could be seen in the exploitation of the undocumented reforestation workers.

THE PLIGHT OF UNDOCUMENTED FOREST WORKERS

Reforestation work is so arduous and exploitative that citizen laborers felt it necessary to respond collectively to their abusive treatment. Without the protections offered by citizenship, undocumented workers suffered at the hands of employers to an even greater degree than their citizen counterparts. Undocumented workers faced maltreatment on the job, arbitrary reductions in pay, exorbitant and unnecessary fees, outright theft of their wages, deportation, and worst of all, the risk of being abandoned in the forest.[22]

Contractors found a multitude of ways to reduce the wages of undocumented workers. They paid piece rates, which meant that workers' earnings depended on the number of trees they were credited with planting, rather than their receiving the hourly wage guaranteed to them under federal contracts. Contractors also manipulated contract terms to punish workers by fining them. The U.S. Forest service randomly reviewed replanted lands and penalized contractors for nonperformance. In order to avoid fines, foremen inspected seedlings at the end of the day. Deceitful contractors arbitrarily made deductions from workers' pay. The Hoedads and other cooperatives avoided this problem and maximized their earnings by inspecting one another's work and assuring that the work was done properly. At the end of the contract the money was evenly distributed among the members of the crew.[23] Undocumented workers could not hope for such an equitable result.

Contractors that sought to make as much money as possible developed numerous ways to scam workers. Tree planting required a wide array of specialized tools, clothing, and other accessories. The cooperatives in the NFWA brought their own equipment. Typically, contractors provided everything a crew would need over the course of the contract. Since the cooperatives were their own contractor, members shared, borrowed, and bought the necessary accouterments to do the job properly. Undocumented workers, by contrast, came ill-prepared. Contractors forced undocumented immigrants to buy their own equipment. The hoedads, planting sacks, plot rope, knives, special boots, rain gear, snow gear, gloves, tents, and sleeping bags all came out of the worker's pay.

Staging areas are far away from any highway or major road and are accessible only by private logging roads. A long hike, from one to fifteen miles, then commences, with workers carrying hundreds of pounds of seedlings and work supplies. Since the work is done almost exclusively in isolated areas in stints lasting between two and eight weeks, workers also had to provide and lug their own shelter. All tree planters normally stayed in tents and sleeping bags while on the job, but only undocumented workers had the cost of "housing" deducted from their wages. The isolation also meant that workers had to depend on the contractor for food. The prohibitive cost of food often forced workers to go days without eating. One tree planter recalled, "For $25 I received a jar of peanut butter, bread, canned beans, and a jar of Tang" (a powdered orange drink).[24]

By the early 1980s the NFWA had lost ground, and undocumented immigrants were doing most of the reforestation work. As Brigido Reyes discovered, however, being documented did not necessarily make life any easier. He earned only $170 for 120 hours of work in his first tree-planting venture, a rate of $1.42 an hour when the minimum wage in Oregon was $2.90 an hour. Still, Reyes looked for more work in reforestation. His next stint proved too disheartening. After planting hundreds of acres near the Oregon-Washington border, Reyes and his coworkers received no pay. Believing that his being a resident alien with a green card would bolster their chances of getting paid, Reyes's coworkers urged him to take legal action. He heeded their call and complained to the US Department of Labor, but it did nothing. At that time the Labor Department only had two Spanish-speaking agents to investigate claims in the entire Pacific Northwest. Reyes continued working while his case remained unresolved. Over the next few months, he was twice the victim of nonpayment. Completely disheartened, he left the industry.

Undocumented workers faced exploitation in whatever line of work they chose. Harassment, wage theft, long hours, overwork, and payroll deductions for equipment were common. Reforestation workers sometimes were not paid, but undocumented reforestation workers faced the possibility of being abandoned. Foremen could deal with workers' insubordination by leaving them in the mountains. For the workers, simply walking off the job was not a viable option. One worker recalled, "We tried to leave several times but we couldn't find a way back."[25] After returning to civilization, he attempted to claim his unpaid wages: "We tried to locate him [the contractor] but it took us weeks to find him. Once we found him he gave us each $150 in cash after he had promised us $2,000."[26] Undocumented workers had little chance of challenging their bosses on the mountain and less of a chance of recouping wages directly from the contractor. According to the deputy district director of the INS, Carl Houseman, undocumented workers in the forest were widespread. In 1979, for instance, his office deported approximately 250 undocumented workers a month, and during the winter months 73 percent of those came from the forests, where they worked on tree planting projects.[27]

Fortunately, undocumented workers are entitled to sue employers for back wages.[28] By the spring of 1980, the Oregon Legal Services farmworker office had almost sixty pending cases of back wage claims for that year.[29] In Jackson County, for example, Ray Smith, a legal services attorney, sued reforestation contractor Alfonso Gonzales for withholding the pay of Ramon Ramos, Gabriel Gamboa, and Genaro Gamboa. Circuit Court Judge Merryman ordered Gonzales to pay $500 in back wages to each of the three workers and an additional $1,500 in fines. Smith told the local paper, "This is the first time the court has enforced a penalty against a migrant labor contractor in the Rogue Valley."[30] Smith's cocounsel, Jim Work, added, "Because the contractor has been paid by the State Forestry or by the US Forest Service for work done by the whole crew, he can easily pay back the wages of the few who complained and then pocket the rest."[31] Work went on to add that of the twenty contractors in the Medford area; they knew only three or four who were legitimate. Smith explained that violations took place more frequently in the reforestation industry than in the orchard industry. The case was an important victory for the workers and the attorneys, but Work's words pointed to the larger problem. Director J. L. Skolaut of the federal Wage and Hour division in Oregon estimated that anywhere from $200,000 to $300,000 in unpaid wages to reforestation workers was reported that year, but believed that it made up a small percentage of the actual violations because most went unreported.[32]

In addition to miserable living conditions, backbreaking work, nonpayment, and the possibility of abandonment, undocumented workers encountered a number of health risks. Like farmworkers, reforestation workers are constantly exposed to pesticides and herbicides.[33] The Environmental Protection Agency turned a blind eye to the pesticides and herbicides being sprayed in the nation's forests. Dow Chemical Company had invented an herbicide, 2,4,5-T, to kill fast-growing hardwood in order to create more sunlight for the merchandisable Douglas fir. During the Vietnam War, 2,4,5-T and 2,4-D were combined to create the deadly toxin known as Agent Orange. Despite its harmful effects on humans, the EPA approved the use of 2,4,5-T for foresters. While the EPA restricted and prohibited the use of chemicals on "food crops intended for human consumption," it was not concerned about workers.[34] The lumber companies' unfettered use of 2,4,5-T spurred several legal challenges from citizens, environmental groups, and the Hoedads, but spraying 2,4,5-T remained commonplace. In 1980, several newspapers reported that women who lived near national forests had an inordinate number of miscarriages. After congressional hearings, the EPA placed a moratorium on 2,4,5-T. Still, several pesticides that have been prohibited or severely restricted on food crops are still allowed in the forestry industry, demonstrating that concern about toxic chemicals has more to do with consumer protection than with workers' health.[35]

Tree planters faced a variety of other physical, biological, chemical, and ergonomic hazards. Insect bites or stings, Lyme disease, rabies, allergic reactions to plants, and extreme temperatures all posed serious risks to workers. Chainsaws and other equipment used to thin acres for planting posed a safety risk, especially without proper training and precautions. If an undocumented worker fell ill or was injured there was little recourse, as the case of Francisco Diaz Bernal demonstrates. On April 11, 1978, this reforestation worker fell down a flight of stairs at the Holiday Village Motel in Beaver Marsh, Oregon, where the workers were staying. Diaz appeared to be paralyzed and was taken to Charles Medical Center in Bend, seventy miles away. When Diaz arrived at the hospital, Dr. John C. Bell came to the conclusion that Diaz was an undocumented immigrant and refused to treat the young man for his injuries.

A day later, Diaz was moved another seventy miles to Presbyterian Community Hospital in Klamath Falls, where he was diagnosed with a neck-level spinal fracture. The neurosurgeon who tended to him told the *Oregonian*: "When he arrived here, he was totally without function of arms or legs. . . . He had a distended abdomen from gases that had accumulated and a full bladder."[36] After twenty-four days, hospital officials decided to move him elsewhere for rehabilitation, claiming that they did not have the facilities to care for Diaz. One vocal administrator doubted that claim: "If he were able to pay, there wouldn't have been a squawk. Klamath Falls was perfectly able to rehabilitate."[37] Having been rejected from all the hospitals in the area, Diaz was put on a chartered flight back to Mexico. Six weeks later he died from his injuries.

The Diaz family filed a $1.77 million wrongful death suit against Dr. John C. Bell and the hospital, the first of its kind in Oregon on behalf of an undocumented immigrant. The suit claimed that Bell failed to "institute treatment" and that Diaz consequently "sustained further damage to the spinal cord, which resulted in a change from partial paraplegia to quadriplegia."[38] The case was settled out of court and the settlement remains sealed, but the suit was an important milestone on behalf of undocumented workers. A few days later a class action suit was filed in Ontario, Oregon, against Holy Rosary Hospital on behalf of "poor people and migrant workers" in Malheur County for failing to provide "a reasonable amount" of free health care. The hospital was obligated to provide care in return for federal construction assistance. The suit sparked a major controversy in Oregon over whether undocumented workers could receive health care, a debate that predated the California debate over Proposition 187 by fifteen years.[39]

Diaz's death demonstrates the many hazards faced by undocumented workers. Despite its difficulties, tree planting promised better wages and steadier work than agricultural labor. But the reality was more dreadful than anything workers encountered in the fields. They confronted the same hardships as field workers, but the isolation of forest work allowed abuses to go unchecked. It was very difficult for anyone to voice their grievances and nearly impossible for anyone to hear them. Dreams of lucrative wages and consistent employment quickly turned into a nightmare. The WVIP decided to begin its battle for unionization among reforestation workers.

AGENTS OF CHANGE

In 1980, some members of the NFWA persuaded representative Jim Weaver, chairman of the forest subcommittee of the House Agriculture Committee, to hold hearings concerning the hiring of undocumented workers in the national forests. Jerry Rust, a former tree planter himself, testified to what many in the immigrant community already knew: "They [undocumented workers] are often arrested and deported before they are paid—to the benefit of the contractor. They are charged exorbitantly for their travel, for their room, and board. Often times they find themselves owing their soul to the company store. They have no health or accident insurance—and no unemployment benefits."[40] Rust made two other very important points in his testimony. First, he had observed that the importation and deportation of undocumented workers was systematic; many of the same workers were repeatedly imported and deported. Second, and most damningly, Rust stated, "It appears to me that the federal government through its contracts is quite possibly the largest single employer of undocumented workers in the Northwest."[41] Pointing the finger at the federal government and contractors, he argued that a methodical system of exploitation existed in reforestation.

Rust's testimony was largely sympathetic to immigrant workers, but Representative Weaver took a decidedly less understanding stance. After the hearing, Weaver told reporters, "If the recession [in the early '80s] deepens, we're going to have lots of people unemployed and I want Americans right here who would otherwise be on unemployment rolls to be able to get jobs."[42] Prior to being approached by the NFWA, Weaver had already made numerous public statements that were hostile to undocumented workers. Despite the NFWA's proclamation of solidarity with undocumented workers, some members launched their own campaign to save "their" jobs. At a tree planters' protest against government hiring practices, Weaver stood in the crowd holding a sign that read "Employ A U.S. Citizen, Not An Illegal Alien."[43] He gave an impromptu speech and promised to fight until the reforestation workers in the crowd got their jobs back. The rogue group of NFWA members prodded him to "do something about the illegals in the woods"[44] by stepping up deportations. The NFWA launched a letter-writing campaign and enlisted the aid of not only Weaver but forty members of the Oregon legislature, aimed at the Forest Service to pressure them into doing something.[45] The sudden change in attitude toward undocumented aliens, in particular the use of the term *illegal alien*, is marked by the appearance of Weaver as an ally. Prior to the hearings, the NFWA documentation, such as minutes, newsletters, and correspondence, does not use the term. This suggests that Weaver's politicization of the situation pushed the NFWA into more vehement racist and nativist attacks.

Weaver responded to these demands by creating an "interagency taskforce" comprised of the US Forest Service, Bureau of Land Management, Department of Labor, Immigration and Naturalization Service, and Oregon Bureau of Labor and Industries. The task force recommended that the Forest Service adopt new regulations intended to keep unscrupulous contractors from underbidding legitimate employers. They included a certified payroll, a 20 percent bond, bilingual contracts, and a requirement of a state labor license.[46] The task force operated under the premise that deporting workers could eliminate unscrupulous contractors. As a result, INS raids became the focal point for interagency cooperation. INS agents received all contract bids and award notices that were 10 percent below government estimates, reasoning that any bid that low must employ undocumented immigrants, making them targets for raids. This despite the fact that the NFWA's bids often came in well below the government estimate. But perhaps the most egregious and offensive regulation provided "training" to Forest Service and BLM planting inspectors on "how to spot an illegal alien."[47] President of the NFWA Gerry Mackie applauded the changes and thanked the Forest Service for being responsive to their concerns.

Although immigration raids had taken place in the reforestation industry in Oregon since at least 1969, the number and frequency of apprehensions increased sharply. Later that year the INS began a series of raids of reforestation sites, using the 10 percent benchmark that Weaver had encouraged. In Waldport, Oregon, the

INS targeted a reforestation site because of the low bid won by Andres Sharipoff of Woodburn. Sharipoff had won the contract by bidding $92 an acre for a 501-acre tract, while the next closest bid stood at $225 an acre. The raid resulted in the deportation of thirty-seven undocumented workers, but the NFWA's Dean Pihlstrom was unimpressed; the bids, he said, "were too low to be done."[48] In other words Pihlstrom felt that the acreage of the awarded contract was too small to be consequential. A second raid a few weeks later "netted" twenty-seven more undocumented immigrants in Reedsport, elicited a similar response from Rick Koven and Bob Leach of the Hoedads, who both said it was too early to tell.[49] Led by NFWA president Gerry Mackie, the workers' cooperative developed a more intimate relationship with Representative Weaver. The NFWA became increasingly hostile towards undocumented workers, in striking contrast to their resolution of just a few years before. Despite the NFWA's claim that they were "not about the money," once the money stopped flowing everything changed.

In response to the growing hostility from the taskforce and the NFWA, the WVIP took the offensive. Both Kleinman and Ferrel accused the NFWA publicly of instigating racist attacks on immigrants, by which they meant INS raids. Ferrel warned that white reforestation workers were ultimately setting the workers' struggle back. Michael Muniz, an attorney with Oregon Legal Services, added that his office continued to see the same number of complaints as before: "it's been our experience that the rules have had little, if any, effect."[50] The WVIP correctly predicted the increase of INS raids, as the following year saw raids in the Gifford Pinchot National Forest, Chelatchi Prairie, Carson, Hood River, Falls Creek, and the Olympic National Forest.[51]

One of the most public attacks on the contractors, the task force, and the NFWA came in a series of investigative articles in Salem, Oregon's *Statesman Journal*. The WVIP alerted *Statesman Journal* reporters Phil Manzano and Michael Walden to the horrific conditions that undocumented workers encountered in the reforestation industry. They followed a group of undocumented workers crossing the border and traveling to Oregon and related their experiences in reforestation. The hard-hitting exposé earned the duo a Bruce Baer award for excellence in the profession. The series sparked community organizations into action. The Lawyers Guild and other legal services agencies pursued back wage claims on behalf of reforestation workers, the Benedictine Sisters provided affordable housing at Mt. Angel College, and numerous other social services agencies provided assistance.

What the WVIP knew about the conditions in the forest was mainly anecdotal. Larry Kleinman recalled the horror stories that were brought to the organization. For example, "We heard persistent rumors of a Mexican crew being killed on Mount Saint Helens during the eruption but could never get anywhere trying to prove it."[52] This and other rumors attested to the terror that immigrant workers felt, but WVIP needed more concrete evidence. Staffers decided to address the problem by starting the Reforestation Worker Education Project. The educational project served a dual purpose: to educate their supporters about working conditions in the forests and to educate each other about the reforestation industry. The WVIP consciously borrowed this tactic from the UFW, which had used it in its early organizing campaigns.[53]

The educational project confirmed the WVIP's suspicions. A survey they conducted of all the immigration cases that came across their desk revealed that reforestation workers made up the majority of the people seeking help. Staffers then interviewed three of the reforestation workers who came into the office. They also interviewed hundreds of additional workers at local hangouts and passed out the survey to other workers to fill out and bring back to the office. The questionnaire asked about workers' experiences, living conditions, pay, and job-related illness and injury. The results confirmed the stories of low wages, long hours, six-day workweeks, being injured in the forests with no access to health care, and being left in the middle of the forest with no way home. As the UFW had done with field workers, the WVIP used the survey results to address the most pressing demands of tree planters.

Fully 80 percent of Oregon's and Washington's estimated 15,000 reforestation workers were Mexican; 78 percent knew little or no English. Their average age was thirty. Most had been doing reforestation work for an average of three years, and 72 percent also worked in the fields. Most (71 percent) lived on the job site, in tents and campers or out in the open, while a few commuted. A majority (51 percent) worked six days a week and 19 percent worked seven days a week. Almost all (93 percent) were allowed less than half an hour for lunch, and almost one-third (30 percent) did not receive more than one break per day. Most were severely underpaid, paid late, or not paid at all. Others received cash payments with no record of deductions and were threatened with deportation if they complained. One-third of the workers had some type of work-related injury, and nearly one-half reported unusual illness (i.e., any sickness more severe than the flu or the common cold).[54]

These findings inspired the WVIP to combat the wave of immigration raids in the forest. Raids are inherently destructive and disruptive, but the isolation of the wilderness made them even more frightening and dangerous. Being caught by the INS meant deportation to Mexico and having to cross a perilous border and make the trek back to Oregon all over again. Trying to escape the INS entailed potentially life-threatening situations. Workers who managed to evade the agents faced hypothermia, starvation, dehydration, and sometimes death. Finding a way back to a main road or a town was nearly impossible.

The WVIP initially pursued a partnership with the NFWA in hopes of building a united front against the INS raids. Project managers believed that the progressive politics of the NFWA made them a natural ally and that the group would be receptive to their proposals. The NFWA pointed out that in the previous year they had passed a strongly worded resolution at their annual conference in support of the rights of undocumented workers. But the WVIP found the resolution insufficient. WVIP members believed that the NFWA was actively working with the INS and pointed to certain members' relationship with Representative Weaver as evidence. The NFWA insisted that it did not intend to aid in the increasing numbers of immigration raids.

One incident after another drove the WVIP and the NFWA apart. For the NFWA these were misunderstandings, but the WVIP read them as blatant racism. According to the minutes from an NFWA meeting on February 21, 1983, the Hoedads placed an advertisement in the *Eugene Register Guard* for tree planters. Shortly thereafter Pat Brenner, a member of the Hoedads, received a call from the INS inquiring about the number of applications that had been submitted. Brenner reported the information to the INS, which used it to argue publicly that qualified American citizens had lost jobs to undocumented workers. When the WVIP discovered this "collaboration" between the Hoedads and the INS, the project demanded that the Hoedads explain themselves. Later, at a face-to-face meeting, the NFWA argued that it was a simple misunderstanding that resulted from a certain amount of naiveté. There was no way, they argued, that Brenner or any other member could have known what the INS was up to. The WVIP was dissatisfied with this explanation.[55]

The two groups also disagreed about legislative responses to undocumented workers in the forests. At the meeting Gerry Mackie explained the NFWA's legislative strategy and reiterated its support for full compliance with payroll certification.[56] Mackie believed that requiring contractors to operate with a state-issued license would deter them from hiring undocumented workers. If a contractor "knowingly" hired undocumented workers, its license would be revoked. The WVIP was not convinced that a license would keep contractors from exploiting workers. Members believed that even if a contractor had its license revoked, it could simply refile under a relative's or a corporation's name. The WVIP argued that this measure did little to affect undocumented workers other than potentially putting them out of work.

The WVIP insisted that the NFWA comply with three demands. First, the NFWA must decide where it stood on the issue of illegal immigration and clarify its position on cooperation with Weaver's interagency task force. Second, it must write a letter disclaiming the validity of the statistics Brenner provided to the INS. Finally, the NFWA should work closely with the WVIP to develop a long-term legislative fix for the contracting problem.[57] The NFWA passed resolutions disclaiming the statistics and on noncooperation with the INS, and agreed to work with the WVIP. There was only one no vote on the first two resolutions and one abstention on the third. The WVIP had extracted the promises they demanded, but when the raids continued they continued to suspect the NFWA of cooperating with the INS.[58] Indeed, WVIP members began to suspect that the collaboration went far beyond sharing statistics. Rumors circulated that the NFWA had begun tipping off INS agents as to the location of work camps. Despite the NFWA's protestations of innocence, Kleinman was unmoved: "Of course they [NFWA] knew [about the INS]. They snitched them [immigrants] off. Who else knew where these workers were? The INS sure as hell didn't know. The Hoedads [NFWA] knew those mountains and where people were."[59] In subsequent years the NFWA worked against the stated goals of their resolutions, which made rumors of their cooperation with the INS increasingly believable.

Yet the WVIP continued to try and find common ground with the NFWA. In the fall of 1984, the NFWA and the WVIP jointly filed a mandamus action intended to force the Department of Labor to include reforestation workers under the Migrant Seasonal Agricultural Workers Act. The act protected workers by requiring employers to provide pay stubs, make certain disclosures about the type of work to be performed, and have the housing they provided for workers inspected. Attorneys Mary Lewis and Michael Dale successfully argued the case in front of Judge Burns in US District Court. On September 30, 1985, Judge Burns ruled that reforestation work was covered under "agricultural employment" and that the protections of the act should be extended to reforestation workers. He wrote, "These individuals have been victimized by contractor exaggeration of conditions of employment, deceived about the length of employment and wages, transported in unsafe vehicles to remote forestry camps, furnished with unsanitary and substandard housing and paid in cash, net of unexplained deduction.... I conclude that these are precisely the evils at which Congress was taking aim when it broadened the definition of agricultural employment in 1974 when it intended to include all contractors."[60] Burns identified forestry work with other forms of agriculture: "It is inconceivable that Congress intended to protect workers planting trees in orchards and to disregard workers planting trees on a hillside, when both groups suffer the same clearly identified harm."[61] Both the NFWA and WVIP viewed Judge Burns's ruling positively. Tree planters no longer lived in a legal limbo between industrial and agricultural work. The decision made it possible for advocates to challenge the treatment of reforestation workers.

The brief moment of collaboration between the WVIP and NFWA temporarily reduced the gap between the two organizations, but in the spring of 1983 they clashed over proposed Senate Bill 525. The NFWA lobbied Margie Hendriksen, a state senator, to introduce a bill curbing the use of undocumented workers in the forest. The main point of contention was a provision that imposed large fines and jail sentences for contractors hiring undocumented workers. The NFWA continued to contend that employer sanctions would discourage contractors from hiring undocumented workers and that depressed wages were caused by the contractors' hiring practices. Speaking to an *Oregonian* reporter, an NFWA spokesperson argued that "most of these contractors will only hire illegal aliens. . . . They want an exploitable work force. . . . Exploited illegal labor is displacing legally-paid labor."[62]

Conversely, the WVIP had long opposed employer sanctions that were already on the books, and in this case they characterized the proposed law as "super sanctions." In a letter to Margie Hendriksen, Ramon Ramirez reiterated this position: "In reality, the unscrupulous contractors exploitation and abuse of labor—US citizens, documented and undocumented alike—is the overwhelming cause of the industry's poor condition."[63] Ramirez explained that employer sanctions would lead to discrimination against Hispanics. To avoid prosecution without burdensome record keeping, he argued, employers would simply refuse to hire anyone who looked Hispanic or "foreign," and those workers would be left without recourse. Ramirez cited a General Accounting Office study that determined that in ten other states where employer sanctions had been introduced, sanctions "were unenforceable and ineffective. Yet their potential for fanning racial discrimination is immense."[64] A coalition of organizations that represented ethnic Mexican interests, including the WVIP, lobbied against the bill, which resulted in the removal of the "super sanctions." The removal was a success, but the WVIP pushed even further by trying to add an amendment that would repeal the employer sanctions already in existence. The original drafters of the bill, the Bureau of Labor and Industries and the NFWA, vehemently opposed the repeal of employer sanctions and Margie Hendriksen saw it as a "different issue."[65] The WVIP reasoned that ultimately an amendment would be an uphill battle and that they should focus their energies on the interagency task force. "In our opinion the present employer sanctions does not represent a threat anywhere near as great as the effects of the NFWA and Rep. Weaver . . . for almost two years, the Bureau of Land Management, the US Forest Service, the Oregon Department of Forestry, and the Immigration and Naturalization Services have collaborated to step up raids against Mexican tree planters in Oregon and Washington."[66] The growing number of raids prompted the WVIP to begin gathering evidence of harassment of US-born Mexican workers by the INS. They thus shifted their focus from the bill to the dismantling of the interagency task force.

The WVIP accused the NFWA of being motivated by racist attitudes, while the NFWA was adamant that its actions were not motivated by race. The NFWA continued to lobby on behalf of employer sanctions, arguing the UFW was also in favor of employer sanctions, despite the fact the UFW was actively lobbying against them at the federal level.[67] In a memo to the Weaver task force, Mackie added, "I want to immediately dispel the impression that our concerns are motivated by racism. That some of our people were out in the woods and saw some Mexicans and got mad."[68] The motivations of the NFWA were clearly more complicated than this, but the NFWA's stated intentions were inconsistent with its actions. The NFWA grew increasingly hostile towards undocumented workers. What began as a careful and measured response to undocumented workers, devolved into racist caricatures and abusive and dehumanizing images in their newsletters. Suddenly words such as "illegal" and "wetback" started making their way from NFWA members' mouths and into the public debate.[69]

A year after Jim Weaver's initial hearing, the group's concern for workers started to fade as its concern for jobs grew. Its arguments were couched in nativist rhetoric. Signs at protests read "Keep the hoedad in American Hands"; "American Citizens Si, Illegal Aliens No"; "Hire Americans to Plant Trees."[70] A Hoedads representative told the *Oregonian*, "With the high rate of unemployment here and tree planting already reduced to forty percent of normal, it is going to be increasingly difficult to tolerate the outlaw sort of contractor who hires illegal aliens and underpays them. . . . From our workers' observation, half the state's tree planters come from Mexico."[71] The NFWA even backtracked from its successful effort to classify reforestation workers as agricultural workers. The newsletter warned, "This is a different case than the farmer who hires illegal aliens; they often cannot find American workers who will work for the wages they pay. But Americans do want to plant trees. With wages running from $8.50 to $12.00 an hour, it is possible to make a living planting trees."[72]

While it was true that some American citizens worked and made a living planting trees, the reality was that the work was so difficult and strenuous that the turnover rate was enormous. The NFWA's numbers vacillated constantly, with the average tree planter lasting less than thirty days.[73] The original Hoedad members often bragged about the turnover rate and understood that not everyone was cut out for the job. In their office they proudly displayed a sign from the Oregon State Employment Service that testified to the rigors of the job:

"It is the hardest physical work known to this office. The most comparative physical requirement is that of a five-mile cross-country run, daily. If all body joints are very good condition, a person has excellent persistence and at four-and-a-half miles of your self-trial run, you know you can do it, and can persuade the foreman, you may make it the three weeks it takes to really learn how to be a team member on a planting crew . . . of those who adequately persist to get on the two hour crummy [a dilapidated motor vehicle] ride for a trial, one person in fifty succeeds for the three week period. It actually is a good job for some."[74]

Members often remarked about all the difficulties that the announcement missed, the forty-pound sack of trees, the weather, and the wildlife, but agreed that this was not a job for most. Yet when undocumented immigrants entered the tree-planting arena, the talk of lost jobs for Americans became a rallying cry. But in actuality very few people were cut out for the job and the State Employment Service had difficulty filling labor needs in the forest.

In the end the WVIP lamented the lost opportunity to build a multiracial movement of workers in the forests. As Anglo reforestation workers moved out of the sector, undocumented workers came to dominate.[75] Concurrently, the reforestation industry in Oregon declined as the recession plunged commercial spending on thinning and seedling planting; the percentage of acres replanted fell from 7.6 percent to 0.42 percent. As the recession ended the spending did not return; the never-ending quest for cheaper labor sent lumber companies fleeing to the American South.[76] At the same time the WVIP ceased to organize workers in the forest but did not give up on the workers themselves. In fact many of those workers went on to play a crucial role in the formation of Oregon's first farmworker union.

FIGURE 1. Mexicans lined up and waiting for registration and assignment to farmers in Hood River County. (From the Braceros in Oregon Photograph Collection, OSU Libraries Special Collections & Archives Research Center.)

FIGURE 2. Flag-raising ceremony, Columbia County Mexican farm labor camp. (From the Braceros in Oregon Photograph Collection, OSU Libraries Special Collections & Archives Research Center.)

FIGURE 3. Josefa and Mercedes Rivera in the fields near Nyssa, Oregon. (From the author's personal collection.)

FIGURE 4. Rivera family at a migrant labor camp in Oregon. (From the author's personal collection.)

FIGURE 5. Children working in the onion fields near Ontario, Oregon. (From the author's personal collection.)

FIGURE 6. Demonstration to support Colegio Cesar Chavez in SE Portland circa 1975. (Courtesy of Pineros y Campesinos Unidos Noroeste.)

FIGURE 7. ¡Ya Basta! Willamette Valley Immigration Project poster. (Courtesy of Pineros y Campesinos Unidos Noroeste.)

FIGURE 8. One of the first groups accompanied by the Service Center to successfully apply for legalization. Larry Kleinman second from the left. July 1987. (Courtesy of Pineros y Campesinos Unidos Noroeste.)

FIGURE 9. Cipriano Ferrel, May 1, 1995. (Courtesy of Pineros y Campesinos Unidos Noroeste.)

FIGURE 10. Conference at Genn Zielinski Farms in Brooks, Oregon, June 1995. Workers renamed the Zielinski labor camp after winning the right to live there. (Courtesy of Pineros y Campesinos Unidos Noroeste.)

FIGURE 11. Workers playing the guitar after work. (From the Braceros in Oregon Photographs Collection, OSU Libraries Special Collections & Archives Research Center.)

5 ❧ "NOW I CAN HOLD MY OWN WITH ANYBODY"

IRCA, Immigrant Organizing, and the Pineros y Campesinos Unidos Noroeste (PCUN)

As the immigration debate began to take center stage around the country, the WVIP's members had already become seasoned veterans. Their position on employer sanctions, immigration raids, and the guest worker programs presaged the developing opinion of Mexican American civil rights groups and immigrant rights organizations. Thanks to their decade-long struggle with the INS, the WVIP was firmly positioned to deal with the challenges of the coming immigration law and turned that it into an opportunity. The group's battles with the INS, contractors, growers, and the NFWA all contributed to the move into labor organizing, and on September 15, 1985, the Willamette Valley Immigration Project gathered its constituency and announced its plan to form a union. Project members picked Mexican Independence Day to draw parallels between the two struggles: "It was on this day in 1819 that the Mexican people demanded their independence. In this same spirit, we will come together to also demand our legitimate right as workers."[1] The WVIP became the Pineros y Campesinos Unidos Noroeste (United Tree Planters and Farm Workers of the Northwest) or PCUN. The foundation of this union had been laid in the immigration work that the WVIP had done in the previous decade, which positioned it to be uniquely prepared for the passage of the Immigration Reform and Control Act of 1986. The amnesty provided PCUN its initial membership base, which grew concurrently with a non-farmworker base that included students, activists, clergy, and laity. For almost a decade the new union built relationships and organizational capacity by developing innovative grassroots strategies and providing services to the immigrant community.

THE NATIONAL DEBATE

The debate surrounding immigration reform involved so many competing interests that settling on a reform bill seemed impossible. In response to numerous legislative failures in addressing immigration reform, President Carter created the US Select Commission on Immigration and Refugee Policy (SCIRP) in 1978. By the 1980s two considerations drove conversations about legalization. On the one hand, proponents advocated for legalization out of a sense of fairness. They believed that undocumented immigrants contributed to the American economy and had developed social and economic equity (built homes, opened businesses, and started families) in this country. They had a stake in the country and should therefore be allowed to participate fully as citizens. On the other hand, others saw legalization as an economic problem, arguing that undocumented workers cost the country money through increased border patrol expenditures, taxes, and jobs. They ignored the fact that immigrants, whether legal or not, paid taxes. The sixteen-member commission spent two years evaluating the immigration question and setting an agenda for reform. On March 1, 1981, SCIRP submitted its report to President Reagan and Congress. Its recommendations defined the terms of the debate and resulted in the passage of IRCA.

After two years of public hearings, congressional testimony, research, and investigations, the primary recommendation was simple: "The Select Commission recommends that a program to legalize undocumented/illegal aliens now in the United States be adopted." SCIRP recommended a cutoff date for eligibility of January 1, 1980, reasoning that undocumented immigrants seeking legalization would be discouraged from entering the country after legislation had been enacted. Despite arguments over the particulars of the legalization program, one thing was certain: a legalization program was necessary. SCIRP concluded that any legalization program had to deal with four central issues: eligibility standards; strategies to maximize participation; new enforcement efforts; and a policy towards undocumented immigrants who did not qualify for amnesty. The SCIRP report lit a fire under Congress and President Reagan, and it triggered a wave of immigration bills.

During his time as the Republican governor of California and as a presidential candidate, Reagan rarely mentioned immigration. When he did broach the subject, it was clear that he did not consider it imperative to address undocumented immigration: "I wonder about the illegal alien fuss. Are great numbers of our unemployed really victims of the illegal alien invasion or are those illegal tourists actually doing work our own people won't do?" As a longtime friend of agribusiness interests who had once famously denied the existence of the UFW grape boycott, Reagan preferred to allow undocumented immigration to continue unchecked. Pressure from the SCIRP report, politicians, and the public, along with the sudden influx of Cuban and Haitian refugees, forced the president to establish an interagency task force to review the SCIRP report and make recommendations.

The issue was a thorny one for Reagan, who had to balance the Republican coalition, which favored a stringent law-and-order approach, with libertarians, who resisted the encroachment of governmental power—and still respond to the demands of agribusiness. The House and the Senate held joint hearings on immigration reform for the first time since 1951. The Immigration Reform and Control Act of 1982, known as the Simpson-Mazzoli bill, included employer sanctions, legalization programs, and an expanded guest worker program. The mishmash of varied opinions and interests the bill included made it a target for derision from all sides. After numerous deaths and reincarnations, the bill passed and was signed into law by President Reagan on November 6, 1986. The newly formed PCUN considered the passage of the bill a defeat. It staunchly opposed employer sanctions, guest worker programs, and increased funding for the border patrol. Yet the opportunity to legalize scores of workers infused the union with new members and new life.

Immigration reform proposals offered PCUN an opportunity to form coalitions with other groups concerned with immigrants' well-being. PCUN joined with other groups to form the Oregon Coalition for Immigrant and Refugee Rights (OCIR) as a collective advocate for immigrants. OCIR voiced strong opposition to IRCA, especially its provision for employer sanctions. The coalition saw employer sanctions as an excuse for wholesale discrimination against Latinos or anyone who "looked illegal," regardless of their citizenship status.[2] Four years later, a study done by the GAO (a politically neutral arm of Congress, now called the Government Accountability Office and formerly the General Accounting Office) confirmed those fears: discrimination against Hispanics and other "foreign-looking" individuals had skyrocketed in the wake of IRCA. Yet employer sanctions did not stop employers from hiring undocumented workers.[3] More than a year after the passage of IRCA, only thirteen citations had been issued in Oregon, and no one had been fined. One company was found to have 750 undocumented workers on its payroll and was issued a citation, but it avoided paying the fines.[4]

In addition, PCUN thought that the proposed amnesty program was too stringent. The legalization program had a number of provisions that PCUN found objectionable. First, immigrants had to demonstrate evidence of unlawful entry before January 1, 1982, and prove that they had lived continuously in the United States since then. Two other provisions required applicants to file within a year of IRCA's enactment and to maintain residence in the United States during the application process. These provisions were intended to prevent a rush of unauthorized entrants looking to take advantage of the amnesty.

PCUN members thought that asking undocumented people to document their presence in the United States was laughable. They had been careful to shield themselves from scrutiny and were ineligible for most public programs, so what official documents could they produce? Additionally, PCUN believed that asking people to stay in the country throughout the legalization process placed an unnecessary financial burden on those who migrated back and forth across the border for their livelihood.

Despite the provision's intent, it ended up causing more confusion for undocumented immigrants, their advocates, and the court. The vagueness of key terms such as "continuous residence" and "known to the government" led to a flood of lawsuits on behalf of undocumented immigrants. Evidentiary problems became an even greater concern for administrators. The general legalization regulations called for three types of documents: proof of identity, proof of residence, and proof of financial responsibility. Acceptable documents included a driver's license, a rent receipt, utility bills, and paycheck stubs. Administrators could easily verify the documents if undocumented immigrants could produce them. But the question remained: what constituted a "preponderance of evidence"? The failure to define the term left the task of interpretation up to individual INS inspectors, which often led to very similar cases being treated very differently. In practice, the process was highly subjective and the results were quite arbitrary. As a direct result of these inconsistencies, various nonprofit organizations filed class action lawsuits on behalf of those whose applications were denied. The INS's inability to define "preponderance of evidence" resulted in an overwhelming number of its denials being overturned.[5]

"LUCKY FOR US THERE WAS SAW"

Legislators crafted IRCA for immigrants like Damian Alvarez-Arias. Alvarez had come to Oregon nearly seven years before the enactment of IRCA and had been living in hiding ever since. Not wanting to be permanently separated from his family in Mexico, Alvarez regularly risked deportation or worse by traveling back and forth. He used a fake social security number and maintained his employment over the course of seven years. These circumstances made it relatively easy for him to prove his residence and duration of residence despite his regular trips back to Mexico.[6] For many other undocumented immigrants, however, the process proved too difficult to navigate. The Special Agricultural Workers (SAW) provision of IRCA proved to be a blessing in disguise for many immigrants who could not meet the eligibility requirements of the general amnesty.

Although SCIRP explicitly rejected a guest worker program in its report, guest worker programs already existed. Growers had long exploited the vulnerable position of guest workers by paying them substandard wages and using their temporary status against them. The bracero program ended in 1964 in name only. In practice, the United States continued to import guest workers through the H-2 section of the Immigration and Nationality Act.[7] Grower representatives, especially the Agricultural Employers Association, pushed to have a new version of the guest worker program in every version of IRCA. President Reagan also tried to advance growers' interests by proposing to admit 50,000 Mexicans annually for two years.

Senator Alan K. Simpson (R–Wyoming), Representative Romano L. Mazzoli (D–Kentucky), Representative Peter W. Rodino (D–New Jersey), Representative Charles N. Wilson (D–Texas), and Senator Ted Kennedy (D–Massachusetts) all introduced versions of a new guest worker program, but none passed until a last-minute amendment was introduced by Representative Chuck Schumer (D–New York) in June 1986. Many have credited the Special Agricultural Worker provision with being the compromise that enabled IRCA to pass. Through the SAW program, undocumented immigrants who could demonstrate sixty days of seasonal agricultural work in qualifying crops between May 1985 and May 1986 were eligible to apply for immediate permanent resident status. Congress eventually decided on a ninety-day work period and temporary resident status until legalization was completed.

As part of IRCA, the H-2 visas were split into H-2A for agricultural workers and H-2B for nonagricultural workers. While IRCA implemented limits on the number of H-2B visas, it placed no such limits on H-2A visas, effectively creating a never-ending supply of exploitable agricultural workers for growers. The Special Agricultural Worker provision of IRCA gave workers without visas, and those hoping to skip out on their visas, an avenue to adjust their status.

The same rights awaited the applicants of the SAW program and the legalization program, but standards of proof vastly differed. General legalization applicants had twelve months to apply for temporary residence, while SAW applicants had eighteen months. General applicants had to demonstrate five years of continued unlawful residence, versus only six months for SAW applicants. Even more significant, SAW applicants could apply from outside the United States. SAW proponents argued that agricultural workers were disproportionately Mexican and poor. They worked in the United States during the summer and returned to Mexico during the off-season, so they should be allowed to apply wherever they were.

The INS created an affidavit for SAW applicants that only needed to be signed by the applicant and a grower, contractor, or farmworker union official swearing that the worker met the requirements of the program.[8] The burden of approving or disproving the application fell to the INS.[9] Initially, the slow stream of applicants in Oregon mirrored the trend nationwide, but as numbers steadily climbed the task became increasingly difficult to manage.[10] Nearly two months after the implementation of IRCA, the Portland office was receiving over one hundred applications for amnesty per day. By the end of the summer, undocumented immigrants had filed 2,580 amnesty applications in Oregon.[11] Close to 60 percent were SAW applications. Oregon was among the top ten states in SAW applicants. The overwhelming number of applicants in Oregon came from Mexico; the remainder came from Central America.[12]

The number of applications continued to rise dramatically. Elizabeth Godfrey, legalization adjudicator for the Portland INS office, saw as many as three hundred people waiting in lines seeking a temporary residence card.[13] Oregon INS records show that by March 1988, there had been 9,000 SAW applications filed in the Portland office, compared to only 200 for general legalization. By the end of the amnesty period, undocumented workers had filed 25,000 SAW applications.[14]

The estimated number of undocumented immigrants working in agriculture was significantly lower than the number of SAW applicants. None of the INS officials in Oregon expected such a huge number of SAW applicants, and many wondered how the numbers climbed so high. Fraud was the obvious explanation for the discrepancy. The hope of attaining amnesty encouraged many undocumented immigrants to obtain false papers and apply to the SAW program. Maria Lourdes Hernandez, for example, came to Oregon to escape the watchful eye of her mother-in-law and to join her husband, who had come in the early 1980s. But briefly after she had reunited with her husband, he abandoned her in Oregon. Hernandez secured employment as a housekeeper, but after a few months of work her employer refused to pay her. In fact, Hernandez and her daughter were forced to live in a doghouse in her employer's backyard. Hernandez borrowed $50 from friends to buy falsified documents to apply for SAW. Although her effort failed, many others like her succeeded in becoming permanent residents through the SAW program.[15]

The large number of SAW applicants can be traced back to the growers themselves. Growers speculated that SAW portended an exodus from the fields once workers attained legalization.[16] In the summer of 1987, their worries seemingly came true. Growers complained that they faced a severe labor shortage in harvesting their bumper crops. Those who were surveyed reported that up to one-third of SAW workers were leaving the fields.[17] One grower, Peter Dinsdale, reportedly rented a school bus and drove to Los Angeles in search of workers.[18] Growers' anxiety confirmed the fact that they relied heavily on undocumented workers. State Agriculture Department director Bob Buchanan blamed the shortage of workers on IRCA and lobbied for the broadening of the H-2A program. In confidential surveys, growers clamored for the return of the bracero program.[19] Ray Malensky, a berry grower from Hillsboro, speaking on behalf of many growers, argued for the return of the bracero program: "That way we could transport workers [from Mexico] here, have them work and transport them back. . . . But nobody wants that because it's too simple."[20] Representative Les Aucoin agreed that a bracero-type program would be ideal, but acknowledged that it would be "a tough sell" because policy makers in Washington, D.C. "see a bracero program totally different[ly] than we see it in the West."[21]

The INS saw the labor shortage in a different light. Regional commissioner James Buck contended that the real culprit was an early crop in Oregon and a late strawberry crop in California that weighed in at 96.3 million pounds, a 47 percent increase from the previous year.[22] Yet growers continued to push for a new guest worker program and issued dire warnings of labor shortages and crops drying up in the fields, while making questionable claims of thousands of acres going unpicked. These conditions, they asserted, would insure rising wages for workers and rising prices for consumers. Growers threatened to leave agriculture altogether or switch to less labor-intensive crops.[23] Seeking other sources of labor, some met with the Chiangri Manpower Center of New York and proposed to import Chinese laborers; the Chinese government would fly the workers into San Francisco, where the growers would pick them up and transport them to Oregon.[24] The scheme never came to fruition. Growers continued to be enamored by Mexican labor. When the Oregon State University extension office surveyed growers to ascertain their labor needs, "nearly all were definite in naming alien Mexicans as the most productive."[25] Growers were determined to use nonresident labor, persistent in their beliefs about the workers' inherent nature and defiant of federal laws. One survey respondent put it bluntly: "it is critical for us to have seasonal help. I need migrant work to harvest trees. If I have to hire illegals, then I'll just have to tell them when to run."[26]

The H-2A provision of IRCA allowed for the importation of foreign workers, but the requirements made such plans impossible. Growers had to pay foreign workers an adverse-effect wage, which in Oregon was $5.26 an hour, $2 more than the minimum wage at the time. They also had to pay for workers' transportation to and from the country and for their lodging, as well as guarantee 75 percent of wages that could be earned during the contract period regardless of the actual amount of work done. Most importantly, growers were required to prove a shortage of labor. Unable to do so, growers turned instead to SAW. Contractors and growers alike used SAW as their own personal recruiting tool by spreading rumors of their willingness to sign papers for anybody. They became notorious for charging undocumented workers exorbitant fees for their signature. Others promised to sign only after the workers had completed their work for the season.[27] The affidavit became a moneymaker for contractors and growers, and it trapped some workers for an entire picking season. Growers' willingness to sell their signatures inflated the number of workers in the field. The promise of a signed affidavit brought massive numbers of workers to Oregon. David Beebe, district director of the INS, estimated that fraud in Oregon ran "anywhere from twenty to twenty-five percent and on up."[28] Yet six months before the close of the amnesty period, the INS had investigated only eight cases of fraud out of 7,200 applications.[29] Most growers feigned ignorance and complained of the increased paperwork and their new role as document inspectors. Typical responses followed along the lines that "growers should not be in a position of having to judge the authenticity of documents."[30]

At the same time, the number of people looking for work in agriculture swelled, just as growers had intended. The shortage that existed was not of labor but of jobs, and housing, and at local food banks. Many of the amnestied men began to bring their families over without papers, and it was often they who ended up working in agriculture. Housing demand increased as housing units that were previously used to house four or five single men now only housed one family. The situation had become so difficult for the new arrivals that Representative Aucoin called on the Federal Emergency Management Agency (FEMA) to provide assistance. FEMA refused to send aid on the grounds that "they had not thought of criteria for evaluating emergency requests for funding."[31] An estimated 35,000 migrants, or 10,000 more than during the previous year, arrived in Oregon that summer.

The situation became so dire that state officials were forced to improvise solutions. Overcrowding and homelessness ran rampant. Local agencies like the Centro Cultural in Cornelius scrambled to feed migrants and help them find their way home. Concerned about the plight of its citizens, the Mexican government sent numerous fact-finding missions to Oregon.[32] That winter, between 6,000 and 10,000 workers decided to stay in Oregon because they believed that leaving would jeopardize their legalization. Many of the migrants slept in their cars, in tents, and in parks, precipitating a spike in homelessness and deaths from exposure. The influx of undocumented immigrants exposed a critical flaw in the legalization process.

Meanwhile, the INS found itself facing a shortage of funds. Congress had set aside monies to help the agency handle the rush to legalization, but the INS declined the extra money and decided to fund the program with fees it collected from applicants. When the expected number of early applicants did not materialize, the INS hurried to find funding for IRCA procedures. The INS closed offices, laid off workers, and implemented other cost-cutting measures. When the rush of SAW applicants hit Oregon, the INS office in Portland had a staff of eight. Workers waited for months to get an appointment, and officials had to scramble to interview sixty people per day. A last-minute expansion bumped the number of interviews up to 180 a day.[33] But the backlog became so serious that the local INS stopped requiring applicants to make an appointment. Overwhelmed by the situation, local INS officials pleaded with the state for help.

Oregon's Legislative Emergency Board granted the local INS office an additional $500,000 to open a new office and hire more staff.[34]

PCUN AND IRCA

Despite its opposition to the final legislation, PCUN had been preparing for the possibility of legalization since the early 1980s. The staff's involvement in immigration cases and its roots in the National Lawyers Guild meant they were well versed in the language of immigration law. As a result, PCUN instituted an efficient process for people to apply for legalization, which strengthened its position in the community.[35]

The passage of IRCA led to mass confusion and skepticism among immigrants. Having foreseen the panic, PCUN held informational meetings every day at 5:00 in the afternoon for anyone looking to apply for amnesty. Led by Javier Ceja, the meetings laid out the requirements for legalization and emphasized the importance of joining the union. They argued that citizenship alone could not protect the immigrants; they had to unionize themselves and their brothers and sisters who did not qualify for amnesty. PCUN attempted as best it could to keep the community informed, but it also offered to help new members with legalization.[36]

The maneuver paid off brilliantly. Applicants made appointments with staff members after the meeting and began their journey towards legalization. Kleinman recalled the process: "We were pretty thorough. We made sure people had the proper evidence. That was one way we avoided a lot of fraud and ensured that people who applied through us were going to receive legalization."[37] After the initial screening, PCUN referred the applicants to medical clinics for their physical exams. Then applicants returned to PCUN to have their applications typed and birth certificates translated, while Kleinman prepared them for their interview. PCUN and the chief INS legalization official, Lilia Araujo, reached an agreement to bring in applicants twice a week in order to streamline the process. Kleinman remembered, "We would carpool from Woodburn and be in Portland by 7:30 in the morning and be done by 11. It was an extremely efficient process"—perhaps too efficient.[38]

Kleinman was concerned that the union would become a victim of its own success as it focused most of its attention on immigration work and did very little labor organizing. Larry Kleinman recalled, "It was making it hard to organize. Wages in strawberries dropped from an already low nine cents per pound to seven cents. It took us a long time to recover from that. We decided to stop doing SAW altogether."[39] The summer before the SAW deadline expired, Kleinman witnessed conditions in the field worsening. He saw "one field with nearly one hundred workers in it. There couldn't have been more than an acre of strawberries there.

They [farmworkers] finished it in half an hour."⁴⁰ In contrast to the growers' predictions that the new immigration law would inflate wages, the number of workers seeking the SAW amnesty pushed wages even lower than before.

On the one hand, the number of workers in the fields had created a problem; on the other, the strategy of recruiting SAW applicants to bolster PCUN's membership proved a resounding success. By the November deadline, 25,000 applicants had filed for legalization in Oregon under the SAW provision of IRCA. PCUN's staff of six people processed 1,300 applicants in a twelve-month period with a 95 percent success rate. The dues-paying membership rose from about 150 to 2,000. Kleinman affirmed, "SAW gave us a lot of credibility. People saw the good work we were engaged in and wanted to be a part of it."⁴¹ Growers seemed to notice it as well. One strawberry grower told OSU extension service agents that "IRCA has affected workers' attitudes. They are less loyal and expect more. Workers are no longer afraid to complain about problems. Now we have to do something about them, rather than ignoring them as in the past."⁴² Building on the momentum that IRCA provided them, PCUN charged straight into a confrontation with growers.

PREPARING FOR A FIGHT

The union's insistence on redefining the meaning of a victory consistently placed the members' needs ahead of the union. While it continued to borrow tactics from the UFW, it nevertheless sought and accepted outcomes other than signing a union contract. To be sure, PCUN often aimed for union recognition, but it just as often desired pay raises for farmworkers. It answered the call for help from both union members and nonmembers, and responded to the workers' demands and desires. While traditional labor unions might scoff at the idea that anything but union recognition is a success, in the nineties PCUN proved that a mix of old and new strategies undoubtedly grew the collective power of farmworkers in the state of Oregon.

PCUN sought to build on the momentum generated by its burgeoning membership and its work in the community. The Immigration Reform and Control Act had a galvanizing effect on immigrants. In addition to the thousands of amnestied PCUN members, thousands more felt empowered to challenge the treatment they received at the hands of growers. Thanks to their adjusted status, others left the fields for better-paying, steadier work. Yet many continued to donate money and time to help the union as organizers and volunteers. Together, farmworkers, organizers, and volunteers launched an organizing effort the likes of which Oregon growers had never seen.

From its inception, PCUN opened its membership to both documented and undocumented workers and structured the organization to give farmworkers a voice in the union. They charged three dollars a month for dues and provided bilingual support services, burial insurance, and a vote. In 1988, the union leadership consisted of a three-person executive committee: president Cipriano Ferrel, vice president Ramon Ramirez, and secretary-treasurer Larry Kleinman. The executive committee reported to a nine-member board of directors made up entirely of farmworkers elected directly by the membership. The board met monthly to determine the direction of the union, while subcommittees, typically made up of volunteers and farmworkers, oversaw the union's other concerns, such as support services, compliance with minimum wage laws, pesticide usage, immigration concerns, and an organizing committee.[43]

Ferrel believed strongly that the union belonged to its members and thought the committees gave farmworkers an opportunity to develop their leadership skills. He hoped that the leadership of the union would eventually come from farmworkers themselves: "We are developing farm workers that are coming through our ranks, that are becoming leaders. . . . The only training we have is our struggle."[44] Ferrel believed that each battle, whether or not it achieved its stated goal, taught workers valuable lessons about their own power as well as strategies. The history of PCUN's labor actions demonstrates a dynamic ability to learn and try new things. The system required significant participation from the membership, and in the post-IRCA days PCUN finally had enough members to function as Ferrel had envisioned. IRCA had boosted PCUN's membership by nearly 4,000 members and brought PCUN into the spotlight.

The union developed a multipronged approach to attacking the injustices in the field. Despite some philosophical differences between the United Farm Workers (UFW) and PCUN, Ferrel maintained a close relationship with the UFW and borrowed tactics it had developed: filing lawsuits, calling strikes, initiating pickets, and organizing sustained boycotts. More importantly, PCUN also understood the importance of building a large base. The UFW had successfully organized in the fields thanks in large part to the efforts of those who were not farmworkers, and PCUN, too, reached out to students, labor unions, and religious organizations. PCUN knew that without them, growers had an advantage over farmworkers and could continue to exploit them without recourse.

PCUN began its battle against the growers by going straight at the institutional discrimination against farmworkers embedded in state labor law. In California, the UFW had successfully lobbied for the passage of perhaps the most favorable labor law in the country in 1975. The Agricultural Labor Relations Act guaranteed collective bargaining rights to farmworkers and even oversaw and certified elections on farms. For many, the passage of the law signified an ultimate triumph for the UFW, so PCUN decided to start there.[45] Through the efforts of friendly state senators, PCUN submitted a collective bargaining law to the Oregon legislature in 1989. The bill had little chance of becoming law (though it did have the support of half the state senate and key legislative leaders), but PCUN knew from the beginning that it did not have the political clout to get the bill passed. Rather, PCUN sought to raise awareness about institutionalized discrimination against farmworkers and to show that PCUN had attempted to remedy it via legislation; and, since these attempts had been unsuccessful, this would give PCUN more compelling justifications to employ other strategies.

PCUN faced a more formidable obstacle in Oregon's long-standing antipicketing law. Enacted in 1963, the "Strangers Picketing Law" prohibited any picketer who had not worked six days at the targeted farm. At that time no other state had such a stringent antipicketing law, and no other industry in Oregon was protected from picketing. The picketing efforts of the UFW made it clear that farmworkers needed allies on the picket lines who were not susceptible to grower intimidation. The law made it impossible for PCUN supporters to be anywhere near potential picketing targets, and PCUN had to remove this obstruction in order for a strike to be successful.

On September 1, 1989, PCUN, with the support of the AFL-CIO and various religious organizations, filed suit in federal district court against Governor Goldschmidt, seeking to invalidate the antipicketing law as an unconstitutional limitation on free speech. At a press conference, Cipriano Ferrel declared that this "lawsuit transcends farm workers' rights by asking whether our Constitution protects only harmless speech and whether it favors the interest of the economically influential by allowing the court's power to be placed at the growers' disposal."[46] Oregon's attorney general, Dave Frohenmayer, sought to have the case dismissed on procedural grounds, claiming that the governor was not the proper defendant and that "no immediate controversy" existed because no one was actually picketing at the time. On May 4, 1990, U.S. District Court judge James Redden denied the state's motion to dismiss the case and issued a four-page ruling stating that the governor was the correct defendant, and that waiting for a situation to arise would unnecessarily put picketers at risk of litigation and criminal prosecution.[47]

Nearly a year and a half later, on September 24, 1990, Judge Redden heard oral arguments from the plaintiffs for a summary judgment. PCUN lawyer Gene Mechanic opened by getting right to the heart of the matter: "This law is saying, 'we the State, wish to protect agricultural profit at the cost of free speech rights.'"[48] Mechanic argued that a ban on picketing would effectively eliminate protest and allow the power of the agribusiness lobby in Oregon to remain unchecked. Mechanic pointed to the lack of such a law in California as evidence that protests and picketing would not lead to the catastrophic downfall of the agricultural economy that the Oregon Farm Bureau predicted. During the hearings, the assistant attorney general, Patricia Bridge Urquhart, renewed the state's motion to dismiss on procedural grounds and added that the spirit of the law should be taken into consideration. The law, she argued, "was meant to protect small growers . . . and outlaw physically disturbing the harvest." She added that the farmworkers and their supporters "have ample opportunity to protest elsewhere." Finally, she contended that the law protected farmworkers by ensuring a strong and healthy economy.

The judge, however, was concerned that "the purpose of this law is to keep farm workers picking and not picketing."[49] When PCUN supporters heard the judge's statements, they felt confident that the law would be struck down. Ruling in the case of *PCUN et al. v Goldschmidt* on September 26, Judge Redden declared the antipicketing law unconstitutional. Oregon governor Neil Goldschmidt declined to appeal the case, and on October 11 he wrote to Irv Fletcher, the president of the Oregon AFL-CIO: "I have never had a personal stake in the PCUN case, but I believe it was appropriate for the court to resolve the serious constitutional issues involved. . . . No purpose would be served in taking the case any further."

Understandably joyful, PCUN was also cautiously optimistic, knowing that more intense struggles lay ahead. Because a favorable decision would clear the way for PCUN to unleash a flurry of activity, it spent the time awaiting the decision by preparing for a large-scale organizing campaign. After the ruling, Cipriano proclaimed, "we've been fighting on many fronts, collective bargaining, minimum wage, workplace picketing, [all] to attain equal labor rights for farm workers. One of the key discriminatory barriers has now fallen."[50] At the press conference, Cipriano described various ways PCUN members had been working to alleviate the oppressive working conditions in the fields.

PCUN used the media very effectively, utilizing frequent press conferences as a way of garnering support and measuring its opponents' reactions. On June 9, 1989, for instance, PCUN, the Oregon Public Employees Union (SEIU), and Clergy and Laity Concerned held a joint press conference to announce the creation of a strike fund. Given that the challenge to the antipicketing statute was still making its way through the courts, it seemed like an odd maneuver. PCUN did not name a strike target but listed a series of demands: union recognition; a grievance procedure to resolve disputes; a seniority system for hiring, promoting, and laying off workers; a closed shop; and a provision allowing workers to be dismissed only for just cause.[51]

The press conferences put growers in the public spotlight and forced them to respond to PCUN's accusations. Growers unaccustomed to the scrutiny of the press and public often answered with threats and profanity-laced tirades that confirmed their intransigence in the eyes of the media. On one occasion, an anonymous Marion County grower told reporters that PCUN's efforts would "eventually . . . force us out of these highly specialized, labor-intensive crops. . . . If this union thing gets to be a pain, we'll just quit—they can all go on welfare."[52]

STRATEGIES IN THE FIELDS: LA TARJETA COLORADA

Before the ruling, the legal limitations on picketing had forced PCUN members to create innovative organizing strategies. The most notable was the "Red Card" campaign, which aimed to document minimum wage violations in the fields by urging workers to keep track of their own hours and output on little red cards that they would turn in to PCUN. In 1989 the Oregon legislature raised the minimum wage to $4.25 an hour and included provisions to ensure that piece-rate workers and restaurant workers received minimum wage. Majorities of farmworkers worked for piece-rate wages and were largely unaware that the minimum wage law applied to them. PCUN set out to resolve that.[53]

In typical PCUN fashion, the union announced the start of this campaign at a press conference on December 29, 1989. PCUN vice president Ramon Ramirez told the media, "If the minimum wage violations we are seeing in the fields this year had occurred at McDonald's, it would be a national scandal."[54] For months, cucumber and berry workers had urged PCUN to investigate wage theft in their harvests. The union investigated and released its findings in a "Report on Wage Survey of Willamette Valley Farm Workers." By interviewing over 200 farm workers during the 1989 harvest, the authors found that 50 percent of berry and cucumber harvesters did not receive the minimum $3.35 per hour on their average workday and 95 percent were underpaid at least once during the season. Although cucumber and berry growers paid on piece rates, Oregon law required that total wages be at least 85 percent of the minimum wage. The PCUN survey determined that despite the law, the pay rate had not increased in over ten years. PCUN timed the release of the report to coincide with Oregon's minimum wage increase, which went into effect a few days later. The report estimated that farmworkers harvesting cucumbers and berries lost nearly $2,000,000 because of minimum wage violations. The report called attention to the consistent underpayment of farmworkers and helped to launch PCUN's minimum wage campaign.[55]

In the summer of 1990 PCUN began monitoring wage violations by focusing on a single crop in a single area. Organizers believed that if they could put enough pressure on a specific target, they could force growers to comply, thereby creating a minimum wage "safe zone." That achievement would motivate workers to seek compliance from other growers, creating a domino effect. One way growers cheated workers out of pay was by miscounting the number of hours they worked, so PCUN instructed farmworkers to keep track of their hours on the little red card. The other major source of contention was deceitfulness at the scales. Growers either covered or manipulated scales and lied about the amount of produce that workers had picked. This type of fraud was more difficult to expose, but organizers encouraged workers to keep track of what the scales said they had picked. If the resulting wage did not adhere to Oregon's minimum wage laws, the red card could be used to support their wage claims.

PCUN targeted 25 strawberry, cane berry, and cucumber farms and handed out over 10,000 time cards. This campaign, literally, paid off for the workers. By mid-summer, 40 PCUN members had received $3,000 directly from growers without state intervention. Keeping track of their wages and deductions enabled another 75 union members to force labor contractors to return $9,000 they had collected in inflated deductions, and in the end documented over 240 minimum wage violations. The immense success of the campaign forced wage compliance in the targeted harvests and, as PCUN predicted, had ramifications for non-union farmworkers as well.[56] By August 1990, farmworkers on nonunion targets had collected $155,538 in back wages.[57]

Word of PCUN's efforts reached beyond its members and its targets. For example, a group of recent migrants from Eagle Pass, Texas, called on the union for help. In Eagle Pass, labor contractor George San Miguel recruited forty men to come to Coleman farms in St. Paul, Oregon, with promises of free rent, full kitchen facilities, forty-five-hour workweeks, and good conditions. Upon their arrival, however, the workers quickly realized that conditions failed to live up to the promises San Miguel had made. The workers were housed in a dilapidated dormitory with only two refrigerators and an outdoor grill to cook on. They worked fewer than thirty hours a week and failed to make enough money to send home. When six of the workers complained about the lack of hours, absence of rain gear, and unsanitary toilets and drinking water, Coleman had them fired. Three of their coworkers left the field and walked seven miles to the PCUN offices in Woodburn.

The workers' conversation with PCUN led to the discovery that the workers had been recruited under the US Department of Labor's Interstate Clearance System. Set up to distribute US agricultural workers "from labor supply areas," it actually required fewer guarantees and assurances than the H2-A guest worker program. PCUN discovered a twelve-page job order that spelled out the conditions of employment and highlighted the portions that San Miguel had misrepresented.[58] PCUN encouraged the three men to bring in the other workers, but only twenty-five of the original forty remained at Coleman farms. Still, twenty of them came to the meeting with PCUN to discuss further action.

In addition to the poor working and living conditions, the workers reported that Coleman had forced them to pick strawberries for his friend Joseph Lambert, a violation of the Interstate Clearance System. Just two days later, news that the workers had met with PCUN forced Lambert to voluntarily pay the workers $1,500 in back wages. Later in the week, US Employment Services officials met with Coleman and the workers to renegotiate the terms of the contract and apologize to the workers. The meeting, however, had little effect on working conditions and even less effect on living conditions.

Despite being run by Benedictine Sisters, the dormitory the workers lived in left much to be desired, and the sisters rebuffed PCUN's attempts to inspect the premises. The Benedictine Sisters claimed that the dormitories were private property and refused to budge when PCUN organizers pointed out that the contract allowed workers to have visitors. One of the sisters replied to PCUN's assertion vehemently: "Farm workers don't need a written contract. . . . They can't even read."[59] One by one the workers abandoned Coleman Farms in search of other jobs. PCUN failed to gain any further concessions for the workers and did not incorporate them into the union, but PCUN did not think of this campaign as a failure.

While winning or losing contracts has been the traditional way of measuring success or failure of a union, PCUN had a broader definition of success. For Ramon Ramirez, developing the consciousness of farmworkers was as important as winning contracts: "We wanted to make farm workers' lives better— sometimes with contracts, other times in less traditional ways."[60] The union saw a growth in the willingness of farmworkers to come to them for help as a positive step in the growth of the union. Even when direct results were elusive, Ferrel believed that PCUN played a crucial role in helping farmworkers win battles over the minimum wage: "It is obvious to the workers that [wage increases are] a buy-off and the workers understand completely that without the organization [PCUN] . . . this would never happen."[61] Farmworkers no longer saw growers as invincible.

CONCLUSION

PCUN built a successful union in an antiunion decade and an antiunion industry thanks in large part to its strong relationship with the immigrant base. For PCUN, the passage of the Immigration Reform and Control Act in 1986 brought challenges and opportunities. The project's history of immigrants' rights work proved to be the catalyst that launched the union into political power. In other words, its connection with the immigrant community positioned it as a place of trustworthy advice and information about the new immigration law. Based on the strength of that relationship, the newly formed PCUN would begin the 1990s with the first agriculture strike in decades.

6 ❧ HUELGA!
PCUN Organization of Farmworkers in the Willamette Valley

The empowerment of farmworkers became tangible a year later as PCUN members launched the first strike in Oregon agriculture in over twenty years. Even after overturning the antipicketing law, PCUN still lacked a sufficient strike fund and a viable target. Cipriano Ferrel wanted to ensure that PCUN was prepared for consistent action: "We don't want to go out on strike, make a big bang and not be able to follow up."[1] The union also wanted to protect its workers in case of a failed strike. Ferrel told an interviewer that they wanted the strike to be focused on a single target so that only a portion of the union would be out of work. Working members could still pay into the strike fund and, if something went wrong with the strike, unemployed workers could seek jobs elsewhere in the valley. A year after announcing the creation of a strike fund and launching the "Red Card" campaign, PCUN picked a target for its first strike.

Harold Kraemer's farm began as a small berry farm in the 1950s and over the years developed into one of the largest in the Willamette Valley. By 1990 the farm had over 2,000 acres in strawberries, cane berries, rhubarb, cucumbers, broccoli, cauliflower, wine grapes, zucchini, wheat, beans, grass seed, and Christmas trees. Kraemer Farms boasted thirty-five pickup trucks, six semitrailer trucks, and eight labor camps. In comparison, the average Oregon farm had 442 acres in 1992, and only 4 percent of farms were larger than 2,000 acres.[2] Oregon State University, the agricultural college in Corvallis, acknowledged his success by naming his operation the "1991 Family Business of the Year" and calling it "one of the most innovative and successful multigenerational family farms in the Pacific Northwest."[3] His son, Dan, had taken over the daily operations, but all members of his family were involved in one way or another.

Notwithstanding the enterprise's image as the quintessential family farm, Kraemer Farms was a large corporation and a decidedly unpleasant place for workers. The Kraemers employed the area's most notorious labor contractor, ran a company store,[4] and operated abysmal labor camps. The largest housing unit, an enlarged trailer, housed nearly sixty workers in bare bunks without mattresses. Charging $50 a week per person, the Kraemers collected $3,000 in rent a week from workers. One of the major complaints farmworkers had about Dan Kraemer was his tendency to hire more workers than he needed. In the summer of 1990 he hired three hundred more workers than he had hired the previous year in order to drive down the cost of labor.

During the Red Card campaign, farmworkers flooded PCUN with complaints about Kraemer Farms. Organizers stepped up their monitoring of minimum wage compliance there, and PCUN's vigilance forced Kraemer to comply with the law. Emboldened by this success, thirty workers, none of them PCUN members, staged an impromptu work stoppage, demanding an increase in wages from 15 cents to 20 cents per pound of strawberries. Fearing PCUN interference, Kraemer immediately conceded, and the workers returned to the fields.

Nonetheless, PCUN felt that the Kraemers had not done enough to alleviate workers' concerns and continued trying to meet with the workers. Two weeks after Kraemer conceded to strawberry workers, workers in the cucumber harvest invited PCUN organizers into the camps to discuss immigrant rights, unionization, and wage demands. Over the course of those meetings, workers unanimously voted to form a workers' committee, elected representatives, and demanded a $6.50 hourly minimum wage. At the time Oregon's minimum wage was only $4.75, yet workers felt emboldened and empowered enough by other workers' success to ask for more.

At the heart of their demand was a belief that a negotiated minimum wage could alleviate the harshest aspects of their work. Dan Kraemer instituted what he described as a "profit-sharing" system that PCUN called "sharecropping." In the harvest, teams of ten workers picked cucumbers that overseers graded by size, with the smallest being the most valuable and the largest being the least. Those cucumbers were sold to picklers, and the crew split 30 percent of the profit. This arrangement was not in the workers' interest. First, organizing workers into crews forced faster workers to subsidize slower ones. Second, workers had no way of verifying their own production. Finally, they had no guarantee that they could earn adequate wages since they depended on the word of an overseer.

Elected representatives from the labor camp traveled to other Kraemer camps to seek support from the other workers before approaching the Kraemers with their demands. After the workers at other labor camps agreed to join them, representatives approached PCUN organizers to negotiate on their behalf. On Friday, August 9, 1991, organizers approached Kraemer Farms' chief of operations, Dan Kraemer, to negotiate a contract. But Kraemer categorically rejected PCUN's offer. Dan's father Harold cursed organizers and disparaged farmworkers: "The workers don't deserve more money because they will just spend it on booze and whores."[5]

The Kraemers' obstinacy was the beginning of a long struggle. Harold Kraemer, Dan Kraemer, and the county sheriff intercepted the organizers who arrived at the labor camp to meet with the workers. But PCUN had the law on its side. A few years earlier, PCUN allies in the state legislature had passed a law guaranteeing farmworkers the right to invite anyone into farm labor housing. Armed with a copy of the law, organizers forced the sheriff and the Kraemers to retreat. Organizers met with the workers in their camps to discuss the next steps. After a brief discussion, the workers voted overwhelmingly to go on strike.

Meanwhile, PCUN staff members worked busily into the night preparing for a strike. They mobilized supporters, notified the press, and assembled banners, signs, and flags. At 6:00 AM on Saturday morning, over one hundred workers and hundreds more supporters lined the fields of Kraemer Farms. PCUN and the workers had initiated the first union-organized strike in Oregon agriculture since 1971.[6] Aware of the upcoming strike, Kraemer had already arranged to hire strike-breakers. He brought in carload after carload of scabs, but the striking workers dissuaded the replacement workers from staying, and some of them even joined the protest. Out of at least eight carloads of scabs, only eight individuals got past the picket lines.

The Kraemers and their allies grew increasingly irritated and resorted to intimidating the strikers with physical violence, but the strikers were not deterred. Poli Guerrero, a relative of the Kraemers' labor contractor, fired a pistol into an empty bucket near the strikers. When the state police arrived, they halfheartedly interviewed the suspect and confiscated the gun but declined to arrest or cite him. Despite Guerrero's threats, organizers entered the field to speak with replacement workers.[7] One strike leader, Timoteo Lopez-Garcia, a Zapotec Indian from Sola de Vega, Oaxaca, was also the leader of his hometown association. He demonstrated a militant streak that other organizers found inspiring, and at the height of the strike he was arrested for trespassing onto the cucumber fields. The majority of the workers at Kraemer Farms were *Zapotecos* from Oaxaca, and Lopez-Garcia wielded significant influence in the group's decision-making process. Dan Kraemer understood the importance of Lopez-Garcia's role in the Zapotec community, because when he saw Lopez-Garcia cross into the fields Kraemer moved immediately to intercept him and began negotiating. According to Lopez-Garcia, Kraemer was ready to settle until a Kraemer crew boss named Juan Diego Sanchez arrived. Sanchez reportedly told Dan Kraemer not to settle and said that he would break the strike by noon the following day. Sanchez, known as "El Ruso" (The Russian) for his light complexion and bushy beard, had a violent streak and was considered by workers to be a goon. Although the Mexican national failed to break the strike, El Ruso managed to sneak fifteen strikebreakers into the fields that day and another fifteen the following day. Adding to the violence of Guerrero and "El Ruso," two different henchmen drove their pickup trucks through the picket line, forcing strikers, organizers, and volunteers to dive out of the way, barely escaping serious injury. Even though witnesses videotaped both incidents, law enforcement officers refused to arrest the drivers.

Fearing a loss of momentum, Cipriano Ferrel and fifteen strikers entered the fields even after they had been threatened with arrest. Infuriated, Dan Kraemer began stomping the ground excitedly and screaming obscenities at Ferrel. Rather comically, he even resorted to throwing cucumbers at Ferrel. The county sheriff arrested Ferrel, Kleinman, and Lopez-Garcia, but the trio were released on their own recognizance and returned to the field later in the day. Their reappearance reinvigorated the strikers. Despite the efforts of "El Ruso," his henchmen, and the entire contingent of Marion County sheriffs' deputies, seventy-five of the original one hundred workers remained on strike.[8]

As the pressure mounted and the workers showed no signs of giving in, Dan Kraemer capitulated and agreed to negotiate with PCUN vice president Ramon Ramirez. After a three-hour meeting, Kraemer and Ramirez settled on 75 cents per bucket of cucumbers, union recognition, and a promise not to retaliate against the strikers. They agreed to meet the next morning with the strike committee to hammer out other aspects of the contract. At dawn on Monday, the strikers met, unanimously ratified the agreement, and headed out to work.

It appeared that PCUN had won its first contract, but when the strikers arrived in the fields at 6:00 in the morning they saw scabs already in the field under police escort. They staged an impromptu strike and ran the scabs out of the fields. Nothing had happened after nearly two hours of sitting in the fields; there was no sign that Kraemer was going to honor the contract, and some workers left the field. Publicly, Kraemer and his attorney, Douglas Brown, claimed that no strike had taken place, but away from the media spotlight Kraemer eventually returned to the fields to negotiate a pay raise and eliminate the "profit-sharing" system. Still, he refused to sign a union contract. Timoteo Lopez-Garcia negotiated the settlement on behalf of the strikers and agreed to the raise, so the workers returned to the harvest the same day.

With help from Marion County extension agent Dan McGrath, the Kraemers continued to downplay the importance of the strike. McGrath told the *Oregonian* that the Kraemers "really do everything they can do to take care of their workers. . . . It was tremendously ironic that the group would choose the Kraemer farm to do the strike. . . . PCUN totally blew it and the Kraemers have been exonerated."[9] McGrath defended the Kraemers' pay system as "innovative" and "brilliant" and contended that the few workers who were complaining simply did not understand the concept. McGrath also claimed that "Hispanics" would now be hesitant to join the union after its "lies and betrayal." Douglas Brown echoed these sentiments and declared, "My personal opinion is that the union actions were one more form of field worker abuse."[10]

For PCUN and the workers, the strike was an important success regardless of what Dan Kraemer and his allies told the media. Kleinman answered critics by pointing out that Kraemers' employees had come to PCUN seeking its aid; in other words, the workers rather than the union chose the target. Workers on that farm had a specific grievance, and PCUN responded to their requests. Although the strike did not result in a union contract, in light of the long history of oppression in Oregon agriculture, workers and union organizers saw the strike as a step in the right direction. PCUN demonstrated the ability to mobilize workers, union members, and supporters. At a meeting in PCUN's union hall a few days later, one of the strikers, Rafael Delgado, offered a poignant reflection on the strike:

> We will continue our struggle to maintain our families who await us in Mexico: our children, our brothers and sisters, our parents, and even our grandparents. We fight to win for our elders everything they deserve because they have passed on to us a strong tradition. Others may put us down because we're short and brown-skinned, but we have a strong spirit. Kraemer Farms has exploited us and treated us badly. All we ask is just wages and fair treatment. We must not lose heart because we will win this struggle so that tomorrow, our children and our countrymen who come to work at Kraemer Farms will be treated more justly![11]

Delgado summed up everything PCUN believed: that the struggle would eventually pay off, that the workers no longer feared growers, and that their commitment extended beyond their own needs. Delgado acknowledged that he belonged to a larger community that included not only his family and his ancestors, but also future generations and his fellow citizens in Mexico.

In the aftermath of the strike, PCUN's response to the strikebreakers was a major departure from the typical reaction of organized labor. PCUN acknowledged the difficult position of the nonstriking workers and continued to encourage them to join the union. It did not inform the Immigration and Naturalization Service about the largely undocumented workforce, but rather demonstrated sympathy. In official statements, PCUN announced: "organizers will continue to work closely with strikers and help win over others at the farm, who now benefit from the hard-fought raises, even though they gave in to threats of firing and eviction and crossed the picket line. The morale at Kraemer Farms remains high. The workers know—better than anyone else—that we won the strike."[12]

Workers continued to show support for PCUN and for each other. A few weeks after the end of the strike, both scabs and strikers united against the deplorable living conditions on Kraemer Farms. Their newfound sense of empowerment led to a decision to stop paying the $50 per week rent for the rest of the season, an opportunity created by Dan Kraemer's denial that the Kraemers operated former farmhouses on their properties as "labor camps." PCUN organizers made sure that the workers knew about Kraemer's statements to the press, but the workers made their own decision, demonstrated their own initiative independent of any union or employer.

Although Kraemer did not retaliate against the strikers that season, PCUN worried that retaliation awaited them the following season. Juan Diego Sanchez confirmed those worries on the very first day when he told a group of workers not even to bother applying for work. He also warned workers not to communicate with PCUN or with the "troublemakers" or else he would evict them or fire them. "El Ruso" went as far as telling workers that PCUN would report them to immigration. Organizers countered his efforts by maintaining a presence in the adjacent fields and leafleting at Kraemer Farms. Taking a page out of the UFW handbook, organizers passed out a comic book narrating the struggle, complete with an unflattering and amusing depiction of Sanchez. Once again, Dan Kraemer responded by calling the Marion County sheriff and instructing him to arrest PCUN organizers for "harassing" workers. This time, perhaps recalling the bad press they had received the previous year, Sheriff's Lieutenant Raul Ramirez, the son of Tejano contractors, did not arrest them but simply instructed workers that they had the right *not* to talk to union organizers.

As before, Kraemer offered to negotiate with PCUN organizers and designated his attorney, Douglas Brown, as his authorized representative to solicit proposals from the union. On June 24, 1992, PCUN submitted a contract proposal containing five major points: increased wages; establishment of a grievance procedure; firing and discipline based only on just cause; respect for seniority; and the creation of a workers' council to help administer company-owned housing. Brown summarily rejected the plan and stormed out of negotiations. PCUN did not expect Kraemer to concede, so it already had a back-up plan in mind.

ORGANIZING A BOYCOTT

Like the UFW before it, PCUN believed that farmworkers needed the help of a broad community base. Although Ferrel believed in building workers' power, he realized that farmworkers "are never going to win a strike by themselves."[13] PCUN began to build partnerships with other progressive organizations in order to create a network for a boycott of Kraemer Farms.

A few weeks after Brown rejected the workers' proposal, PCUN wrote to SteinfeldPickles and NORPAC foods, two of Kraemer Farms' biggest buyers, to persuade them to force Kraemer back to the bargaining table.[14] PCUN asked the two companies to sever ties with Kraemer Farms if Kraemer failed to negotiate within thirty days. Kraemer sold cucumbers, cabbage, berries, corn, and broccoli and other vegetables directly and exclusively to Steinfeld and NORPAC. Steinfeld had contracts with 25 growers in the Northwest, produced 40 million pounds of pickles annually, operated 2 pickling plants, and dominated the pickle industry in Oregon. NORPAC was a giant cooperative owned by 250 growers that generated over $210 million in annual revenue. Operating six plants in Oregon, it distributed under such major labels as Flav-R-Pac, Santiam, and Stone Mill Foods. Both companies were highly visible, and PCUN believed that it could leverage the public image of the companies against Kraemer Farms.[15]

NORPAC and Steinfeld both flatly rejected PCUN's request. NORPAC threatened to file a lawsuit against PCUN, while Steinfeld claimed they had no responsibility for the conditions in the fields. In a letter to PCUN, NORPAC attorney John Zenor wrote, "As a matter of good business practice, NORPAC is unwilling to interfere in the independent affairs of its suppliers." Steinfeld asserted, "We really don't understand this attempt to involve Steinfeld in a third party labor dispute."[16] PCUN countered by arguing that if Kraemer, NORPAC, and Steinfeld had agreements over the standard for quality produce, they should have similar agreements concerning the quality of labor conditions. It is unclear whether PCUN ever believed that Kraemer could be forced to the negotiating table; almost from the start, it had been preparing to launch a boycott.

On September 13, 1992, PCUN held a rally and press conference to formally announce its call for a nationwide boycott of Steinfeld and NORPAC food products. At the rally, farmworker representative Timoteo Lopez-Garcia expressed the sentiments of many Kraemer employees: "We have returned year after year to Kraemer Farms and worked hard, but we're paid wages which don't support our families and we're fired if we speak up. The boycott is the only way we will win [the] respect and better working conditions we deserve."[17] Within days of the announcement, the boycott received endorsements from the National Farm Worker Ministry and the Fellowship of Reconciliation.[18]

Once again, the PCUN borrowed tactics from the UFW, setting up boycott committees in urban centers across the country. Rather than focusing on national chains, however, the committees targeted neighborhood stores that ostensibly had a commitment to social justice, environmentalism, and local products. The strategy paid dividends when stores like Nature's Fresh Northwest and others closed out their stock of Flav-R-Pac products and pledged not to stock any more. Students played a major role in the boycott effort. On March 10, 1993, sixty students at Reed, a small liberal arts college in Portland, marched into the president's office to deliver a signed petition from over half the student body (about 1,400 at the time) demanding that the school cease buying these products.[19] The president, Steven Koblik, denied the request, citing the college's policy of "avoiding political stands on anything not directly relating to the University or higher education."[20] The students refused to take no for an answer. They continued to protest, leaflet, and put pressure on the administration until seven months later, when the college's food service signed an agreement with the Reed Boycott Committee to cease purchasing NORPAC and Steinfeld products. Soon other colleges and universities followed suit. Over the ten-year course of the boycott, educational institutions across the country and abroad severed their ties to NORPAC.[21]

In response to mounting pressure, Kraemer Farms took the offensive, sending letters to boycott supporters reiterating its claims that there had been no strike on the farm and that farmworkers loved working there. The letter included an article from the Salem-based weekly, the *Capital Press*, which claimed that Kraemer treated his workers well, provided them with decent housing, and paid them well, as well as stating that the workers were rabidly opposed to PCUN. The main source for the article, Poli Guerrero, claimed that Kraemer treated his workers as equals and that only lazy workers sided with PCUN. The *Capital Press* failed to mention that Poli Guerrero was the same "worker" who had fired his .357 Magnum at protestors the year before. The article also quoted Linda Moreno Beaird, identified by the paper as Kraemer's bilingual consultant, but failed to mention that she was an employee of the Farm Labor Employment Services, an enterprise that PCUN believed was formed to engage in union-busting.

Farmworkers responded by sending a public letter of their own to the Kraemers refuting these assertions. The Kraemers' letter claimed that workers averaged more than $7 an hour and earned over $16 an hour in the cucumber and zucchini harvests. Farm workers testified, "We often work ten to twelve hours a week in cucumber harvest. . . . None of us has ever earned sixteen dollars per hour. . . . We average five to seven dollars per hour . . . and we don't get time and a half for hours over forty. . . . Most of us barely made $2,000 to $4,000 in four months." The Kraemers' letter also claimed that Beaird educated and assisted workers, but none of the workers had ever heard of her, much less met her. Finally, Kraemer made the outrageous claim that he provided free housing to his workers, but failed to mention that he was not collecting rent because the farmworkers were still on a rent strike.[22]

Kraemers' efforts failed to slow down the boycott, which by March 1993 had been endorsed by 23 organizations and 650 households across the nation. The boycott attracted the support of celebrities such as the legendary folk singer Pete Seeger. Seeger and his grandson, Tao Rodriguez Seeger, held a fundraising concert in the summer of 1993.[23] That September, the UFW unanimously voted to endorse the boycott. Its secretary-treasurer, David Martinez, wrote, "We are convinced that you will win the NORPAC and Steinfeld boycott because we see the same determination and sprit in PCUN that it has taken the UFW to win in the past." Yet PCUN did not receive any kind of financial or organizational support from the UFW. It remained fiercely independent and saw the UFW mainly as a consultant; staff members asked questions and solicited advice, but the relationship remained largely informal.

While the boycott gained momentum and garnered national attention, it also emboldened workers on neighboring farms. In early July 1993, over one hundred workers from Haines Farms in nearby Salem approached PCUN for help. Workers at Haines Farms harvested cherries for twelve straight days, up to twelve hours a day, and received on average only $30 for the whole twelve-day period. Haines also withheld 25 cents per bucket of cherries and paid it out as a bonus at the end of the harvest.[24] This deduction took away one of the only weapons workers had in their arsenal, the ability to walk away. Led by Alfredo Morales, workers went to foreman Wilfredo Hernandez and demanded that Haines end this exploitative practice and begin paying by the hour. Haines responded by shutting off the water to the camps, firing all the workers, and evicting them. At that time, the garage-like dormitory housed eighty workers and ten children; almost everyone slept on the floor.[25]

PCUN's commitment to undocumented workers led the union to acknowledge that immigrants could employ a myriad of tools to attain justice. The meeting between the workers and PCUN organizers demonstrated the group's flexibility and its commitment to democracy. On the one hand PCUN felt that the outrages at Haines Farms merited a strike. On the other hand, Haines workers feared deportation and did not feel comfortable pursuing this strategy. Instead, the workers decided to hold a press conference and begin legal actions for wage claims and other violations. The bad publicity prompted Haines to back off the eviction notice and restore water to the labor camps, but he also hired Kraemer Farms' attorney, Douglas Brown.

Part lawyer, part public relations man, Brown immediately began asserting that Haines pickers earned far more than the press conference claimed. He declared, "The longest working days in this two-week period were nine hours, and Mrs. Haines said that the average picker—not the best, but the average—picks thirty to thirty-two buckets a day. In a nine-hour day, the pay for 32 buckets would amount to $6.22 an hour."[26] Brown asserted that Alfredo Morales had lied about the hours worked and about the 25-cent deduction. In an Orwellian maneuver, Brown turned the practice upside down, asserting that workers had agreed to work for $1.75 a bucket and that the 25 cents per bucket was in fact a bonus. At the time, state law required employers to post notices of such bonuses at the worksite. Conveniently, Brown claimed that it had been posted until that weekend. Brown continued his efforts on behalf of growers throughout the state by holding hour-long information sessions for growers around the valley. At these sessions he instructed growers on how to handle the union. He informed growers that because of a lack of state law that applies to farmworkers, "there's nothing to stop you from firing a worker and replacing them."[27] He also misinformed them, referencing the picketing law that PCUN had successfully challenged in 1990, and claiming that only employees or former employees of the farm could picket during a dispute.

PCUN's long-standing relationship with Oregon Legal Services continued to play a crucial role in winning victories for farmworkers. Attorney Michael Dale took on the wage claim against Haines Farms. The case never made it that far, however, as Haines settled out of court and paid $3,000 to the 100 workers, adding $30 to the pay of each farmworker for the two-week period they complained about. Brown claimed that the payment was simply a "matter of expediency." Farmworkers saw it as a victory.[28]

Meanwhile, a new set of workers on Kraemer Farms was protesting their low wages and working conditions. In 1994, Kraemer set the price for the strawberry harvest at 12 cents per pound, 2 cents less than most farms in the area. Instead of leaving to find better jobs, farmworkers initiated three different work stoppages until Kraemer finally decided to raise the piece rate. Then, on August 6, 1994, nearly half of the one hundred cucumber workers halted the harvest when they received checks averaging $80 to $150. While refusing to return to the fields, the workers negotiated with Kraemer until he conceded and agreed to pay them what amounted to a minimum wage of $200 per week. In response to workers' repeated complaints about the scales on Kraemer Farms, the Oregon Department of Agriculture finally investigated and eventually fined Kraemer for covering the scales used to weigh blackberries. The ODA discovered that Kraemer Farms paid workers for 38 pounds per crate regardless of the crate's actual weight. While the Kraemers, Haines, and their attorneys continued to claim that farmworkers were opposed to PCUN, the evidence suggests that workers used PCUN as a weapon against the growers, exactly as organizers had intended.

¡AUMENTO YA! PCUN AND THE TENTH ANNIVERSARY ORGANIZING CAMPAIGN

This flurry of worker activity, both organized and spontaneous, inspired PCUN to plan another campaign. On November 6, 1994, PCUN members meeting at the union hall decided to target the upcoming strawberry harvest. A substantial number of PCUN members picked strawberries. While wages had remained stagnant since the 1980s, retail had risen over 40 percent in the ten years since PCUN's founding, generating 40 million dollars in profits that farmworkers had not shared in. PCUN estimated that "even if we calculated only according to cost of living, this ten-year wage freeze had cost farm workers at least 15 million dollars."[29] California at the time was the nation's leader in strawberry production, with Oregon following a distant second; the difference in the cultivars is significant. Strawberries had grown in importance thanks in large part to specific cultivars that performed well in Oregon's rainy seasons. These cultivars, while not as large or as prolific as those used in California, nevertheless are esteemed by food processors for their strong taste and deep internal color. They are used extensively in jams, jelly, ice cream, yogurt, and fruit juice blends, and are frozen and canned as well.[30] As a result the majority of Oregon's annual crop, as much as 95 percent in some years, is processed with a small percentage being sold fresh, whereas California's are overwhelmingly meant for fresh consumption. California's high-yielding cultivars are harvested annually, while as much as one-fourth of the Oregon crop is replanted every year. California's long growing season, almost six months a year, stands in stark contrast with Oregon's very short three-week-plus season. Because of the short growing season, labor demands are extraordinarily high early in the season. In 1990, for instance, experts estimated that the 5,700 acres required 28,186 workers to pick the crop.[31] The short season made the strawberry harvest susceptible to work stoppages, which could be twice as damaging because workers often left the harvest early when the harvest for more lucrative crops like cherries began.

In the aftermath of IRCA, the workforce in the strawberry fields had also changed dramatically. By 1990, Mexican nationals made up over 79 percent of the total workers hired. A study conducted by Oregon State University's Agricultural Extension reasoned that the majority of the workers were undocumented relatives of SAW applicants.[32] PCUN knew this to be true as well. About one-third of the amnestied farm workers that PCUN aided came from Oaxaca and belonged to the Mixtec indigenous group. These male heads of household brought their families to Oregon and created a more stable permanent community. It was not uncommon for groups of as many as twenty families to take up residence in the Willamette Valley and live in increasingly mixed-status households, that is, households that had both documented and undocumented members.[33]

The presence of a large number of families in the fields meant that women took up the mantle of organizing as well. Yet their undocumented status forced them into the shadows, often in their own homes. PCUN saw a rise in complaints of sexual assault, harassment, and spousal abuse among its membership and saw the need for developing a space for farm-working women. In 1995, PCUN launched the Farmworker Women's Leadership Project. PCUN surveyed the women to ascertain their desires and found that the top responses were the need to learn how to drive and to make extra money. PCUN began offering driving lessons and created a co-op so that the women could sell handcrafted goods. The project taught the women practical skills, like driving, balancing a checkbook, and project planning, but more importantly it gave them self-confidence, public speaking skills, and a safe space to talk among themselves. The group proved especially helpful to newcomers, who often arrived harboring feelings of isolation and loneliness.[34] After awhile many women in the group took up leadership positions in the community as well as in the union.

It was these farmworkers, with their family's previous connection to PCUN, who shaped the course of this campaign from the outset. They designed and implemented the organizing strategy and told PCUN volunteers and staff what they expected of them. Workers recommended that organizers be kept in the field throughout the harvest and that volunteers and farmworkers make door-to-door visits to farmworkers' households. They told PCUN to hold a major rally before the harvest began and raise enough money to support the strikers and hire more organizers. Over the next few months PCUN tapped into the base it had been building and raised enough money to hire or recruit as full-time, short-term volunteers, twenty-four new organizers from among its own members and college students. The money also helped to build its strike fund. The notion that workers deserved a fair share of the profits reflects the influence that radical organizations like Centro de Acción Social Autonomó (CASA) had on PCUN. With that shot fired, PCUN announced its "Tenth Anniversary Organizing Campaign," "the biggest farm worker organizing drive ever attempted in the Northwest."[35]

PCUN used the fundraising drive as an opportunity to develop a large coalition of progressives. Widening its appeal by describing itself as a "movement" rather than just another interest group, PCUN said it sought to do more than just "redress . . . a specific economic injustice . . . the campaign aims to broaden the movement, strengthen dignity, self-worth, and class identification of the individuals who comprise it, and develop new leadership for the struggles that lie ahead."[36] PCUN embraced language that was easier for Oregon progressives to accept and identify with, speaking in terms of social justice as distinct from a labor conflict. Yet PCUN continued to engage in the "meat and potatoes" work of union organizing, focusing on contracts and wage negotiations.

At the same time, PCUN developed volunteers to take leadership positions in the community and in sister organizations that dealt with other issues. In the following years the union launched a PCUN support committee in Portland and helped establish the Oregon Coalition for Immigrant and Refugee Rights, as well as a Police Oversight Board in Portland.[37] Taking yet another lesson from the UFW, PCUN understood that it needed to build a political base in urban areas. PCUN called on the various organizations to contribute during the strikes by doing research, raising funds, mobilizing picketers, and promoting unionization in the fields. PCUN believed that expanding the base was essential to reframing farmworkers' struggle and inspiring coalition-building. The newsletter asked readers, "If immigrant farm workers can organize and take on the state's most powerful industry, what's stopping the rest of us from doing likewise in our workplace?" The newsletter encouraged workers to think of themselves as united regardless of immigration status by repeatedly invoking CASA's credo of "Con o sin papeles, tenemos derechos porque hacemos la riqueza"— With or without documents, we have rights because we create wealth.

PCUN reached out to many different coalition partners, including gay and lesbian organizations in Portland, especially Basic Rights Oregon (BRO). Founded in 1996, BRO had formed in an effort to consolidate forces that had fought off numerous antigay initiatives that had been placed on Oregon ballots since 1988. Given the tradition of the farmworkers' movement, especially Cesar Chavez and the UFW, to forge close connections with the Catholic Church and utilize religious iconography, reaching out to the gay and lesbian community seemed counterintuitive. Despite the perceived homophobia within the farmworker community, PCUN's commitment to fairness and equality was a matter of principle. The decision to partner with BRO was not an easy one; it even divided the leadership. Ramirez recalled, "Cipriano saw the growth of an anti-gay alliance and [to him] it had overtones of racism and anti-immigrant rhetoric. Even though his position at the time was very homophobic . . . he was able to overcome that."[38]

The force that brought BRO and PCUN together was the conservative Christian political organization, Oregon Citizens Alliance (OCA). Founded in 1986 by Lou Mabon, the OCA placed numerous initiatives on the ballot in the late 1980s and early 1990s that ranged from requiring parental notification for teen abortions to eliminating protections for gay and lesbian employees. The opportunity to forge this alliance came when organizers of "For Love and Justice: A Walk Against Hate" approached PCUN about helping with the action. Organizers designed this two-week trek from Eugene to Portland to counter the OCA's effort to place an antigay rights initiative on the ballot later that year. Measure 9 would have amended the state's constitution to read, "The state recognizes homosexuality, pedophilia, sadism, masochism, as abnormal, wrong, unnatural and perverse."[39]

Walkers along the route needed hosts, and the PCUN union hall seemed like an obvious place to stop. At most locations along the route, walkers rested and ate, but the union organizers saw it as a chance to meet with supporters. Ramirez recalled, "In most places church leaders would give them a place to stay, hand them the keys and leave. Not us! We got farm workers waving the 'Huelga' flags and we met them outside of town and marched together to the union! It was an emotional moment!"[40] PCUN saw this as an opportunity to educate the gay and lesbian community about farmworkers' struggles and to educate its own membership about homophobia.[41] Ramirez recalled, "We had some hard conversations that night. We challenged them to get more involved in our movement, and we promised to help them defeat Measure Nine."[42]

The relationship between BRO and PCUN solidified in the coming years as they repeatedly joined forces to defeat anti-immigrant and antigay bills in the state. In March 1995, for instance, the Oregon legislature introduced House Bill 2933, described by critics as "Oregon Prop. 187" because of its similarity to the California initiative that barred undocumented immigrants from receiving social services and health care services and excluded them from public education. PCUN relied on one of its sister organizations, an immigrant rights organization called CAUSA ("The Cause" in English, an Oregon immigrant rights group), to put political pressure on lawmakers. CAUSA succeeded in stalling the bill in the House, but a few years later an offshoot of the OCA, Oregonians For Immigration Reform, circulated a new version of the bill for signatures to qualify it for the Oregon ballot. Initially CAUSA board members wanted to travel to California to receive training from organizations there in how to defeat the bill. Ramirez had a different idea: "California lost, man! They did not have a winning strategy. I was against going down there. We had the gay and lesbian community right here. They have already fought the measure here and won!"[43] Ramirez convinced the CAUSA board to work with BRO. CAUSA launched a thirty-five-city tour across the state and met with gay and lesbian groups in each city. The grassroots effort proved effective, and the initiative failed to attract enough signatures to qualify for the ballot.[44]

The decision to build broad-based coalitions depended largely on Ferrel's vision. Throughout his education, Ferrel saw similarities between the farmworkers' struggle and the struggles of oppressed peoples all over the world. He spent time in Puerto Rico and became familiar with the nationalist independence movement on the island. He traveled to Nicaragua to observe the Sandinistas' electoral victories, and as a Brown Beret he actively opposed the war in Vietnam. Ferrel argued that farmworkers must "start understanding that their whole situation . . . is connected to a larger picture. It's a system that survives and breeds on the exploitation of oppressed peoples. . . . They start realizing they are not different than a lot of people in the black community, Mexico, Latin America; we can even relate to what's happening in South Africa."[45]

Ferrel foresaw a larger struggle looming on the horizon and he tried to impart this message to the membership as best he could. The coalition sought to construct a wider base and expand the political consciousness of its members. PCUN depended on its sister organizations to fight legislative efforts and to help educate its members, while PCUN focused on organizing.

With spring approaching, PCUN set specific demands at its tenth annual convention. More than 330 farmworkers gathered on April 30, 1995, and established a crop-wide wage demand for strawberries. After three hours of discussion, they decided on 17 cents per pound.[46] This price represented a significant jump from the 10–12 cents per pound that growers had paid the previous decade.[47]

UFW president Arturo Rodriguez, who came to the convention, urged workers to fight for the raise: "Each of you here today is like a match that will ignite a movement throughout Oregon!"[48] As mandated by the assembly, PCUN sent a letter to area strawberry growers informing them of the wage demand and inviting them to discuss it before the harvest began in late May.[49] They received no response. The *Farm Bureau News* warned its readers of the coming strike and offered the contact information of Don Schellenburg, a lobbyist for the Farm Bureau.[50]

PCUN put to work in this campaign the lessons they had learned in the Kraemer Farms struggle about the importance of indigenous workers' information networks. Before the strawberry harvest began, PCUN bought radio spots and produced trilingual (Spanish, Mixtec, and Triqui) messages to promote the organizing campaign, and sent organizers to Madera, California to distribute information about the wage demands to indigenous workers. They knew the migration route that indigenous workers traveled and decided to get a jumpstart on organizing by reaching out to them before they came to Oregon for the harvest. They gathered 2,500 support pledges from workers in the Central Valley before the campaign in Oregon had even started. The union also hired organizers who spoke indigenous languages as well as Spanish and sent them to Mexico to visit the home communities of workers. Thus PCUN stretched the organizing turf of the union from Oregon to Mexico and maintained contact with workers on their migratory circuit. PCUN's efforts resulted in close ties to indigenous communities that made up the backbone of their organizing effort. When the dust settled, the campaign resulted in two major strikes, dozens of work stoppages, and a raise in wages.[51]

The first strike began only one hour into the harvest at Moorhouse Farms, a small operation of about sixty acres just northwest of Molalla. Richard Moorhouse paid only 13 cents per pound. This low rate, coupled with a poor crop, meant that workers stood no chance of making a decent wage. By 6:30 AM on June 2, PCUN had dispatched fifteen organizers into the fields.[52] Workers asked PCUN to represent them in talks with Moorhouse Farms, but Moorhouse refused to participate and ignored the organizers. Instead, Moorhouse attempted to talk to the workers directly, but they returned the favor by ignoring him. Then 170 workers promptly left the fields chanting, "Huelga! Huelga!" (Strike! Strike!) Only crew bosses and their families remained in the fields.[53]

Moorhouse called in some faces familiar to PCUN: the sheriffs and the goons who had worked for the Kraemers. Six minutes after the strike began, Clackamas County sheriffs' cruisers appeared on the scene claiming that they had received calls about armed protestors.[54] After finding no evidence of anyone being armed, they left as quickly as they had arrived. This response marked a major departure from their reaction just four years earlier. PCUN had become a prominent and well-known organization, so law enforcement officers responded to calls more cautiously, apparently tired of answering growers' hysterical phone calls. Then Moorhouse turned to "El Ruso," the Kraemer Farms employee and expert strike-breaker. This time "El Ruso" had help from Jorge Vasquez, a Moorhouse farm labor contractor known as "El Diablo" (the Devil). In addition to being a labor contractor, El Diablo owned and operated three labor camps in the area. They housed close to 150 workers and charged $80 a month plus $3 a day for transportation to and from the fields. On top of the money he made operating the camps, "El Diablo" also earned the typical contractor's fee of 2.5 cents on every pound picked by his workers. On any given day, 200 workers picked 40,000 pounds of strawberries, so El Diablo stood to make nearly $1,200 a day without lifting a finger. In contrast, the average worker picked 200 to 250 pounds per day at 13 cents per pound, earning $35 for a 10–12-hour workday. In sum, El Diablo and other contractors made a fortune, while farmworkers toiled for a pittance.[55]

The wage inequity and poor housing conditions led the workers to walk out of the fields and into PCUN offices. At 4:00 AM the next day, PCUN organizers and supporters traveled to various labor camps owned by Vasquez and another contractor, Lazaro Ruiz. They arrived to find both El Ruso and El Diablo in wait with their henchmen, a group that had clubs in their hands and attempted to intimidate workers by threatening to fire and evict them. Yet farmworkers held steadfast. Only thirteen workers crossed the picket line and jumped into the contractors' van. At the end of the second day of the strike, El Diablo had thirty-three workers in the field, including twenty day-laborers he had picked that morning. Almost two hundred workers remained on strike. El Diablo did not give up, however; he continued to pressure workers and eventually put together a whole crew. Nonetheless, sufficient damage had been done.[56] The first pick of the harvest is short, lasting no more than two weeks. Workers who decided to return worked slowly and inefficiently, and many left altogether after the first week. Vasquez became so nervous about the crop failing that he actually began to pick himself, to the great amusement of the picketers. The combination of the three-day strike and the slowdown devastated Moorhouse's crop and his profits despite the growers' contentions otherwise.[57]

As the action at Moorhouse Farms was winding down, workers on another farm geared up for an even more intense battle. On Monday, June 5, at 6:00 AM, three workers walked to the PCUN office to inform staff members that sixty-five workers had refused to enter the fields on Zielinski Farms near Brooks. Just days earlier PCUN had met with many of the workers at the Zielinski labor camp to discuss wage rates and the organizing campaign. The workers' chief complaint, however, was the housing. As at most labor camps, it was in serious disrepair. Workers paid $2.50 a day to sleep on wooden planks in unheated plywood cabins. PCUN convinced the farmworkers that they should demand not only better housing but also a raise.[58] When organizers left the meeting they remained unsure whether the workers were on board. Unbeknownst to PCUN, the workers held a meeting at the labor camp and resolved to refuse to work on the first day of harvest, and they dispatched leaders to PCUN offices again.[59]

As before, PCUN mobilized its base and brought dozens of supporters to support the workers picketing in a line along River Road, the major artery adjacent to Zielinski's fields. Strikers and supporters carried red PCUN strike flags and PCUN jackets adorned with the symbol of a closed fist over the silhouette of mountains on the back. Along with their supporters, workers hung a banner over the nearby Interstate 5 overpass that read, "Zielinski: Strawberry Workers Demand a Raise." They also plastered strike posters over a three-mile stretch of River Road (well traveled by workers and growers) and even picketed Zielinski's home. "This time," PCUN's newsletter promised, "they wouldn't be able to say there was no strike."[60] The Oregonian profiled worker Bartolome Garcia, a rarity given the risk of retaliation. Garcia, one of the one hundred on strike, told the newspapers that the strikers were restless, "they are wondering what they are doing in the United States. They came to make money but you can work as hard as you can and still make poor wages."[61] Garcia testified that he picked around eighty pounds of strawberries an hour, which equaled about $9.50 an hour, a wage that was rarely reflected in his paychecks. He complained that Zielinski pocketed deductions and kept their wages artificially low. His biggest complaint, however, was about his treatment at the hands of the farmers: "they don't notice that you work hard . . . maybe as the strawberries go bad they'll notice. Maybe now that the union is helping us they'll stop taking us for granted."[62]

Unfortunately Zielinski continued to disregard his employees' desires. He drove up and down River Road personally removing all the posters and refused to deal with the union. PCUN volunteers documenting the strike on video said to Zielinski, "Your workers demonstrate that they want PCUN to represent them, so how can you presume to dictate otherwise?" Zielinski responded, "If my workers want a union, I'll bulldoze the camp and plow under my strawberry fields."[63] Workers responded to the threat by chanting "Aumento de precio o aumento de presion" (Raise the wages or we raise the pressure!). Zielinski continued to resist, however. PCUN organizers facilitated a meeting of strikers to assist them with their internal organization and negotiating strategies. Workers formed a council with fifteen representatives (one from each cabin), and they met with Zielinski without the presence of PCUN staff in order to test Zielinski's claim that the only issue was PCUN's presence. The workers felt he was negotiating in bad faith when he would not budge beyond a one-cent raise. When the negotiations broke off, Zielinski brought in eighty scabs to finish the harvest and continued trying to evict the workers. According to PCUN, Zielinski lost an estimated $75,000 rather than bargain in good faith with the farmworkers.[64] PCUN's network of lawyers challenged Zielinski's right to evict the workers and eventually forced him to pay damages and make repairs. This small victory prompted workers to rename the place "Campo Benito Juarez." Juarez was a Zapotec Indian born in Oaxaca in 1806 who became the first indigenous president of Mexico, serving from 1861 to 1872.

CONCLUSION

Despite their failure to win raises at Zielinski Farms, many of the workers from "Campo Benito Juarez" went on to lead strikes on other farms in Oregon. Addressing the Oregon Public Employees Union in the state capital, strike leader Manuel Rivera summed up the effects of their struggle: "What we did at Camp Benito Juarez made possible victories at many other farms because it showed workers that when we unite and have support, we can defy grower power."[65] Numerous work stoppages and wildcat strikes erupted over that summer, securing wage increases at Krahmer Farms (not to be confused with Kraemer Farms), Norwood Farms, Meneyev Farms, Kutsev Farms, Lucht Farms, Haener Farms, Eder Farms, Wuringer Farms, Bryant Farms, and Kalugin Farms. Ironically, Kraemer Farms raised its wages from 14 to 20 cents per pound, more than workers had demanded of neighboring farms, without any strike threat. Growers continued to assert that their strawberries got picked and that strikes had little effect on their production, yet the numbers belied their contention. In 1990, Oregon growers harvested 71 million pounds of strawberries and during the strike year harvested 53 million pounds, representing around $8 million lost.[66] The crop bounced back in 1994 to 63 million pounds valued at $27 million and fell again during the strike year of 1995 to 52 million pounds valued at $23.4 million. Growers blamed other factors, such as an early rain, but PCUN organizers proudly claimed to have made an impact on growers' pocketbooks.

Regardless of the causes and although the campaign failed to win a contract on Zielinski Farms, the union walked away with collective bargaining agreements on five other farms. Despite the fact that workers in contact with PCUN members and organizers rarely belonged to the union, PCUN assisted them in every way it could, bringing in supporters, picketing, informing them of their rights, filing lawsuits on their behalf, and occasionally representing them in negotiations. PCUN came to see itself as a "wedge in the workers' hands" that not only drove up the wage rates but also gave farmworkers a sense of empowerment that they carried with them wherever they went. Beyond the fields of Oregon, PCUN and its organizing campaign left an indelible mark on the workers. Ramon Ramirez recalled an encounter with workers he met fifteen years after the Kraemer strike: "They were four brothers and they told me they had been looking for me and wanted to tell me thank you. They said we taught them how to organize. How to stand up for themselves."[67] The four brothers had consistently organized walk-outs in the strawberry harvest in California. They did not have the backing of a union, picketers, or boycotters; all they had was an old worn-out business card: "Whenever anyone tried to take advantage of them they would pull out this card I had given them with my name on it. They would show it to contractors and say 'Hey you better not mess with us. We are from PCUN. We will strike you!'"[68] The brother told Ramirez about the numerous times they had used this tactic, and they all got a good laugh out of it. They asked him for another card. Finally, Ramirez thought to himself, "we feel like winners."[69]

PCUN regarded this campaign as a victory for the union, but the death of founder and former president Cipriano Ferrel a few months later left the union in shock. Cipriano passed away suddenly from a heart attack just days before his forty-sixth birthday.[70] Many in Oregon and California loved "Cip," and people packed the PCUN hall in Woodburn and, days later, the UFW's hall at "Forty Acres" outside of Delano to pay their respects at his memorial services. Donations and condolences poured into the PCUN office. In many respects "Cip" was the soul of the union. His previous connections with the UFW facilitated a shift into labor organizing, but his compassion for the immigrant community never let PCUN forget about the undocumented. The militant style that he brought with him from the Brown Berets emboldened many union members, and his relentless commitment to social justice opened up the movement to everyone. His insistence on leadership development enabled the union to live on after his death.

❧ EPILOGUE
La Lucha Sigue

Mexican guest workers, Mexican Americans, and Mexican immigrant labor played a major role in the development of agriculture in the Northwest. In this book I have sought to demonstrate the different ways that ethnic Mexican labor tried to resist exploitation. At various moments in history different avenues were available and the methods changed, but one thing remained constant: they fought to improve their lives. They skipped out on contracts, loaded down bags, naturalized, went on strike, marched, boycotted, and even danced. They did everything within their power to carve out a space for themselves in the Pacific Northwest.

The struggles of braceros, Tejanos, and undocumented workers laid the groundwork for the emergence of PCUN. PCUN has become the voice of the disenfranchised farmworker whose programs achieved short-term and long-term change by combining membership services with grassroots organizing. PCUN sees itself as part of a larger movement for social justice and is dedicated to building not just organizations but the infrastructure for success well beyond the scope of traditional labor unions. Throughout the rest of the '90s and into the 2000s, PCUN continued to rack up victories large and small. In 1997 they launched a boycott against Gardenburger because they purchased the vegetables for their burgers from NORPAC. The boycott lasted ten years before they capitulated and began purchasing from a different company. In 1998 PCUN signed contracts with three growers, and in 2002 it signed two more contracts.[1] Also in 2002, the Farmworker Women's Leadership Project became its own self-sustaining organization, known now as Mujere Luchadores Progresistas.

On a sunny day in June 2005, my sister and I, along with a couple of friends, pulled into the parking lot of Colonia Libertad. The grand opening of the farmworker housing project was a joyous affair, with supporters, farmworkers, and politicians in attendance. After decades of dealing with squalid conditions, farmworkers could now look to the Farmworker Housing Development Corporation as a shining example of what is possible. The FHDC, in cooperation with PCUN and other organizations, opened five separate farmworkers' housing units in Oregon. Nuevo Amanecer (New Dawn), Colonia Libertad (Liberty Colony), Colonia Amistad (Friendship Colony), Villa de Sol (Village of the Sun), and Esperanza Courts (Hope Courts) are all modern apartment complexes with amenities, community programs, child care, and most importantly, dignity. On the grounds of Nuevo Amanecer stands the Cipriano Ferrel Education Center, a multiuse space intended to provide services and after-school activities for farmworker youth.

In the years since the death of cofounder Cipriano Ferrel, the union has grown bigger and stronger. As Danny Santos, senior political advisor for the former governor of Oregon, told me, "We don't do one thing without first thinking about how PCUN is going to react."[2] PCUN took on the issues of police brutality in Woodburn, substandard education for the ethnic Mexican community, voter registration, and farmworker housing. They have built their union as part of a movement, and not the movement itself. They now work in conjunction with eight other sister organizations known as CAPACES (Abilities or skills). CAPACES acts as an umbrella organization for FHDC; Voz Hispana, a Latino voter education project; Mujeres Luchadoras Progresistas (MLP); Latinos Unidos Siempre (LUS), a Latino youth leadership project; Mano a Mano, a provider of social services; and Salem-Keizer coalition for equality, which empowers Latino families to take an active role in their children's education and in advocating for equity in the public education system. PCUN has succeeded in creating and maintaining a progressive movement in Oregon.

In March 2007, with the aid of the Prometheus project, PCUN launched Radio Movimiento, a twenty-four-hour low power FM station. The radio station has trilingual radio programming including cultural shows, organizing shows, and music. PCUN continues to attack labor problems on the legislative front, organize workers, sign collective bargaining agreements, and organize for immigrant rights. The current development of a Leadership Institute will formalize the on-the-job training that organizers previously received with PCUN. The union's membership holds steady at just over 5,000 dues-paying members and is a leading example of what organizing in the immigrant community can look like.

Yet the struggle in Oregon is far from over. As many farmworking families move out of the fields and into service sector work, the migrant stream is once again largely undocumented; increasingly indigenous; often monolingual in a language other than Spanish, such as Triqui, Mixteco, or Zapoteco; young; and male. These new workers are facing some of the same exploitative conditions that existed when the first braceros arrived, and some of them, unbelievably, live in the same facilities. As the founding staff of PCUN moves on and retires, the union's dedication to leadership development has ensured that it will not miss a beat in confronting these new challenges.

NOTES

INTRODUCTION

1. James Scott, *Weapons of the Weak: Everyday Forms of Peasant Resistance* (New Haven: Yale University Press, 1987).

2. William G. Robbins, *Landscapes of Promise: The Oregon Story, 1800–1940* (Seattle: University of Washington Press, 1999); and *Landscapes of Conflict: The Oregon Story, 1940–2000* (Seattle: University of Washington Press), 2004.

3. Richard White, "American Environmental History: The Development of a New Historical Field," *Pacific Historical Review* 54, no. 3 (1985): 297–335.

4. William Cronon, "Modes of Prophecy and Production: Placing Nature in History," *Journal of American History* 77 (Winter 1990); Andre Hurley, *Environmental Inequalities: Class, Race, and Industrial Pollution in Gary, Indiana, 1945–1990* (Chapel Hill: University of North Carolina Press, 1995); Richard White, *The Organic Machine: The Remaking of the Columbia River* (New York: Hill and Wang, 1995); Richard White, "Are You an Environmentalist or Do You Work for a Living," in *Uncommon Ground: Toward Reinventing Nature,* ed. William Cronon (New York: W.W. Norton, 1995); Donald Worster, "Seeing Beyond Culture," *Journal of American History* 77 (Winter 1990).

5. Gunther Peck, "The Nature of Labor: Fault Lines and Common Ground in Environmental and Labor History," in *Environmental History* 11 (April 2006): 212–238.

6. For instance, see the Coalition of Immokalee Workers, a community-based workers' organization.

7. Mike Davis, *Prisoners of the American Dream: Politics and Economy in the History of the US Working Class* (London: Verso, 1986).

8. Jennifer Gordon, *Suburban Sweatshops: The Fight for Immigrant Rights* (Cambridge, MA: Belknap Press of Harvard University Press, 2005); Pierrette Hondagneu-Sotelo, *Doméstica: Immigrant Workers Cleaning and Caring in the Shadows of Affluence* (Berkeley: University of California Press, 2001).

9. Gary Okihiro, "Oral History and the Writing of Ethnic History: A Reconnaissance into Method and Theory," in *The Oral History Review* 9 (1981): 27–46.

10. I use the term "ethnic Mexicans" frequently in the introduction to refer to the three waves of immigrants to the Pacific Northwest. I employ this term as shorthand to describe the totality of immigrants discussed in this book. It is not meant to homogenize the diverse racial makeup, class makeup, or citizenship status of the subjects of this book. In the text I argue that the class, racial, and citizenship status of each distinct wave affected not only the decisions they made but also the outcome. Thus the term is not intended to be a theoretical category but a marker of a shared experience, with a full acknowledgment that those identities are different at various times.

11. Donald Cutter, "The Other Explorers: Alcada Galiano and Vladez," *Columbia* (Summer 1991); Iris H. W. Engstrand, "Jose Mariano Moziño: Pioneer Mexican Naturalist," *Columbia* (Spring 1991); Erasmo Gamboa, "Chicanos in the Northwest: An Historical Perspective," *El Grito* 6, no. 4 (Summer 1973): 57–70; James Watt, *Journal of Mule Train Packing in Eastern Washington in the 1860s* (Morgantown, WV: Galleon Press, 1978).

12. Carlos S. Maldonado, "An Overview of the Mexicano/Chicano Presence in the Pacific Northwest," in *The Chicano Experience in the Northwest,* ed. Gilberto Garcia and Carlos S. Maldonado (Dubuque, IA: Kendall/Hunt, 2001).

13. I use the term *Mexican* to describe the population in the region because the number of non-Mexican Hispanics was less than 2 percent of all Hispanics until the 1980s and 1990s, when the number of non-Mexican Hispanics reached 18 percent. I adjust the numbers accordingly, starting with those decades.

14. The census did not enumerate Mexicans in most states and excluded Idaho from the figures collected.

15. Richard W. Slatta, "Chicanos in the Pacific Northwest: A Demographic and Socioeconomic Portrait," *Pacific Northwest Quarterly* 70, no. 4 (October 1979): 155–162.

CHAPTER 1   MANY MILES FROM HOME

1. Ernesto Galarza, *Merchants of Labor: The Mexican Bracero Story* (McNally & Loftin, 1972); Richard Steven Street, *Beasts of the Field: A Narrative History of California Farmworkers. 1769–1913* (Stanford, CA: Stanford University Press, 2004).

2. Dorothy B. Fujita-Rony, *American Workers, Colonial Power: Philippine Seattle and the Transpacific West, 1919–1941,* 1st ed. (Berkeley: University of California Press, 2002).

3. Clete Daniel, *Chicano Workers and the Politics of Fairness: The FEPC in the Southwest, 1941–1945* (Austin: University of Texas Press, 1991).

4. Manuel Garcia y Griego, "The Importation of Mexican Contract Labor to the United States, 1942–1964," in *Between Two Worlds: Mexican Immigrants to the United States,* ed. David G. Gutierrez (Lanham, MD: Rowman and Littlefield, 1996).

5. Erasmo Gamboa, *Mexican Labor and World War II: Braceros in the Pacific Northwest, 1942–1947* (Austin: University of Texas Press, 1990).

6. Ibid.

7. Malheur County Historical Society, *Malheur County History,* 2 vols. (Malheur County Historical Society, 1988).

8. Gamboa, *Mexican Labor and World War II.*

9. Ibid.

10. Ibid.

11. *Yakima Daily Republic,* August 18, 1941.

12. *Idaho Statesman,* August 25, 1942; *Oregonian,* June 13, 1943.

13. *Idaho Statesman,* May 10, 1943.

14. "War Relocation Authority Sets Up Three Offices in Gem State," *Idaho Statesman,* April 30, 1943.

15. *Idaho Statesman,* June 1, 1942.

16. *Monmouth Herald,* June 17, 1943.

17. *Northwest Farm News,* February 4, 1943.

18. During this period, growers across the country also experimented with importing Jamaican guest workers. Oregon and Washington never imported Jamaicans while Idaho brought small numbers. At their peak they never accounted for more than 10 percent of all imported labor in Idaho. For more on Jamaican guest workers, see Cindy Hahamovitch, *No Man's Land: Jamaican Guestworkers in America and the Global History of Deportable Labor* (Princeton, NJ: Princeton University Press, 2011).

19. *Northwest Farm News,* February 4, 1943.

20. *Idaho Statesman,* June 9, 1942.

21. Galarza, *Merchants of Labor.*

22. Mae Ngai, *Impossible Subjects: Illegal Aliens and the Making of Modern America* (Princeton, NJ: Princeton University Press, 2005).

23. *Yakima Daily Republic*, April 27, 1943.
24. Interview with Juan Contreras, May 26, 2006, in Perris, CA. Conducted and translated by the author.
25. Ibid.
26. Ibid.
27. Ibid.
28. Ibid.
29. Ibid.
30. Ibid.
31. Ibid.
32. Ibid.
33. *Oregon Statesman*, July 18, 1943.
34. *Ontario Argus*, May 22, 1947; *Ontario Argus*, May 29, 1947.
35. Johanna Ogden, "Race, Labor, and Getting Out the Harvest: The Bracero Program in World War II Hood River Oregon," in *Memory, Community, and Activism: Mexican Migration and Labor in the Pacific Northwest*, ed. Jerry Garcia and Gilberto Garcia (East Lansing, MI: Julian Zamora Research Institute, Michigan State University Press, 2005).
36. Interview with Juan Contreras, May 26, 2006.
37. Ibid.
38. Ibid.
39. *Idaho Statesman*, May 4, 1945.
40. Interview with Atanacio Jimenez Lopez, May 24, 2006, in Heber, CA. Conducted and translated by the author.
41. Ibid.
42. Ibid.
43. Ibid.
44. Ibid.
45. Paul S. Taylor, "Some Aspects of Mexican Immigration," *Journal of Political Economy* 38, no. 5 (October 1930).
46. Gamboa, *Mexican Labor and World War II.*
47. Interview with Atanacio Jimenez Lopez, May 24, 2006.
48. Ibid.
49. Ibid.
50. Ibid.
51. Interview with Augustin Bautista, May 20, 2006, in Coachella, CA. Conducted and translated by the author.
52. Ibid.
53. Ibid.
54. Interview with Atanacio Jimenez Lopez, May 24, 2006.
55. *Oregon Statesman*, September 19, 1943.
56. Interview with Atanacio Jimenez Lopez, May 24, 2006.
57. Matt Garcia, *A World of Its Own: Race, Labor, and Citrus in the Making of Greater Los Angeles, 1900–1970* (Chapel Hill: University of North Carolina Press, 2002).
58. Interview with Juan Contreras, May 26, 2006, in Perris, CA. Conducted and translated by the author.
59. Ibid.
60. Ibid.
61. Interview with Augustin Bautista, May 20, 2006.

62. Ibid.

63. Interview with Juan Contreras, May 26, 2006.

64. Ibid.

65. Ibid.

66. Ibid.

67. *Northwest Farm News*, April 27, 1944.

68. *Northwest Farm News*, July 13, 1945.

69. *Oregonian*, September 12, 1944; October 9, 1944; October 11, 1944.

70. This tactic had been used by other groups of farmworkers who were paid by the pound of crop they picked, and inspection systems had been set up to combat it in the cotton fields and row crops.

71. Interview with Atanacio Jimenez Lopez, May 24, 2006.

72. Ibid.

73. Ibid.

74. Gamboa, *Mexican Labor and World War II*.

75. Interview with Atanacio Jimenez Lopez, May 24, 2006.

76. Interview with Juan Contreras, May 26, 2006.

77. Ibid.

78. *Hood River News*, June 4, 1963; July 23, 1943; September 17, 1943; July 28, 1944; August 6, 1943; July 28, 1944; August 14, 1944.

79. Ogden, "Race, Labor, and Getting Out the Harvest."

80. David Berman, *Radicalism in the Mountain West, 1890–1920: Socialists, Populists, Miners, and Wobblies* (Boulder: University Press of Colorado, 2007).

81. *Idaho Statesman*, May 14, 1937; April 6, 1938; June 13, 1938; June 22, 1938; March 13, 1942.

82. *Idaho Statesman*, June 6, 1945.

83. Ibid.

84. *Idaho Statesman*, June 10, 1945.

85. *Idaho Statesman*, June 1, 1946.

86. Gamboa, *Mexican Labor and World War II*.

87. *Northwest Farm News*, December 1, 1946.

88. Gamboa, *Mexican Labor and World War II*; Ogden, "Race, Labor, and Getting Out the Harvest."

89. Gilbert G. Gonzalez, *Mexican Consuls and Labor Organizing: Imperial Politics in the American Southwest* (Austin: University of Texas Press, 1999).

90. *Idaho Statesman*, October 13, 1948.

91. *Idaho Statesman*, May 30, 1946.

92. *Idaho Statesman*, June 19, 1946.

93. Gamboa, *Mexican Labor and World War II*.

94. Ibid.

95. Manuel Garcia y Griego, "The Importation of Mexican Contract Labor to the United States, 1942–1964," in *Between Two Worlds: Mexican Immigrants to the United States*, ed. David G. Gutierrez. (Lanham, MD: Rowman and Littlefield, 1996).

96. *Idaho Statesman*, June 12, 1945.

97. Ibid.

98. *Idaho Statesman*, October 30, 1945.

99. *Idaho Statesman*, June 17, 1945.

100. *Oregonian*, July 23, 1944.

101. Patricia K. Ourada, *Migrant Workers in Idaho*. Unpublished manuscript. Boise State University, 1980.

102. *Northwest Farm News*, August 23, 1945.

103. Interview with Francisco Murillo Almaraz, May 22, 2006, in Ripley, CA. Conducted and translated by the author.

104. *Idaho Statesman*, July 27, 1947.

105. Pesqueira was involved in strikes in Caldwell, Nampa, Preston, and Walla Walla.

106. *Idaho Statesman*, June 15, 1946; June 18, 1946; June 25, 1946; June 26, 1946.

107. Kitty Calavita, *Inside the State: The Bracero Program, Immigration, and the INS* (New Orleans: Quid Pro Books, 2010); Alicia Camacho, *Migrant Imaginaries: Latino Cultural Politics in the US–Mexico Borderlands* (New York: New York University Press, 2008); Deborah Cohen, *Braceros: Migrant Citizens and Transnational Subjects in the Postwar United States and Mexico*. (Chapel Hill: University of North Carolina Press, 2011); Mae Ngai, *Impossible Subjects: Illegal Aliens and the Making of Modern America* (Princeton, NJ: Princeton University Press, 2005).

108. Legislative Interim Committee on Migratory Labor. *Migratory Labor in Oregon*, 1958.

109. Oregon Bureau of Labor, *Vamonos Pal Norte (Let's Go North): A Social Profile of the Spanish Speaking Migratory Farm Laborer*, 1958; Joe Bianco, "Impending Halt of Bracero Labor Poses Knotty Problems for Farmers," May 14, 1964; *Oregonian*, May 17, 1953.

110. Oregon State College Extension Service Annual Report of Harry R. Sundquist, Malheur County Extension Agent, December 1, 1945–November 30, 1946.

111. *Northwest Farm News*, September 5, 1946.

112. *Hood River News*, September 24, 1943.

113. *Farm Labor News Notes*, August 16, 1945.

114. *Oregonian*, January 11, 1948.

115. Ibid.

116. Ibid.

CHAPTER 2   LOS TEJANOS

1. I utilize the term *Tejano* in the same manner that Marc Simon Rodriguez does in his work *The Tejano Diaspora*. Rodriguez argues that the term does not simply imply Spanish and Mexican settlers in Texas and their descendants, but "migrants that increasingly became 'Tejano' as a result of these labor networks, which thrust Texas-based workers into the North American migrant labor market."

2. Antonia I. Castañeda, "Que Se Pudieran Defender (So You Could Defend Yourselves: Chicanas, Regional History, and National Discourse," "Women's West" issue, *Frontiers: A Journal of Women's Studies* 22, no. 3 (2001), 116–142.

3. A similar process in Wisconsin is described by Marc Simon Rodriguez. Rodriguez also argues that a social movement developed in both Crystal City and Milwaukee which informed the emergence of a Chicano consciousness, while I see little evidence of such a development in Oregon.

4. Legislative Interim Committee on Migratory Labor. *Migratory Labor in Oregon* (1958).

5. Josue Quesada Estrada, "Texas-Mexican Diaspora to Washington State: Recruitment, Migration, and Community, 1940–1960," Master's thesis, Washington State University, 2007.

6. Estrada, "Texas-Mexican Diaspora to Washington State"; Marc Simon Rodriguez, *The Tejano Diaspora: Mexican Americanism and Ethnic Politics in Texas and Washington* (Chapel Hill: University of North Carolina Press, 2011).

7. *Oregon Journal*, June 5, 1958.

8. David Peterson del Mar, *Oregon's Promise: An Interpretive History* (Corvallis: Oregon State University Press, 2003).

9. Janet Seiko Nishihara, "Japanese Americans in Eastern Oregon," in *Seeing Color: Indigenous Peoples and Racialized Ethnic Minorities in Oregon*, ed. Jun Xing, Erlinda Gonzalez Berry, Patti Sakurai, Robert D. Thompson Jr., and Kurt Peters (Lanham, MD: University Press of America, 2007).

10. The first generation of Japanese immigrants or "Issei" who came to Oregon worked in a variety of occupations, including railroad work, lumber mills, and cannery work. The second generation made the transition to truck farming and farm work.

11. 50th Anniversary of Snake River Chapter of the Japanese American Citizens League, Four Rivers Cultural Center, Ontario, Oregon. Interviewer anonymous, 1992.

12. Ibid.

13. Interview with Robert Komoto, August 13, 2009, in Ontario, Oregon. Conducted by the author.

14. Robert C. Sims, "The Free Zone Nikkei: Japanese Americans in Idaho and Eastern Oregon in World War II," in *Nikkei in the Pacific Northwest: Japanese Americans and Japanese Canadians in the Twentieth Century* (Seattle: University of Washington Press), 2005.

15. 50th Anniversary of Snake River Chapter of the Japanese American Citizens League. Interviewer anonymous, 1992.

16. Sims, "The Free Zone Nikkei."

17. Eichiro Azuma, "A History of Oregon's Issei, 1880–1952," *Oregon Historical Quarterly* 94 (1993–1994): 315–367.

18. In total, 33,000 "free-zoners" worked across Montana, Utah, Idaho, and Wyoming. Louis Fiset, "Thinning, Topping, and Loading: Japanese Americans and Beet Sugar in World War II," *Pacific Northwest Quarterly* 90, no. 3 (Summer 1999).

19. Historian Louis Fiset relates a similar situation in the assembly centers in Portland. The first call for workers garnered only fifteen volunteers, who decided to leave for Vale, Oregon. Eventually word reached internees and fifty more signed up for the next round. Fiset, "Thinning, Topping, and Loading."

20. Sims, "The Free Zone Nikkei."

21. Ibid.

22. 50th Anniversary of Snake River Chapter. Interviewer anonymous, 1992. Original interviewee said "fearsome." I have made the change to correct her English.

23. Interview with Robert Komoto, August 13, 2009.

24. Eichiro Azuma, "A History of Oregon's Issei, 1880–1952."

25. *Oregon Journal*, October 22, 1950.

26. Paul S. Taylor, "Hand Laborers in the Western Sugar Beet Industry," *Agricultural History* 41, no. 1 (January 1967): 19–26.

27. *Oregonian*, August 11, 1956.

28. Legislative Interim Committee, *Migratory Labor in Oregon*, 1958.

29. "Typical Migrant Picker Family Heads North for Better Wages," *Oregonian*, August 3, 1958.

30. *Ontario Argus*, May 5, 1949.

31. Interview with Josefa Rivera, August 8, 2009, in Ontario, Oregon. Conducted and translated by the author.

32. Tom Current and Mark Martínez Infante, *Final Report of the 1958–1959 Migrant Farm Labor Studies in Oregon Including Material from the Preliminary Report of the Bureau of Labor: "We Talked to the Migrants . . . and Migrant Problems Demand Attention."* Oregon Bureau of Labor, Migrant Labor Division, 1959.

33. Current and Martínez Infante, *Final Report of the 1958–1959 Migrant Farm Labor Studies in Oregon.*

34. *Oregon Journal,* October 22, 1950; *Oregon Statesman Journal,* June 5, 1948.

35. Legislative Interim Committee, *Migratory Labor in Oregon.*

36. *Oregon Journal,* June 5, 1958.

37. *Interagency Committee Report on Migratory Labor, 1965,* to Mark O. Hatfield, governor of Oregon.

38. *Oregonian,* July 19, 1962.

39. *Oregonian,* July 7, 1972.

40. "Shocking Conditions in Migrant Labor Camp Revealed in Survey Team Report," *Oregonian,* July 21, 1958.

41. Ibid.

42. "Migrant Labor Survey Indicts Contractors," *Oregon Journal,* July 20, 1958.

43. Interview with Josefa Rivera, August 8, 2009.

44. Interview with Mercedes Rivera, August 8, 2009, in Ontario, Oregon. Conducted and translated by the author.

45. Ibid.

46. Oregon Governor's Task Force, *OSU Report on Seasonal Agricultural Labor in Oregon,* Office of the Governor, 1969.

47. Oregon State College Extension Service Annual Report of Harry R. Sandquist, Malheur County extension agent, December 1, 1948–November 30, 1949; December 1, 1949–November 30, 1950; December 1, 1953–November 30, 1954; December 1, 1956–November 30, 1957.

48. Oregon State College Extension Service Annual Report of Harry R. Sandquist, Malheur County extension agent, December 1, 1956–November 30, 1957.

49. Interview with Robert Komoto, August 13, 2009.

50. Ibid.

51. Oregon Bureau of Labor, *"Vamanos pal Norte" (Let's Go North): A Social Profile of the Spanish Speaking Migratory Farm Labor* (1958). Ruvacables was later investigated for permitting the use of child labor but was cleared of any criminal charges because the state could not prove that he knew the children were underage.

52. Ibid.

53. Legislative Interim Committee, *Migratory Labor in Oregon,* 1958.

54. Oregon Law ORS 658, Sections 145–155.

55. Interview with Osvaldo Gonzalez, July 19, 2009, in Ontario, Oregon. Conducted and translated by the author.

56. Ibid.

57. Ibid.

58. Ibid.

59. Ibid.

60. Ibid.

61. Ibid.

62. *Interagency Committee Report on Migratory Labor, 1965.*

63. Interview with Osvaldo González, July 19, 2009.

64. Interview with Adela Menchaca, August 15, 2009, in Ontario, Oregon. Conducted and translated by the author.

65. Interview with Benito Menchaca, August 15, 2009, in Ontario, Oregon. Conducted and translated by the author.

66. Ibid.

67. Rodriguez, *The Tejano Diaspora.*
68. Interview with Adela Menchaca, August 15, 2009.
69. Ibid.
70. Ibid.
71. Ibid.
72. Interview with Benito Menchaca, August 15, 2009.
73. Ibid.
74. Ibid.
75. Interview with Micaela Rodriguez Guijarro, July 30, 2009, in Ontario, Oregon. Conducted and translated by the author.
76. Luis Alfonso Herrera Robles, "Historia de braceros: Olvido y abandono en el norte de Mexico," *Guaraguao*, ano 14, no. 34 (Verano 2010): 38–50; Jesus Tamayo, "Las areas expulsoras de mano de obra del estado de Zacatecas," *Estudios Demograficos y Urbanos* 6, no. 2 (May–August 1991): 347–378.
77. Interview with Aurora Rodriguez Banda, August 9, 2009, in Ontario, Oregon. Conducted and translated by the author.
78. Ibid.
79. Ibid.
80. Ibid.
81. Ibid.
82. Ibid.
83. Oregon Bureau of Labor, "*Vamanos pal Norte.*"
84. Interview with Aurora Rodriguez Banda, August 9, 2009.
85. Ibid.
86. Ibid.
87. Interview with Adela Menchaca, August 15, 2009.
88. Interview with Graciela Olvera Machuca, August 28, 2009, in Ontario, Oregon. Conducted and translated by the author.
89. Ibid.
90. Ibid.
91. Interview with Ernesto Guijarro, July 30, 2009, in Ontario, Oregon. Conducted and translated by the author.
92. Ibid.
93. Interview with Micaela Rodriguez Guijarro, July 30, 2009.
94. *Ontario Argus*, June 2, 1948.
95. *Ontario Argus*, July 19, 1949; June 29, 1950; June 14, 1951.
96. Interview with Jose Machuca, August 28, 2009, in Ontario, Oregon. Conducted and translated by the author.
97. Interview with Jesus Garcia, July 23, 2009, in Ontario, Oregon. Conducted and translated by the author.
98. Interview with Josefa Rivera, August 8, 2009.
99. Ibid.
100. Interview with Mercedes Rivera, August 8, 2009.
101. Manuel Pena, *The Texas Mexican Conjunto: History of a Working Class Music* (Austin: University of Texas Press, 1985).
102. Interview with Ernesto Guijarro, July 30, 2009.
103. Ibid.
104. Interview with Micaela Rodriguez Guijarro, July 30, 2009.

105. Ibid.
106. Oregon Bureau of Labor, *"Vamanos pal Norte."*
107. Ibid.
108. Interview with Mercedes Rivera, August 8, 2009.
109. Interview with Juanita Rivera, August 8, 2009, in Ontario, Oregon. Conducted and translated by the author.
110. Ibid.
111. Interview with Mercedes Rivera, August 8, 2009.
112. Ibid.

CHAPTER 3   THE GENESIS OF THE WILLAMETTE VALLEY
IMMIGRATION PROJECT

1. "New Name Given College: Colegio Cesar Chavez," *Oregonian*, December 13, 1973.
2. Glenn Anthony May, *Sonny Montes and Mexican American Activism in Oregon* (Corvallis: Oregon State University Press, 2011); Carlos Maldonado, *Colegio Cesar Chavez, 1973–1983: A Chicano Struggle for Educational Self-Determination* (New York: Routledge, 2000).
3. José Angel Gutierrez, *The Making of a Chicano Militant: Lessons from Cristal* (Madison: University of Wisconsin Press, 1998).
4. Originally established in 1888 as a female academy of higher education, Mt. Angel Academy was reorganized into a Normal School (teacher training) in 1897. In 1954 it received accreditation from the Northwest Accrediting Association and became Mt. Angel College. After taking out various federal loans to expand the campus, Mt. Angel College suffered a financial crisis. College officials worried that they could not enroll a sufficient number of students to be able to pay back the loan, and eventually filed for bankruptcy in 1982.
5. The Brown Berets modeled themselves after black nationalist groups such as the Black Panthers. Ernesto Chavez, *Mi Raza Primero (My People First!): Nationalism, Identity, and Insurgency in the Chicano Movement in Los Angeles, 1966–1978* (Berkeley: University of California Press), 2002.
6. Interview with Larry Kleinman, July 24, 2007, in Woodburn, Oregon. Conducted by the author.
7. George Lipsitz, *The Possessive Investment in Whiteness: How White People Profit from Identity Politics* (Philadelphia: Temple University Press, 2006).
8. Sitting on the floor, not shaving or bathing, and wearing a black ribbon are traditional mourning customs performed by Jews. His sitting "shiva" for MLK is an expression of a deep sense of kinship.
9. Congregation Solel is a liberal congregation in Highland Park, which was founded in 1957 by the eminent Reform rabbi, Arnold Jacob Wolf.
10. Larry Kleinman, "The Long Road: HUD Dogs Chicano School," *The Portland Scribe*, October 13, 1976.
11. Interview with Ramón Ramírez, July 28, 2007, in Woodburn, Oregon. Conducted by the author.
12. *Oregonian*, October 27, 1969; September 30, 1969.
13. *Oregonian*, May 6, 1977.
14. Ibid.
15. Founded by Bert Corona in 1968 as a mutual aid society, CASA eventually became a Marxist-Leninist organization focused on the ethnic Mexican working class. Their papers and journal *Sin Fronteras* are located at Stanford University.

16. Interview with Ramón Ramírez, July 28, 2007.
17. Ruben Salazar was a *Los Angeles Times* reporter and columnist, military veteran, and US citizen. A coroner's inquest determined that his death was a premeditated homicide. Despite the finding, Sheriff Tom Wilson, the man who killed Salazar, was never charged or prosecuted.
18. As Ian Haney López demonstrates in his book *Racism on Trial*, Ramírez's experience with the police was typical. In fact López argues that maltreatment at the hands of the police forced Mexican Americans to see themselves as a distinct racial minority who had more in common with African Americans than with whites. Ian Haney-López, *Racism on Trial: The Chicano Fight for Justice* (Cambridge, MA: Belknap Press of Harvard University Press, 2003).
19. Interview with Ramón Ramírez, July 28, 2007.
20. Ibid.
21. Chavez, *"Mi Raza Primero!" (My People First!)*; Mario García, *Mexican Americans: Leadership, Ideology and Identity, 1930–1960* (New Haven, CT: Yale University Press, 1991); David Gutiérrez, *Walls and Mirrors: Mexican Americans, Mexican Immigrants, and the Politics of Ethnicity* (Berkeley: University of California Press, 1995).
22. Interview with Ramón Ramírez, July 28, 2007.
23. Ibid.
24. This structure mirrored the NAACP's structure.
25. Interview with Larry Kleinman, July 24, 2007.
26. Flyer, PCUN Archives, Woodburn, Oregon.
27. Interview with Larry Kleinman, July 24, 2007.
28. Larry Kleinman, unpublished manuscript, "Resisting La Migra." Larry Kleinman has graciously and exclusively provided me with a copy of his personal memoirs. These memoirs are unpublished and have been cited here with permission of the author.
29. Ibid.
30. Interim Decision #2778, *Matter of García*, in Deportation Proceedings, A-22290411, Decided by Board, January 16, 1980.
31. Affidavit, Ann Witte, PCUN archives, Woodburn, OR.
32. Ibid.
33. Kleinman, "Resisting La Migra."
34. Ibid.
35. Interview with Larry Kleinman, July 24, 2007.
36. Kleinman, "Resisting La Migra."
37. *Matter of García*.
38. Ibid.
39. Interview with Larry Kleinman, July 24, 2007.
40. Ibid.
41. Ibid.
42. Old Believers are the descendants of a group that rejected Russian Orthodox Church reforms in 1654. They migrated to Oregon in the 1960s and founded a community of about 2,000. There are 10,000 Old Believers in Oregon, the largest concentration in the United States. They dress conservatively, have over forty religious holidays per year, are not allowed to eat from the same dishes as nonbelievers, and generally remain aloof from the mainstream.
43. Robert C. Dash and Robert E. Hawkinson, "Mexicans and 'Business as Usual': Small Town Politics in Oregon," *Aztlan* 26, no. 2 (Fall 2001).
44. Kleinman, "Resisting La Migra."
45. "Immigration Raid Catch 156 Illegals," *Oregonian*, May 17, 1978; "At Least 30 Undocumented Workers Arrested Here, INS Director Reports," *Oregon Statesman*, April 14, 1979.

46. Interview with Larry Kleinman, July 24, 2007.
47. Ibid.
48. Kleinman, "Resisting La Migra."
49. Ibid.
50. "Child Care Director Won't Let Immigration Take Infant, Parents," *Oregon Statesman*, October 21, 1978.
51. Kleinman, "Resisting La Migra."
52. Ibid.
53. Ibid.
54. Noel A. Cazenave, *Impossible Democracy: The Unlikely Success of the War on Poverty Community Action Programs* (Albany: State University of New York Press, 2007).
55. Glenn Anthony May, *Sonny Montes and Mexican American Activism in Oregon* (Corvallis: Oregon State University Press, 2011).
56. *El Malcriado*, June 15, 1968.
57. Interview with Larry Kleinman, July 24, 2007.
58. *Oregon Agriculture*, January 25, 1971; February 25, 1971.
59. Jacques E. Levy and Cesar Chavez, *Cesar Chavez: Autobiography of La Causa*, 1st ed. (New York: Norton, 1975).
60. Ibid.
61. *Oregonian*, July 1, 1971.
62. *Oregonian*, June 12, 1969; *Eugene-Register Guard*, August 30, 1970; *Oregonian*, August 30, 1970.
63. *Oregonian*, June 30, 1971; *Willamette Bridge*, July 8–14, 1971.
64. *Eugene-Register Guard*, October 7, 1971.
65. *Oregonian*, July 4, 1971; letter from McCall to Secretary of State Clay Meyers, July 2, 1971.
66. Levy and Chavez, *Cesar Chavez*.
67. Ibid.
68. Matt Garcia, *From the Jaws of Victory: The Triumph and Tragedy of Cesar Chavez and the Farm Worker Movement* (Berkeley: University of California Press, 2012).
69. Marc Simon Rodriguez, *The Tejano Diaspora: Mexican Americanism and Ethnic Politics in Texas and Washington* (Chapel Hill: University of North Carolina Press, 2011); Dionicio Nodin Valdes, *Organized Agriculture and the Labor Movement before the UFW: Puerto Rico, Hawai'i, and California* (Austin: University of Texas Press, 2012).
70. Frank Bardacke, *Trampling Out the Vintage: Cesar Chavez and the Two Souls of the United Farm Workers* (Verso, 2012); Garcia, *From the Jaws of Victory*; Miriam Pawel, *The Crusade of Cesar Chavez: A Biography* (London: Bloomsbury, 2014).
71. "Fresno County Illegal Alien Documents," Jacques Levy Papers, Box 21, File 83; "Trouble in the UFW," Box 21, File 88.
72. Interview with Ramón Ramírez, July 28, 2007.
73. Gutierrez, *Walls and Mirrors*.
74. Ibid.
75. Interview with Larry Kleinman, July 24, 2007.
76. Kleinman, "Resisting La Migra."
77. Interview with Larry Kleinman, July 24, 2007.
78. Ibid.
79. *The Bulletin*, August 14, 1981.
80. *Tri City Herald*, August 14, 1981.
81. Kleinman, "Resisting La Migra."

CHAPTER 4   WHIP THAT HOEDAD IN THE GROUND

1. Interview with Larry Kleinman, July 24, 2007, in Woodburn, Oregon. Conducted by the author.
2. Interview with Larry Kleinman, August 28, 2009, in Woodburn, Oregon. Conducted by the author.
3. The terms *seedlings* and *saplings* are used interchangeably here.
4. The hoedad is also sometimes called a hoedag.
5. Hal Hartzell Jr., *Birth of a Cooperative: Hoedads, Inc: A Worker Owned Forest Labor Co-op* (Eugene and Roseburg, OR: Hulogos'i Communications, 1987).
6. *Statesman Journal*, March 1, 1988.
7. William G. Robbins, *Landscapes of Conflict: The Oregon Story, 1940–2000* (Seattle: University of Washington Press, 2004).
8. Ibid.
9. Hartzell, *Birth of a Cooperative.*
10. Ibid.
11. Interview with Roscoe Caron, July 24, 2007, in Eugene, Oregon. Conducted by the author.
12. *Eugene Register-Guard*, May 11, 1980.
13. Ibid.
14. *Eugene Daily Emerald*, January 13, 1981.
15. Ibid.
16. *Together*, volume 3, no. 2 (October 1976).
17. Ibid.
18. *Eugene Register-Guard*, February 14, 1981.
19. *Eugene Register-Guard*, October 18, 1980.
20. *Together*, vol. 4, no. 2 (Summer 1977).
21. Nativism is the political position demanding a favored status for native-born workers as opposed to immigrant workers. Historically, nativism is differentiated from racism as it has primarily been aimed at white ethnic immigrants.
22. "Judge Orders Back Pay for Tree Planters," *Mail Tribune*, August 25, 1981.
23. Hartzell, *Birth of a Cooperative.*
24. Anonymous, interview conducted by the author, October 27, 2007. The subject asked not to be identified due to his immigration status. Subject worked as a tree planter in various locations for a two-year period 1980–1982. In addition to this worker's concern about his immigration status, the contractor whom he worked for in 1980–1982 is still a prominent contractor in the area.
25. Anonymous, interview.
26. Ibid.
27. *Springfield News*, February 14, 1981.
28. Author Pierrette Hondagneu-Sotelo highlights the recent efforts of undocumented domestic workers in Los Angeles to reclaim their wages. The same strategy was implemented by the Willamette Valley Immigration Project (WVIP) and Pineros y Campesinos Unidos Noroeste (PCUN) in the 1970s and 1980s.
29. *Oregonian*, May 16, 1980.
30. "Judge Orders Back Pay."
31. Ibid.
32. *Statesman Journal*, May 11, 1982.

33. The fight against pesticides on food crops is well chronicled. The struggle to ban pesticides and herbicides in the fields is by no means over, but the movement has made considerable headway. The arguments against using pesticides and herbicides on food crops drew sympathy from organized labor and environmentalists for farmworkersbut it also had another very strong ally in its corner as well, health-conscious consumers. Less concerned about laborers, many consumers' refusal to buy fruits and vegetables that had possibly been sprayed with DDT or other pesticides and herbicides put an unyielding pressure on the producers to at least make it appear that their foodstuffs were healthy. The health of the middle-class consumer was at stake and that fact as much as any sympathy for workers was instrumental in the anti-pesticide movement.

34. Robbins, *Landscapes of Conflict.*

35. The Hoedad also had internal debates about taking contracts with Thiram-covered trees. Thiram is an anti-fungal chemical sprayed on trees. When inhaled it causes nausea, dizziness, fatigue, and diarrhea. Long-term exposure can interfere with speech and motor skills.

36. *Oregonian*, March 18, 1979.

37. Ibid.

38. Ibid.

39. *Eugene Register-Guard*, March 18, 1979.

40. "Use of Illegal Aliens in Government Reforestation Contracts," *Hearing before the Subcommittee on Forests of the Committee on Agriculture*, House of Representatives 96th Congress, Second Session, May 15, 1980, Eugene, OR.

41. Ibid.

42. *Oregonian*, May 16, 1980.

43. *Oregonian*, February 14, 1981.

44. "Use of Illegal Aliens."

45. *Eugene Register-Guard*, October 26, 1983.

46. *Eugene Register-Guard*, November 4, 1983.

47. Willamette Valley Immigration Project, "Reforestation Workers Education Project," n.d.; PCUN archives and internal memo from Larry Kleinman to signers of March 15 letter on Senate Bill 535, n.d.

48. *Springfield News*, February 14, 1982.

49. *Statesman Journal*, February 25, 1982.

50. Ibid.

51. *Oregonian*, May 17, 1985.

52. Interview with Larry Kleinman, August 28, 2009.

53. Cesar Chavez and the National Farm Workers Association (NFWA) began their organizing campaign through a farmworker survey. Chavez and his volunteers would visit farmworkers in their home and ask them about their needs. The "farmworker census" gave Chavez a sense of the needs and demands of farmworkers. Similarly, the WVIP used the idea of a census to assess the most pressing demands of tree planters.

54. Willamette Valley Immigration Project, "Reforestation Workers Education Project."

55. Cipriano Ferrel to Roscoe Caron, January 24, 1983.

56. Payroll certification, now known as Employment Eligibility Verification, is a process conducted to ensure that all employees on the payroll are eligible to work in the United States.

57. Cipriano Ferrel to Gerry Mackie, February 22, 1983; Cipriano Ferrel to Roscoe Caron, February 22, 1983, PCUN archives.

58. Northwest Forest Workers Association, Minutes, February 21, 1983.

59. Interview with Larry Kleinman, August 28, 2009.

60. *Bresgal v. E Brock*, Nos. 86–3996, 86–4072, United States Court of Appeals, Ninth Circuit.
61. Ibid.
62. *Oregonian*, February 16, 1981.
63. Ramon Ramirez to Gerry Mackie, February 21, 1981, PCUN archives.
64. Ramon Ramirez to Margie Hendriksen, March 15, 1983.
65. WVIP to Recipients of May 3 Letter, May 5, 1983.
66. Internal memo from Larry Kleinman to signers of March 15 letter on Senate Bill 535, n.d.
67. Ramon Ramirez to Dave Papen, March 22, 1983.
68. "Weaver Task Force Recommendations," *Northwest Forest Workers Association*, March 1983.
69. "Use of Illegal Aliens in Government Reforestation Contracts."
70. *Oregonian*, February 14, 1981; *Springfield News*, February 14, 1981.
71. *Together*, vol. 3, no. 3 (Winter 1976).
72. Ibid.
73. Hal Hartzell, *Birth of a Cooperative*.
74. Ibid.
75. Sarathy Brinda, *Pineros: Latino Labour and the Changing Face of Forestry in the Pacific Northwest* (Seattle: University of Washington Press, 2012).
76. Ibid.

CHAPTER 5   "NOW I CAN HOLD MY OWN WITH ANYBODY"

1. Augustine Valle to Willamette Valley Immigration Project supporters and members, August 8, 1985.
2. Lynn Stephens, *The Story of PCUN and the Farm Worker Movement in Oregon* (Eugene: Department of Anthropology, University of Oregon, 2001).
3. Paul Koberstein, "INS Probes Fraud in 8 Illegals' Applications for Residency, Time for Warnings End as Companies, Individuals Face Law," *Oregonian*, November 6, 1987.
4. Robert Olmos, "Attorney Sees 'Good' and 'Bad' in Immigration Law," *Oregonian*, December 31, 1987.
5. See *Ayuda INC v. Meese*; *Catholic Social Services v. Meese*; *Zambrano v. Meese*.
6. Phil Manzano, "Years of Hiding End for Salem Man," *Oregonian*, August 20, 1987.
7. Southern Poverty Law Center, *Close to Slavery: Guest Worker Programs in the United States* (Montgomery, AL, 2007).
8. Unions that had workers under contract were allowed to sign the I-705s. For example, the UFW was able to sign affidavits for workers who belonged to the union and worked under contract. PCUN at the time had no union contracts and therefore did not sign any I-705s.
9. IRCA Sec. 210(3)(B).
10. There was no apparent intended irony in choosing "Cinco de Mayo" as the implementation date.
11. Manzano, "Years of Hiding End."
12. University of Oregon basketball star Greg Trapp was one of the literally handfuls of non-Mexicans to apply for amnesty in Oregon. Trapp, of Belizean birth, was unaware that he was undocumented until he applied for a passport to play basketball overseas. Trapp's parents had never informed him that he was born in Belize before moving to Los Angeles. Trapp qualified for Amnesty under the Registry Update provision of IRCA. Tony Frei, "Talk About Being Caught in a Trapp," *Oregonian*, September 9, 1987.
13. Robert Olmos, "Laborers Take Toll on Agencies Providing Food in Cornelius," *Oregonian*, March 31, 1988.

14. Robert Olmos, "Forest Grove Migrant Housing Project Deemed a Success; Expansion Sought," *Oregonian*, March 12, 1988.

15. *Oregonian*, December 29, 1991.

16. The Replenishment Agricultural Worker (RAW) provision sought to fill the purported shortage caused by the mass exodus of SAW workers. Through RAW, the Department of Labor was given special permission to determine in three years after the closing of legalization whether there was indeed a labor shortage.

17. "IRCA and Oregon Agricultural Industries: Nursery Crops, Christmas Trees, and Strawberries in the Willamette Valley and Pears in the Hood River Valley," Oregon State University Agricultural Experiment Station, Special Report no. 910, revised April 1993.

18. Phil Manzano, "Confusion Surrounds Immigration Rules," *Oregonian*, October 5, 1987.

19. "IRCA and Oregon Agricultural Industries."

20. Robert Olmos, "Aucoin Calls Agency Biased Against Farm Worker Program, Oregon Democrat Urges Farmers to Pinpoint the New Immigration Laws Ills," *Oregonian*, October 13, 1987.

21. Ibid.

22. Phil Manzano, "Growers Won't Face Slim Pickings for Labor," *Oregonian*, August 29, 1987.

23. Robert Olmos, "Worry Over Lack of Workers Keeps Strawberry Growers from Planting," *Oregonian*, January 7, 1988; Jim Kader, "Reforms Trouble Growers/Strawberry Famers Face Labor Uncertainty Over Immigration Law," *Oregonian*, January 28, 1988; Eric Goranson, "Undocumented Aliens to Harvest Strawberries," *Oregonian*, February 23, 1988; "Forum Readied for Agricultural Employers," *Oregonian*, March 11, 1988; Ellis C. Barnes, "Oregon Growers Blast New Immigration Law," *Oregonian*, March 13, 1988.

24. Eric Goranson, "Chinese Labor Pool Studied: Strawberry Growers to Meet with NY Firm Importing Workers," *Oregonian*, February 18, 1988.

25. "IRCA and Oregon Agricultural Industries."

26. Ibid.

27. Lauren Cowen, "New Legals Find Struggle Continues," *Oregonian*, November 28, 1988; Ellis C. Barnes, "INS: Farmer Selling False Papers," *Oregonian*, April 29, 1989.

28. Cheryl Martinis, "Farm Worker Union Says Farmer Lured Migrants," *Oregonian*, June 4, 1988.

29. Paul Koberstein, "INS Probes Fraud," *Oregonian*, November 6, 1987. Washington State also faced large amounts of fraud that led to a few arrests. James Eng, "Immigration Fraud Probe Continues," *Oregonian*, December 17, 1987.

30. "IRCA and Oregon Agricultural Industries."

31. Phil Manzano, "Aucoin Assails Agency for Not Aiding Migrant Workers," *Oregonian*, May 7, 1988. Apparently the State of Oregon had a contentious relationship with FEMA. State officials refused to participate in civil defense drills to prepare them for a nuclear attack, and subsequently FEMA threatened to withhold over a million dollars in federal funding.

32. Jeff Grency, "Mexican Fact Finders Ttour Migrant Farm Site," *Oregonian*, September 15, 1987; Sarah Ames, "Fact Finders Take Close Look at Migrants' Life on the Job," *Oregonian*, September 16, 1987.

33. Lauren Cowen, "New Legals Find Struggle Continues."

34. Ibid. IRCA had set aside an additional funding program for states that required additional resources through the State Legislation Impact Assistance Grant (SLIAG). It is unclear (to the author) if the money granted through the Legislative Emergency Board came from

SLIAG. Although the state did receive a federal grant in January 1988, nearly eight months after the implementation of IRCA to educate the public about legalization. "Grant to Help Publicize INS Changes," *Oregonian*, January 23, 1988.

35. In fact, Larry Kleinman was commissioned by the National Lawyers Guild to write a guide for understanding the new immigration laws. Lawrence Kleinman, *The 1986 Immigration and Nationality Acts* (New York: Clark Boardman, 1987).

36. IRCA and the INS developed a category for community organizations, approved to help undocumented workers navigate the legalization process. They came to be known as QDEs or Qualified Designated Entities. In Oregon those entities were the Oregon Human Development Corporation and the Catholic Church. PCUN refused to register as a DQE because of fear that the INS would attempt to access its records.

37. Interview with Larry Kleinman, August 28, 2009, in Woodburn, Oregon. Conducted by the author; Martinis, "Farm Workers Union Says Farmers Lured Migrants."

38. Larry Kleinman interview, August 28, 2009; "Portland INS Office Quiet as U.S. Amnesty Program Goes into Second Phase," *Oregonian*, November 8, 1988.

39. Interview with Larry Kleinman, August 28, 2009.

40. Ibid.

41. Ibid.

42. "IRCA and Oregon Agricultural Industries."

43. Jean Cecilia Powell, "Entre Dos Mundos (Between Two Worlds): Empowering Oregon's Hispanics," Unpublished master's thesis, University of Oregon, 1990.

44. Ibid.

45. Marshall Ganz, *Why David Sometimes Wins: Leadership, Organization, and Strategy in the California Farm Worker Movement* (New York: Oxford University Press, 2009); Matt Garcia, *From the Jaws of Victory: The Triumph and Tragedy of Cesar Chavez and the Farm Worker Movement* (Berkeley: University of California Press, 2012); Miriam Pawel, *The Union of Their Dreams: Power, Hope, and Struggle in César Chavez's Farm Worker Movement* (New York: Bloomsbury, 2009).

46. *PCUN Update*, issue 1, February 1990.

47. "Judge Refuses to Dismiss Suit By Farm Workers," *Oregonian*, May 5, 1990.

48. "Judge Mulls Farm-Picketing Suit," *Oregonian*, September 25, 1990.

49. Ibid.

50. *PCUN Update*, issue 4, October 1990.

51. "Union Starts Strike Fund to Support Farm Workers, Members Plan to Picket Undisclosed Farms to Get Growers to Discuss Pacts," *Oregonian*, June 10, 1989.

52. Ibid.

53. *Statesman Journal*, June 18, 1990.

54. *Oregonian*, June 17, 1989.

55. *Statesman Journal*, August 17, 1990.

56. Statement to Senate Labor Committee on Minimum Wage Compliance in 1990 Strawberry Harvest, n.d.

57. *Salem Capital Press*, September 28, 1990.

58. *PCUN Update*, issue 3, August 1990.

59. *Oregonian*, June 21, 1989.

60. Oral interview with Ramon Ramirez, March 25, 2010, in Woodburn, Oregon. Conducted by the author.

61. Powell, *Entre Dos Mundos*, 60.

CHAPTER 6   HUELGA!

1. Jean Cecilia Powell, "Entre Dos Mundos (Between Two Worlds): Empowering Oregon's Hispanics." Unpublished Master's thesis, University of Oregon, 1990, 59.
2. United States Department of Agriculture, Economic Research Service, Data Sets, Oregon.
3. "Is Farm Workers Union Taking Root in Oregon?" *Oregonian*, December 23, 1991.
4. Employees were often forced to buy goods from the company store that would then deduct the costs at inflated prices from their paychecks. Effectively the farmer or contractor paid themselves with the money they paid employees.
5. "Is Farm Workers Union Taking Root?"
6. *PCUN Update*, issue 7 (August 1991).
7. *Oregonian*, July 9, 1992.
8. *PCUN Update*, issue 11 (October 1992).
9. "Is Farm Workers Union Taking Root?"
10. Ibid.
11. *PCUN Update*, issue 7 (August 1991).
12. *Oregonian*, September 14, 1992.
13. Powell, *Entre Dos Mundos*, 58.
14. *Salem Capital Press*, August 21, 1992.
15. *Woodburn Independent*, August 7, 1992.
16. *Salem Capital Press*, August 13, 1992.
17. *Oregonian*, August 11, 1992.
18. *PCUN Update*, issue 14 (June 1993).
19. *Reed College Quest*, February 4, 1997.
20. *PCUN Update*, issue 12 (December 1992).
21. *PCUN Update*, issue 13 (March 1993); issue 15 (October 1993).
22. *Oregonian*, September 14, 1993.
23. *PCUN Update* issue 15 (October 1993).
24. "Pickers, Orchardist in Conflict," *Oregonian*, July 7, 1993.
25. *PCUN Update*, issue 15 (October 1993).
26. "Pickers, Orchardist in Conflict."
27. *Capital Press*, January 24, 1992.
28. "Pickers, Orchardist in Conflict."
29. United States Department of Agriculture, Economic Research Service, Data Sets, Oregon.
30. Juan Vicente Palermo, "Farm Labor Needs and Farm Workers in California, 1970–1990"; California Employment Development Department. *California Agricultural Studies*, 91–92 (April 1991), 57–62.
31. Robert Mason, Tim Cross, and David Thomas, "Labor Demand, Productivity, and Overhead Cost Estimates for Harvesting the 1990 Strawberry Crop," Oregon State University Agricultural Experiment Station, Special Report No. 886, revised January 1992.
32. "IRCA and Oregon Agricultural Industries: Nursery Crops, Christmas Trees, and Strawberries in the Willamette Valley and Pears in the Hood River Valley," Oregon State University Agricultural Experiment Station, Special Report no. 910, revised April 1993.
33. Lynn Stephens, *Transborder Lives: Indigenous Oaxacans in Mexico, California, and Oregon* (Durham: Duke University Press, 2007), 246–249.
34. Ibid.
35. *PCUN Update*, issue 19 (1994).
36. *Vanguard*, November 21–27, 1996.

37. *PCUN Update,* issue 8 (November 1991).
38. Interview with Ramón Ramírez, July 28, 2007, in Woodburn, Oregon. Conducted by the author.
39. *Oregonian,* September 2, 1992.
40. Interview with Ramón Ramírez, July 28, 2007.
41. *PCUN Update,* issue 18 (August 1994).
42. Interview with Ramón Ramírez, July 28, 2007.
43. Ibid.
44. *Noticias Latinas,* April 1996; *Catholic News Service,* July 16, 1996.
45. Powell, *Entre Dos Mundos,* 61.
46. *Woodburn Independent,* May 31, 1995.
47. *Northwest Labor Press,* June 16, 1995.
48. *PCUN Update* issue 21 (May 1995).
49. *Oregonian,* May 12, 1995.
50. *Farm Bureau News,* May 23, 1995.
51. Stephens, *Transborder Lives.*
52. *Oregonian,* June 6, 1995.
53. *Statesman Journal,* June 16, 1995.
54. *Oregonian,* June 7, 1995.
55. Interview with Ramón Ramírez, July 28, 2007.
56. *Oregonian,* June 7, 1995.
57. *Molalla Pioneer,* June 7, 1995.
58. *Statesman Journal,* June 7, 1995.
59. *Capital Press,* June 23, 1995.
60. *PCUN Update,* issue 22 (July 1995).
61. *Oregonian,* June 9, 1995.
62. Ibid.
63. *PCUN Update* issue 22 (July 1995).
64. *Vanguard,* November 21–27, 1996.
65. *PCUN Update,* issue 22 (July 1995).
66. *Statesman Journal,* June 6, 1995.
67. Interview with Ramón Ramírez, July 28, 2007.
68. Ibid.
69. Ibid.
70. *PCUN Update,* issue 23 (December 1995).

EPILOGUE

1. *Oregonian,* October 3, 1998.
2. Interview, Danny Santos, February 19, 2009, in Salem, Oregon. Interviewed by Mario Sifuentez.

INDEX

ABOUT THE AUTHOR

MARIO SIFUENTEZ is an assistant professor of history at the University of California, Merced. He is currently at work on his next project on food, water, and labor in California's Central Valley.

Available titles in the Latinidad: Transnational Cultures in the United States series:

María Acosta Cruz, *Dream Nation: Puerto Rican Culture and the Fictions of Independence*

Rodolfo F. Acuña, *The Making of Chicana/o Studies: In the Trenches of Academe*

Xóchitl Bada, *Mexican Hometown Associations in Chicagoacán: From Local to Transnational Civic Engagement*

Adriana Cruz-Manjarrez, *Zapotecs on the Move: Cultural, Social, and Political Processes in Transnational Perspective*

Marivel T. Danielson, *Homecoming Queers: Desire and Difference in Chicana Latina Cultural Production*

Rudy P. Guevarra Jr., *Becoming Mexipino: Multiethnic Identities and Communities in San Diego*

Colin Gunckel, *Mexico on Main Street: Transnational Film Culture in Los Angeles before World War II*

Marie-Theresa Hernández, *The Virgin of Guadalupe and the Conversos: Uncovering Hidden Influences from Spain to Mexico*

Lisa Jarvinen, *The Rise of Spanish-Language Filmmaking: Out from Hollywood's Shadow, 1929–1939*

Regina M. Marchi, *Day of the Dead in the USA: The Migration and Transformation of a Cultural Phenomenon*

Desirée A. Martín, *Borderlands Saints: Secular Sanctity in Chicano/a and Mexican Culture*

Marci R. McMahon, *Domestic Negotiations: Gender, Nation, and Self-Fashioning in US Mexicana and Chicana Literature and Art*

A. Gabriel Meléndez, *Hidden Chicano Cinema: Film Dramas in the Borderlands*

Priscilla Peña Ovalle, *Dance and the Hollywood Latina: Race, Sex, and Stardom*

Amalia Pallares, *Family Activism: Immigrant Struggles and the Politics of Noncitizenship*

Luis F. B. Plascencia, *Disenchanting Citizenship: Mexican Migrants and the Boundaries of Belonging*

Cecilia M. Rivas, *Salvadoran Imaginaries: Mediated Identities and Cultures of Consumption*

Mario Jimenez Sifuentez, *Of Forests and Fields: Mexican Labor in the Pacific Northwest*

Maya Socolovsky, *Troubling Nationhood in U.S. Latina Literature: Explorations of Place and Belonging*